NFL
Moments

NFL Moments

125 Icons and Stories that Define the NFL

Allan Maki and George Johnson

FIREFLY BOOKS

Published by Firefly Books Ltd. 2025

First printing

Library of Congress Control Number: 2025936545

Library and Archives Canada Cataloguing in Publication

Title: NFL moments : 125 icons and stories that define the NFL / Allan Maki and George Johnson.
Other titles: National Football League moments
Names: Maki, Allan, author | Johnson, George, 1957- author
Description: Includes index.
Identifiers: Canadiana 20250192659 | ISBN 9780228105725 (softcover)
Subjects: LCSH: National Football League—Anecdotes. | LCSH: Football players—United States—Anecdotes. | LCSH: Football—United States—Anecdotes. | LCGFT: Anecdotes.
Classification: LCC GV955.5.N35 M35 2025 | DDC 796.332/640973—dc23

Published in the United States by
Firefly Books (U.S.) Inc.
P.O. Box 1338, Ellicott Station
Buffalo, New York 14205

Published in Canada by
Firefly Books Ltd.
50 Staples Avenue, Unit 1
Richmond Hill, Ontario L4B 0A7

Cover and interior design: Hartley Millson

Printed in China | E

We gratefully acknowledge the financial support of the Government of Canada for our publishing program.

To my wife, my friend and my loving caregiver.
Thank you, Jeanne, for all you do.
— Allan Maki

As always, to my wife, Rita, and daughters, Michela and Sabrina, who keep me sane, whole and happy.
— George Johnson

Contents

Early Days | Pre-1960s

No. 1 Birth of a League 11
No. 2 The Ghost Gallops across America 13
No. 3 The Greatest Game Ever Played 15
No. 4 Shamateurism and the Jim Thorpe Story 16
No. 5 Bronko Runs Wild 20
No. 6 It was a Close Game, Until the Opening Kickoff 21
No. 7 The Forgotten Four and the Emergence of Black Athletes 22
No. 8 The Other Half of the Forgotten Four 24
No. 9 The First Black Hall of Famer 25
No. 10 And Still the Undisputed Leader ... 28
No. 11 Bobby Layne and the Detroit Curse 30
No. 12 Viewer Discretion Is Advised 33

The 1960s

No. 13 He Came Clean and Said Yes 35
No. 14 The Last of the 60-minute Men 38
No. 15 Breaking Football's Final Color Barrier 39
No. 16 Where the Immortals Live On 41
No. 17 Wrong Way Marshall 43
No. 18 America's Sweethearts 44
No. 19 Here's Mud in Your Eye 45
No. 20 Ode to a Unique Friendship 47
No. 21 Lucky No. 7 48
No. 22 The GOAT Running Back 50
No. 23 The Lost Weekend 52
No. 24 Have a Drink on Him 53
No. 25 Frozen in Time 54
No. 26 Mr. Lombardi Goes to Washington 56
No. 27 Good Drama, Bad Call 57
No. 28 He Had a Crystal Ball 58
No. 29 The Super Bowl Is Born, Officially 60
No. 30 Now That's a Scorekeeper's Nightmare 61
No. 31 Aaaaaand ... Action! 62

The 1970s

No. 32 Three in the Booth 65
No. 33 Cue the Orchestra and Strike up the Replays 66
No. 34 The Steelers Draft a Beast at Linebacker 67
No. 35 He Had the Leg for It 69
No. 36 Aging Most Splendidly 71
No. 37 Yeah, *That* John Wayne 72
No. 38 "Perfection" Personified 73
No. 39 What's in a Name? Plenty 75
No. 40 America's Team 77
No. 41 The First 2,000-yard Man 78
No. 42 "After Further Reviews ..." 80
No. 43 Heavenly Intervention 81
No. 44 On a Wing and a Prayer 83
No. 45 The Miracle at the Meadowlands 84
No. 46 A Devastating Blow 85
No. 47 Dressed for Success 87
No. 48 The Passing of a Legend 88
No. 49 A Mean Star Is Born 91

The 1980s

No. 50 Forever a Bear 93
No. 51 This, Most Definitely, Is Not for the Squeamish 95
No. 52 Stickum-up 97
No. 53 The Drive, Denver-style 98
No. 54 The Catch 100
No. 55 "An Unspeakable Tragedy" 102
No. 56 Long-distance Delivery 103
No. 57 Chicago's 1985 Bears 105
No. 58 The Iceman Cometh 107
No. 59 The West Coast Offense 108
No. 60 The Drive, San Francisco-style 109
No. 61 When Nothing Made the News 111
No. 62 The New England Snow Job 112
No. 63 Not Good for Business 114
No. 64 The Best, Bar None 115
No. 65 NFL Madden-ess 117

The 1990s

No. 66 Is There a QB in the House? 120
No. 67 The Comeback 121
No. 68 Gridiron Technology 101 124
No. 69 It's All on the Line 125
No. 70 The Steroid Era (1980s to 1990s and Beyond) 127
No. 71 Sanders Calls It Quits 130
No. 72 They Called Him Sweetness 132
No. 73 Did We Really See That? 135
No. 74 The Fake Spike 137
No. 75 Snakebit at the Super Bowl 138
No. 76 The Trade of the Decade 140
No. 77 Elway Cements His Legacy 142

The 2000s

No. 78 Another Crazy Trade 145
No. 79 The Music City Miracle 146
No. 80 One Yard Short 148
No. 81 Laying Down the Law 149
No. 82 Death of a Quarterback 151
No. 83 A Heady Decision 152
No. 84 What the Tuck?! 155
No. 85 Corp. Pat Tillman and the Battle for Truth 156
No. 86 The NFL Network Is on the Air 159
No. 87 A Super Turnabout 160
No. 88 The River City Relay 162
No. 89 The Unstoppable Dante Hall 163
No. 90 Rebirth of a City and Its Team 165
No. 91 Fortune Favors the Bold 166
No. 92 Spygate 168
No. 93 Bountygate 170
No. 94 Overseas Investments 172
No. 95 The Incredible Rise and Fall of Michael Vick 174

The 2010s

No. 96 Deflategate 177
No. 97 Game Changers 179
No. 98 The First Super Bowl OT 180
No. 99 The Super Bore 182
No. 100 It's Up, and He's Good 184
No. 101 Super-ville USA 185
No. 102 Worst. Missed. Penalty. Ever. 186
No. 103 The Magic Mahomes 187
No. 104 Who Really Did What? 190
No. 105 Take a Knee, Lose a Job 191
No. 106 Michael Sam, I Am 194
No. 107 Another Off-field Demise 195
No. 108 Bringing It On 197
No. 109 Everybody Dance Now 198
No. 110 The Top Twosome 200

The 2020s

No. 111 The Pro Bowl: Visual Sominex 202
No. 112 The Resurrection of Damar Hamlin 204
No. 113 Man on Fire 206
No. 114 All Hail the Mighty Tight Ends 207
No. 115 Big-time Stadiums 210
No. 116 Big-money Men 211
No. 117 The End Run 213
No. 118 Jayden Daniels and the Year of the Young Guns 214
No. 119 Kicking Them When They're Up and Down 217
No. 120 Rodgers, Over and Out ... of the Playoffs (Again) 219
No. 121 The Brett Favre Saga 221
No. 122 The T and T Watch 223
No. 123 The Trouble with Tua 225
No. 124 Running to Glory 227
No. 125 Where Eagles Dare 230

Index 234
Photo Credits 240

Foreword

Rose Elizabeth Fitzgerald Kennedy, the matriarch of a fabled political dynasty, once reflected, "Life isn't a matter of milestones, but of moments."

For football fans everywhere, whatever their rooting interest, this sentiment could not be truer. Moments of inspiration. Moments of achievement. Moments of sorrow. Moments of high drama and of low comedy. Moments that survive years, even decades, after they actually occurred. The people, places, innovations and exploits that define a franchise, a league, a sport and the eras that spawned them.

Joe Namath's guarantee. Bobby Layne's "Detroit curse." Vince Lombardi's trademark fedora and camel-hair coat. The Pro Football Hall of Fame's signature Haggar gold jacket.

Norm Van Brocklin's single-game record for throwing, 554 yards, which has lasted over 70 years. Miami coach Don Shula being borne aloft following the Dolphins' "perfect" 17-0 1972 season. Green Bay QB Bart Starr's 1-yard plunge over offensive guard Jerry Kramer in the Ice Bowl, with 16 seconds left to lay claim to the 1967 NFL Championship. David Tyree rising to pin an Eli Manning pass against his helmet for a 32-yard gain, sending the New York Giants on their way to an upset Super Bowl XLII victory over the New England Patriots.

Jim Marshall's wrong-way run. Miami kicker Garo Yepremian's Super Bowl pass "attempt." The River City Relay. Spygate. Bountygate. Deflategate.

The integration of Black players. Steroid use. Concussion dangers. Instant replay. Colin Kaepernick taking a knee. Howard Cosell, Frank Gifford and "Dandy" Don Meredith on Monday nights.

The power of Jim Brown. The elegance of Jerry Rice. The savagery of

Dick Butkus. The unrivaled improvisational skills of Patrick Mahomes. The heft of placekicker Tom Dempsey's toe-less right foot. The death of Sweetness. The birth of the West Coast offense.

Cheeseheads at Lambeau. Taylor Swift at Arrowhead. Rebirth in hurricane-devastated New Orleans. Cheerleaders in hot pants in Dallas.

Those instantly recognizable nicknames: Night Train, Mean Joe, Broadway Joe, Prime Time, Concrete Charlie, the Fearsome Foursome, the Purple People Eaters, the Galloping Ghost, Refrigerator, Crazylegs, Iron Mike, Joe Cool, Too Tall, Beast Mode.

Over the passage of time, from the formation of the American Professional Football Association in 1920 and its name shift to the National Football League two years later, to the Tom Brady–Bill Belichick and Patrick Mahomes–Andy Reid dynasties of a more recent vintage, the NFL has morphed into the most lucrative, most eyeballed sports entity anywhere on the globe, with reported revenues of over $20 billion in 2023. It is, no one can argue, big, *big* business. But for those who rush out to secure the tickets, often braving the elements, to those who religiously set up shop in front of their TVs every week, it's a singularly emotional experience as well.

Which draws us back, as always, to the moments. Extraordinarily public but, conversely, still uniquely personal. Moments caught in time, illuminated in imagination, packed away to be revisited in each fan's keepsake album of memories.

And now, a sampling of 125 of them.

Early Days Pre-1960s

Contents

No. 1 Birth of a League 11

No. 2 The Ghost Gallops across America 13

No. 3 The Greatest Game Ever Played 15

No. 4 Shamateurism and the Jim Thorpe Story 16

No. 5 Bronko Runs Wild 20

No. 6 It was a Close Game, Until the Opening Kickoff 21

No. 7 The Forgotten Four and the Emergence of Black Athletes 22

No. 8 The Other Half of the Forgotten Four 24

No. 9 The First Black Hall of Famer 25

No. 10 And Still the Undisputed Leader ... 28

No. 11 Bobby Layne and the Detroit Curse 30

No. 12 Viewer Discretion Is Advised 33

Birth of a League

NO. 1

THERE WAS A time when U.S. professional football took a back seat to the college game. The pros, it was argued, were too fragmented and volatile. Teams like the Muncie Flyers and Chicago Tigers came and went. There were precious few star attractions and no longstanding traditions to compare with "The Game," Harvard University versus Yale University — a rivalry dating back to 1875.

Such was the reality confronting the American Professional Football Association, a 14-team operation that included the Flyers, the Tigers and the Bulldogs from Canton, Ohio — the future home of the Pro Football Hall of Fame. Jim Thorpe, who played for Canton from 1915 to 1920, was elected as the first league president, though Joe F. Carr would replace him in 1921, when the league ballooned to 21 teams.

The Original 14

These 14 teams were members of the APFA starting in 1920:

- **Akron Pros – Akron, Ohio**
- **Buffalo All-Americans – Buffalo, New York**
- **Canton Bulldogs – Canton, Ohio**
- **Racine Cardinals – Chicago, Illinois**
- **Chicago Tigers – Chicago, Illinois**
- **Cleveland Tigers – Cleveland, Ohio**
- **Columbus Panhandles – Columbus, Ohio**
- **Dayton Triangles – Dayton, Ohio**
- **Decatur Staleys – Decatur, Illinois**
- **Detroit Heralds – Detroit, Michigan**
- **Hammond Pros – Hammond, Indiana**
- **Muncie Flyers – Muncie, Indiana**
- **Rock Island Independents – Rock Island, Illinois**
- **Rochester Jeffersons – Rochester, New York**

The first official APFA game was held on October 3, 1920. The Dayton Triangles hosted the Columbus Panhandles, and the Triangles took the win 14–0.

The APFA morphed into the National Football League in 1922, when the team owners pushed for larger markets and partners with deeper pockets. This paved the way for the game's true titans, the men who would lay the foundation for what we see today: Earl "Curly" Lambeau of the Green Bay Packers, Charles Bidwill of the Chicago Cardinals, George "Papa Bear" Halas of the Chicago Bears, Art Rooney of the Pittsburgh Steelers, George Preston Marshall of the Washington Redskins, Bert Bell of the Philadelphia Eagles and, later, the Steelers, and New York Giants co-founder Tim Mara, who paid $500 for his team. (Today, the Giants are worth more than $7 billion.)

In 1941 Elmer Layden, a former member of Notre Dame's fabled Four Horsemen backfield, was chosen to be the NFL's first commissioner. He lasted five years on the job before being replaced by Bert Bell, the consummate football man who, while he was the owner of the Eagles, pushed for a yearly draft of college players to generate on-field parity.

As commissioner, Bell understood the importance of controlling television rights, permitting only away games to be televised back to home cities as a way of protecting a team's gate revenues while making road games and high-profile match-ups between non-local teams accessible to fans. This was a cornerstone strategy that increased the league's popularity. But it would be through the countless, tireless efforts of the many owners, players, coaches and innovators that the NFL would find its groove and propel itself up to the highest echelon of professional sport.

The First NFL Draft

The inaugural draft was held on February 8, 1936, at Philadelphia's Ritz-Carlton Hotel, where the Eagles picked first, selecting University of Chicago halfback Jay Berwanger. Berwanger was the first recipient of the Heisman Trophy (then called the Downtown Athletic Club Trophy). Uninterested in the pros, he never played in the NFL. His plan was to remain an amateur and compete at the 1936 Berlin Olympics as a decathlete, but he didn't make the U.S. team.

The Ghost Gallops across America

NO. 2

Beginning in the 1920s, Papa Bear Halas did all he could to make his Bears the NFL's standard bearer. It was his plan to have the team barnstorm the country playing university or local club teams to show just how talented his squad was. In turn, that helped enhance the NFL's credibility.

The quickest way to do that was to sign the most-talked-about college player in the nation, University of Illinois running back Harold Edward "Red" Grange, best known as the Galloping Ghost, a nickname hung on him by sports writer Warren Brown.

Grange was box-office dynamite.

At 6 feet and 180 pounds, the Ghost was not an overwhelming physical presence. But his October 18, 1924, tour de force with Illinois against rival Michigan showcased just how dominant he could be. It started with the opening kickoff. Grange caught it and ran 95 yards for his first touchdown. Over the next 12 minutes, he scored on a 67-yard run, a 56-yard run and a 44-yard run. He added another touchdown run and threw a TD pass in the second half.

The Bears' barnstorming tour was ignited by Grange's fame and charisma. The cross-country tour featured both exhibition and NFL league games and ran from early December all the way to January. The first leg was a run of eight games in 12 days and it included two back-to-backs. It was highlighted by a 19–7 conquest of the New York Giants in front of an astounding crowd of 73,000 fans at the Polo Grounds — such was the excitement surrounding the Galloping Ghost.

By the tour's end in January 1926, the Bears had played 30 games, an estimated 400,000 people had attended and Grange had pocketed a tidy $200,000.

The residual effects of publicity surrounding the tour cannot be underestimated. It generated national interest in football, to the point where Halas

Red Grange as a Chicago Bear in December 1925.

and Grange were meeting the President at the White House and hobnobbing with celebrities and sporting legends like Babe Ruth. The 1925 Bears are still considered to be one of the most influential teams in NFL history.

Grange and his agent, Charles C. Pyle, wanted a one-third share of the Bears but were rebuffed, so they started their own team, the New York Yankees (the same name as the baseball team) of the American Football League. It was a short-lived venture. Grange's Yankees were absorbed by the NFL in 1927. Unfortunately for the Galloping Ghost, he suffered a knee injury and had to sit out the entire 1928 season. Newspapers reported that Grange had lost some of his speed, making it sound like he was just another player. After the Yankees folded, Grange returned to Chicago and helped the Bears win NFL titles in 1932 and 1933, but the long-run brilliance that left opponents and fans in awe was no longer prevalent.

The Greatest Game Ever Played

NO. 3

THE NFL ADDED three more teams for the 1950 season, when the San Francisco 49ers, the Baltimore Colts and the Cleveland Browns were pilfered from the All-America Football Conference. It didn't take long for them to make their mark.

The Browns, coached by the legendary Paul Brown and quarterbacked by the famed Otto Graham (a three-time NFL MVP wearing Cleveland colors), won three NFL championships, in 1950, 1954 and 1955. The Browns reached the title game in six-straight seasons from '50 through '55.

"When Paul Brown talked contract, the championship game was part of it," Graham once reflected. "We took the championship game for granted."

The Colts eventually responded, winning the 1958 league title by defeating the New York Giants in what became known as the "Greatest Game Ever Played." With time winding down in the fourth quarter, Colts quarterback Johnny Unitas moved his team to within field goal range to tie the score at 17–17. That forced the first overtime championship game in NFL history. Once again, Unitas went on the attack, dissecting the Giants' defense with a surgeon's touch before fullback Alan Ameche scored on a 1-yard plunge.

In 2019, a voting panel made up of coaches, executives, players and media members listed the game as one of the greatest in the NFL's first 100 years.

Now, everything was aligned in the NFL's favor — the professionalism, the product, rising attendance figures and TV ratings that spiked to 45 million for the Colts' championship win.

By the late 1960s, the NFL was ready for another merger. Tired of losing its players and draft picks to the upstart AFL, the NFL agreed to take in all eight AFL franchises, including the New York Jets (formerly the Titans), the Denver Broncos, the San Diego Chargers (who later moved to LA in 2017) and the Kansas City Chiefs (formerly the Dallas Texans).

Leading up to that merger was an open vault of money. In 1964 the AFL had signed a five-year, $36-million deal with NBC, while CBS paid $14

The Man with the Golden Arm

The 1958 league title also made Unitas a star. The gunslinger of a QB with a commanding presence was so steely-eyed and composed that one of his teammates said, "It was like being in the huddle with God." Unitas was the first quarterback to pass for 30 touchdowns in a season. He set a record of throwing for at least one touchdown in 47 consecutive games. New Orleans' Drew Brees finally broke that record in 2012.

million for the NFL regular-season games for 1964 and 1965. For 1966 and 1967, CBS paid $18.8 million per year for NFL regular-season games; playoffs cost extra.

Just as its forefathers had hoped, the NFL was on its way to being the most popular and lucrative sporting league on the continent. It also became a favorite sport for gamblers. (Nowadays fans can bet on anything from the opening coin toss to how long it takes the singer to get through the national anthem.) Once the Super Bowl was polished and marketed, the NFL had popularity and authority aplenty. The league that was once lapped by college football was now firmly in the lead.

NO. 4 Shamateurism and the Jim Thorpe Story

THERE WASN'T ANYTHING Jim Thorpe couldn't do as an athlete. He was Bo before Jackson "Knew It" M.J. before Michael Jordan "Just Did It." Neon Deion before Sanders split his time between pro football and baseball. For Thorpe, his multi-sport mastery knew few limits and extended well beyond a football field or a baseball diamond.

At the 1912 Stockholm Summer Olympics in Sweden, Thorpe became the first Native American to win a medal, taking gold in both the pentathlon and decathlon by running everything from the 100-yard dash to the 1,500 meters, jumping everything from the long jump to the high jump, and throwing

Jim Thorpe at an athletics meeting at the Parc Pommery in Reims, France, July 1912.

everything from the javelin to the discus. It was more than enough to earn him praise as the world's greatest athlete. And he did it in ill-fitting shoes after his had gone missing on the morning of the decathlon's second day of events. He used two shoes that he found in a garbage can. One shoe was too small, the other too big. And still, Thorpe won the 1,500 meters by a full five seconds.

The problem was that he didn't get to keep the medals for long.

Born in 1887, Thorpe was a member of the Sac and Fox Nation in central Oklahoma. His parents gave him the Sauk name Wa-Tho-Huk, which means "bright path the lightning makes as it goes across the sky." As a youngster, he was a restless, free spirit who hated the school he attended with his twin brother, Charlie. Sadly, Charlie died of pneumonia at the age of nine. Two years later, Thorpe lost his mother to childbirth complications. His father succumbed to gangrene poisoning when Thorpe was just 16.

In 1904 Thorpe made his way to the Carlisle Indian Industrial School in Pennsylvania. It was there that his natural athleticism caught the attention of Glenn Scobey "Pop" Warner, who coached the football and track-and-field teams.

Various books and articles say Warner took an interest in Thorpe when he bettered the school's top high jumpers by clearing 5 feet, 9 inches — in his street clothes. And when he took to the football field, Thorpe proved to be a dynamic force. In 1912 he carried Carlisle to a national collegiate championship, scoring 25 touchdowns and totaling 198 points, according to ESPN.

But it was baseball, not football, his favorite sport, that cost Thorpe his two Olympic gold medals.

It turned out Thorpe had been paid $5 a game to play for the Rocky Mount Railroaders of the semipro Eastern Carolina League in 1909 and 1910. It was a common practice at that time for college ball players to play for pay during the summer months to earn cash for school. Some players used fake names when they signed on, but Thorpe didn't. When the USA's Amateur Athletic Union got wind of Thorpe's deal, it quashed his amateur status, allowing the International Olympic Committee to take away his two gold medals.

What constituted an amateur athlete was open to interpretation. The IOC would often look away from some cases while pursuing others. Case in point: fencing masters were allowed to compete despite openly being professionals, in large part because they were considered "gentlemen." Allowing professionals was a way to preserve the sport for the aristocracy, not the commoners. Such practices would later be dubbed "shamateurism."

Thorpe was also victimized by the IOC's kangaroo-court style of doing business. Thorpe's pro status wasn't revealed until January 1913, roughly four months after the deadline to challenge the results of the Games. It gave his supporters proof of the IOC's mishandling of the matter.

Thorpe's Final Resting Place

Even in death, Jim Thorpe was dogged by controversy. In 1953 his third wife, Patricia, claimed his body the night before an interment ceremony was to be conducted by the Sac and Fox Nation in Oklahoma, where Thorpe was born. Patricia took her husband's casket to protest the state's refusal to fund a proper memorial. She awarded his body to a pair of neighboring towns that merged in 1954 under the new name Jim Thorpe, Pennsylvania. It remains his final resting place, much to the chagrin of Thorpe's children, who filed every legal challenge they could.

As the debate over his Olympic status raged on, Thorpe signed as a rangy outfielder with Major League Baseball's New York Giants. He spent six seasons in the big leagues, helping the Giants win the 1913 National League championship. In 1915 he joined the Canton Bulldogs of the independent Ohio League, a predecessor to the APFA and the NFL. His football heroics took the Bulldogs to three championships and earned him his rightful place in the Pro Football Hall of Fame in 1963.

There were other successes in Thorpe's athletic career. He was the star attraction with a touring basketball team calling itself the World Famous Indians of LaRue, Ohio. He even had a 1913 offer to play pro hockey with the Toronto-based Tecumseh Hockey Club. He turned it down.

Finally, on October 13, 1982, the IOC agreed that taking away Thorpe's medals was a mistake and that they would be returned to his family. IOC president Juan Antonio Samaranch presented them to Thorpe's children prior to the 1984 Los Angeles Summer Olympics. The medals were then given to the Oklahoma Historical Society, which put them on display in the state capitol. A security guard stole the medals but turned them over after being arrested. The medals have also been shown at the National Museum of the American Indian in Washington, D.C.

Thorpe died of heart failure in March 1953. He was 65. Hailed as the greatest athlete of the half-century, he left behind a legacy unmatched in its scope and accomplishments.

NO.

5 Bronko Runs Wild

WHEN IT CAME to smashing into multiple tacklers, the 6-foot-2, 226-pound, Canadian-born Bronislau "Bronko" Nagurski was a bare-knuckled, smashmouth of a fullback on offense and a roughhouse tackle on defense. No ball carrier his size ran faster, no defender hit harder. He became prominent with the Chicago Bears during the Great Depression, sometimes pairing with Red Grange in the offensive backfield and proving to be as dangerous with the football as he was without it.

Born to Ukrainian and Polish parents in Rainy River, Ontario, Nagurski moved with his family to International Falls, Minnesota, where he grew up and worked at his father's sawmill and farm. It was said of Nagurski that his path to football was destined by a chance visit. According to folklore, University of Minnesota football coach Clarence Spears saw the strapping young Nagurski plowing a field without any horses. Spears stopped and asked Nagurski for directions and was surprised when Nagurski picked up the plow and used it to point the way. Spears later acknowledged he had made up the story to give Nagurski a larger-than-life, Paul Bunyan-like quality.

As a Minnesota Golden Gopher, Nagurski was an All-America fullback and defensive tackle. He helped the team win a Big Ten conference championship in 1927. In 1930, during his first season with the Bears, Nagurski established himself as the most dominant player the NFL had ever seen. That produced a series of Nagurski follies — some of them true, some enhanced to the point of ridiculousness. Consider this tale: Nagurski supposedly carried the ball through four tacklers on one play before charging into a goalpost and cracking into a brick wall at Chicago's Wrigley Field. When he returned to the sideline, he told his teammates, "That last guy hit me awfully hard."

Then there's the story of Nagurski running at full speed into a line of mounted policemen. As legend has it, Bronko crashed into a horse, knocking both it and its rider to the ground.

In 1932 Nagurski helped the Bears finish as the NFL's top team by defeating the Portsmouth Spartans with a touchdown pass to Red Grange. Five seasons later, Nagurski retired over a contract dispute, saying he was worth more than $6,500 a year. He became a professional wrestler and a rather good one at that, winning the National Wrestling Association's world title from Lou Thesz in 1939.

The Bears were able to lure Nagurski back to the gridiron in 1943, when many of their players had left to fight in World War II. Even at 34 Nagurski was able to inflict his will on opposing teams. He scored a touchdown against the Chicago Cardinals to put the Bears in the NFL championship game against the Washington Redskins. Nagurski scored again in the league final, lifting the Bears back atop the football world. Nagurski then retired for good. (His son, Bronko Jr., would keep the family name in the news by playing eight seasons as an offensive lineman with the Hamilton Tiger-Cats of the Canadian Football League. The young Nagurski was a member of two Tiger-Cats teams that won the Grey Cup.)

One last Bronko Sr. story: Green Bay defender Cal Hubbard was lined up opposite Red Grange and wanted to make a deal — Hubbard vowed not to block a Chicago punt if Grange promised not to block him. What Hubbard wanted was a clear shot at Nagurski. So Grange let Hubbard go only to see him bounce off Nagurski like a tennis ball off a racket. "Hey, Red," Hubbard fumed. "Don't do me any more favors."

It Was a Close Game, Until the Opening Kickoff

NO. 6

CHICAGO'S MONSTERS OF the Midway became the NFL's first dynasty, a point without argument after the 1940 NFL title game. With a young Sid Luckman at quarterback, Chicago ran the T-formation and two-back offense and recorded the most lopsided victory in NFL history, a 73–0 dismembering of the Washington Redskins. (That score is not a typo.)

The background to this story began three weeks before the slaughter, with the Redskins edging the Bears by a 7–3 score. On the last play of the game, Luckman fired a pass to Bill Osmanski in the end zone that fell incomplete after a Washington defender interfered with Bullet Bill, as he was known. The non-call drove the Bears bonkers.

Redskins' owner George Preston Marshall kept the fires burning by insulting his Chicago counterparts. "The Bears are front runners. Quitters. They are not a second-half team, just a bunch of crybabies," said Marshall. The Bears remembered those comments in the championship clash at Washington's Griffith Stadium. Just seconds into the game, Osmanski scored on a 68-yard run. By halftime, the score was 28–0 for Chicago. And just to prove a point, the Bears showed themselves to be a dominant second-half team by adding 26 points in the third quarter and 19 more in the fourth. Altogether, of the 11 majors scored that day, only one player, Harry Clarke, scored twice — and he did it in the fourth quarter. It was after the bloodletting that Washington quarterback Slingin' Sammy Baugh was asked whether things might have been different if early on one of his receivers had caught the football in the Chicago end zone instead of dropping it.

"Yeah," said Baugh. "It would have been 73–7."

The Bears defended their title in 1941 against the New York Giants with a 37–9 decision.

NO. 7 The Forgotten Four and the Emergence of Black Athletes

With no apologies given, the NFL used to be as white as a starched dress shirt.

While there were Black players such as Fritz Pollard, Bobby Marshall and Duke Slater in the league's pre-World War II era, it wasn't until 1946 that the NFL got serious about integration. That led to the signing of Kenny "Kingfish" Washington, Woody Strode, Marion Motley and Bill Willis — a collection of talent tagged as the Forgotten Four.

Together, the foursome broke the NFL's 13-year barrier for signing African American players, and it happened seven months before Jackie Robinson

A portrait of Woody Strode, Jack Robinson and Kenny Washington when they played for the UCLA Bruins, 1939.

earned lasting fame and did the same for Major League Baseball.

During his time at UCLA, Washington's on-field heroics should have earned him numerous honors. He finished his career as a Bruin by setting a school rushing record of 1,914 yards, with Strode often blocking for him. Instead, Washington was not named a First-Team All-American in 1939 and was ignored for the East-West Shrine Game. He ended up playing for the semipro Pacific Coast Professional Football League's Hollywood Bears, a team Strode also joined.

It was in 1946 that the Cleveland Rams moved to Los Angeles and looked to sign a lease at the Memorial Coliseum, which had been funded by both Black and white taxpayers. That helped create a push to have Black players on the Rams, so Washington and Strode were offered contracts.

Sadly, Rams fans never got to see Washington at his absolute best. He had both knees operated on a total of five times, including two surgeries before his Rams introduction. He was merely a shadow of his former self and opted for retirement in 1948. He died at 52 from heart and lung troubles. Strode secured gainful employment in Hollywood, appearing in more than 65 movies. He also played for the Calgary Stampeders of the Canadian Football League and died at the age of 80 from lung cancer. His last movie was *The Quick and the Dead* in 1995, starring Russell Crowe, Gene Hackman, Leonardo DiCaprio and Sharon Stone.

NO. 8

The Other Half of the Forgotten Four

THE CLEVELAND BROWNS signed Marion Motley and Bill Willis in 1946, just weeks before Kenny Washington and Woody Strode joined the Rams. The Browns were part of the eight-team All-America Football Conference. Both Motley and Willis caught the eye of the Browns' head coach, Paul Brown, who was impressed with the duo's athleticism. Willis played middle guard (now known as the nose tackle position) on defense and was an All-Pro (AAFC and NFL) in each of the eight seasons he played for Cleveland. Little wonder he drew lofty praise from Brown, who called him "one of the most outstanding linemen in the history of professional football." Just days after the Willis signing, Motley became a Brown with a $4,500-a-year contract and began running like few backs before him. At 6-foot-1 and 232 pounds — and wearing No. 76 — he resembled a lineman who had scooped up a fumble and was running to daylight.

Motley's finest statistical season occurred in 1948, when he rushed for a league-leading 964 yards, added another 192 by receptions and scored seven touchdowns. For four consecutive seasons, Motley and Willis helped Cleveland win the AAFC championship. And when the Browns were welcomed into the NFL in 1950, they didn't miss a beat.

In that first NFL season, Motley totaled 961 yards from scrimmage, scored four touchdowns and was named an All-Pro selection. He set what was then a single-game record of 188 yards on just 11 carries for an average of 17 yards per rush. In his first NFL postseason action, Willis showed his amazing skills by chasing down New York Giants receiver Gene "Choo Choo" Roberts, who looked to be en route to the winning TD. Instead, Willis derailed Choo Choo and Cleveland hung on for an 8–3 triumph that propelled the Browns to their first of four NFL titles won between 1950 and 1964.

As Black pioneers, Motley and Willis were subjected to their unfair share of blatant discrimination. They couldn't eat at the same restaurants as their white teammates and couldn't stay in the same hotels. They received hate mail and death threats. It was just as bad on the field, like the many times when opposing players deliberately stepped on Motley right in front of officials, who saw what had happened but chose to turn their backs and refused to call a penalty.

"That kind of crap went on for two or three years," Motley said. "They found out that while they were calling us n★★★★★★s and alligator bait, I was running for touchdowns and Willis was knocking the shit out of them."

But as Motley grew older, his knees began to fail him. He rushed for a meager 273 yards during the 1951 season as the Browns lost the championship rematch with the Rams. He played seven games as a linebacker with the 1955 Pittsburgh Steelers before retiring. In 1968 Motley became the second Black player voted into the Pro Football Hall of Fame. He died of cancer in June 1999. Willis died in November 2007.

Fast forward more than four decades after the Forgotten Four and it was Doug Williams who continued to open doors by becoming the first Black quarterback to start and win a Super Bowl. He was named the MVP of Super Bowl XXII for completing 18 of 29 throws for 340 yards and four touchdowns. It took another 26 years before the Seattle Seahawks' Russell Wilson became the second Black QB to win a Super Bowl.

The First Black Hall of Famer

NO. 9

EMLEN TUNNELL WAS a groundbreaker. He played 14 seasons in the NFL as a safety and punt returner with the New York Giants and Green Bay Packers. His accomplishments were staggering. At retirement in 1962, the man called "Mr. Defense" and the "Gremlin," held NFL records for most interceptions (79), most interception return yards (1,282), most punt returns (258) and most punt return yards (2,209).

But there was more to Tunnell than his impressive compilation of numbers. While playing for the University of Toledo, a block thrown on him while attempting to make a tackle in a game against Marshall University had serious consequences.

Turns out, he'd suffered a broken neck.

After the impact, the next thing Tunnell remembers was a priest standing over him, administering last rites.

"We weren't even Catholic," Tunnell's sister, Vivian Robinson, was quoted as saying in a *New York Times* article. "But they weren't waiting to ask."

The neck injury kept Tunnell out of the U.S. Army and Navy during World War II. He did, however, manage to enlist in the Coast Guard and was stationed on the U.S. cargo ship *Etamin* in Papua New Guinea in April 1944. The *Etamin* was anchored in Aitape Harbor, unloading 6,000 tons of gasoline and explosives, when it was hit by a torpedo from a Japanese airplane. Seeing Machinist's Mate First Class Fred Shaver on fire from the explosion, Tunnell used his hands to douse the flames, which left him with severe burns, too. Not done with that, he hauled the stricken Shaver to safety. Tunnell described the incident in his autobiography *Footsteps of a Giant*: "I really don't know how I knew the horrible figure running toward me in the darkness was Freddy. There was almost nothing recognizable about him. He was covered with fire."

Two years later, it was Tunnell to the rescue again. When shipmate Alfred Givens fell off the Coast Guard cutter *Tampa* docked at the U.S. naval base Argentia in Newfoundland, Tunnell jumped into the icy waters of the Atlantic Ocean to save the day. For that, he posthumously received the Silver Lifesaving Medal, and in December 2017 the Coast Guard announced it would name its 45th Sentinel class cutter the *Emlen Tunnell*. The No. 45 adorned Tunnell's jersey with the Giants and Packers.

It was after the war that Tunnell decided to give pro football a go. With little money to support his pursuit, Tunnell hitchhiked his way from his home in Garrett Hill, Pennsylvania — with $1.50 in his pocket — to New York with a West Indian banana-truck driver. Once at the Giants' Polo Grounds' office, he asked for a tryout. Suitably impressed, the Giants signed him to a $5,000 contract and were immediately rewarded by the rookie safety, who appeared in 10 games and made seven interceptions, including one he returned for a 43-yard touchdown.

"At first I thought he was just lucky," said teammate Frank Gifford. "Then I realized he was just great."

Having set dozens of league and franchise records in 11 seasons with the Giants, Tunnell, in February 1967, became the first Black athlete inducted into the Pro Football Hall of Fame and the first to play solely as a defensive back.

Emlen Tunnell eyes two prospective tacklers while making a short gain in a New York Giants–Cleveland Browns game on October 22, 1950.

During his enshrinement speech in Canton, Tunnell thanked the Mara family, his wife, teammates and friends in attendance.

"But most of all," he said in conclusion, "and the last thing before I get a little choked up here, I'd like to thank the truck driver, wherever he is, that gave me the ride over to New York."

NO. 10

And Still the Undisputed Leader ...

ot Tom Brady. Not Joe Montana. Not Dan Marino or Joe Namath.

Nor any other quarterback who might instantly pop into your head, for that matter.

On September 28, the opening day of the 1951 season, Norm Van Brocklin threw for 554 yards, a record that still stands after more than 70 years. The 554 yards passing eclipsed Johnny Lujack's existing mark of 468 yards.

With designated starter Bob Waterfield sidelined by an injury, Van Brocklin went to work as the Los Angeles Rams' quarterback. LA torched the New York Yanks 54–14, with Van Brocklin completing 27 passes for an average of 20.5 yards per hookup.

Van Brocklin connected that day for five touchdowns — four to Elroy "Crazylegs" Hirsch. He also ran one in himself.

The 6-foot-1, 190-pound Van Brocklin, nicknamed the "Dutchman," was renowned as a hard-edged, hot-tempered athlete. And that style served him well. The product of Eagle Butte, South Dakota, played in nine Pro Bowls during his on-field career and is one of only two quarterbacks to lead multiple franchises to championship titles.

Of the modern-era QBs who have passed for more than 500 yards, Ben Roethlisberger did it four times, three times during the regular season and once in the playoffs. Drew Brees and Tom Brady each managed it twice, with Brady doing it in both a regular-season and postseason game. Brees hit his total in a pair of regular-season matchups. And Atlanta's Kirk Cousins added his name to the list when he threw for 509 yards in a 36–30 overtime win against the Tampa Bay Buccaneers in October 2024.

But Van Brocklin, who spent the first nine of his dozen NFL seasons in LA before moving on to the Philadelphia Eagles, remains the standard for yardage in a single game.

"The word desire," he once said of his success, "is overworked, but a quarterback must have desire. He can't discourage easily. He has to be confident that if he just hangs on, against adversity, he finally can get the job done."

Other Quarterbacks Who've Surpassed the 500-yard Mark

Name	Team	Season	Number of yards
Y.A. Tittle	New York Giants	1962	505
Vince Ferragamo	Los Angeles Rams	1982	509
Phil Simms	New York Giants	1985	513
Dan Marino	Miami Dolphins	1988	521
Warren Moon	Houston Oilers	1990	527
Boomer Esiason	Arizona Cardinals	1996	522
Elvis Grbac	Kansas City Chiefs	2000	504
Drew Brees	New Orleans Saints	2006; 2015	510; 505
Ben Roethlisberger	Pittsburgh Steelers	2009; 2014; 2017; 2021	503; 522; 506; 501
Tom Brady	New England Patriots	2011; 2018	517; 505
Matthew Stafford	Detroit Lions	2012	520
Eli Manning	New York Giants	2012	510
Matt Schaub	Houston Texans	2012	527
Tony Romo	Dallas Cowboys	2013	506
Philip Rivers	San Diego Chargers	2015	503
Matt Ryan	Atlanta Falcons	2016	503
Derek Carr	Oakland Raiders	2016	513
Jared Goff	Los Angeles Rams	2019	517
Dak Prescott	Dallas Cowboys	2020	502
Joe Burrow	Cincinnati Bengals	2021	525
Kirk Cousins	Atlanta Falcons	2024	509

While other quarterbacks have managed to surpass the 500-yard mark, no one has managed to throw for 555.

In retirement, Van Brocklin coached both the Minnesota Vikings and the Atlanta Falcons. In his final years, he suffered from a number of ailments, including a brain tumor. After its removal, he told the press, "It was a brain transplant. They gave me a sports writer's brain, to make sure I got one that hadn't been used."

The Dutchman died of a heart attack, aged 57, in 1983, a dozen years after being enshrined in Canton at the Pro Football Hall of Fame.

NO. 11

Bobby Layne and the Detroit Curse

During eight full seasons in Detroit, quarterback Bobby Layne played a major part in three NFL championship runs.

He played in four Pro Bowls in that span and was selected First Team All-Pro twice.

Layne embodied the pro football player of that era. Two of his nicknames were the "Blond Bomber" and the "Gadabout Gladiator."

"The secret to a happy life," he said once, "is to run out of cash and air at the same time."

Along with this famous line: "If I want a beer or two, I'm not going to sneak around some back-alley joint. I'm going to walk in the front door of the best place in town."

In short, Layne was a hard-playing, hard-living, no-saying-sorry guy. "When Bobby Layne said 'block,' you blocked, and when he said 'drink,' you drank," recalled Lions teammate Yale Lary.

"He demanded only the best and would accept only the best," Detroit halfback/kicker Doak Walker recalled. "Here is a man who was a general on the field and off the field in every way. He was the greatest two-minute quarterback I have ever seen."

Layne took the game personally. And he took the way he was treated by the game personally, too.

So when, following the second game of the 1958 season, on October 6, it was announced Detroit coach George Wilson had traded his future Hall-of-Fame quarterback to the Pittsburgh Steelers, the team that had originally drafted him a decade before (Pittsburgh boss and former Lions coach Buddy Parker was instrumental in setting up the exchange) for QB Earl Morrall and two draft picks, Layne was one unhappy individual. He felt betrayed.

Bobby Layne gets ready to throw the ball in a game against the Green Bay Packers on October 5, 1958. This was Layne's last game as a Detroit Lion.

On his way out of the dressing room after cleaning out his locker at Briggs Stadium, he reportedly snarled a line that has gone into urban NFL legend: "This team will not win for another 50 years."

Bad blood? Spur-of-the-moment sound bite? An utter fabrication?

No one knows for certain.

Why, it's often asked, was Layne traded from a place where he'd had such success? Some blamed an underlying power struggle between coach and star player as the primary reason. Others felt that at 31, coming off an injury — a broken ankle that kept him out of the NFL championship game — and the team receiving a 24-year Morrall in exchange at the position was a step toward the future.

Whatever, Layne would spend four-plus years in Pittsburgh endeavoring to bring that city a championship. But it wasn't to be.

He retired after the 1962 season and died of cardiac arrest in 1986 at the age of 59. He left behind many fans and memories. Many old-timers cite him as the toughest quarterback ever. He won three championships. He threw for close to 27,000 yards. He was inducted at Canton in 1967.

Yet the legend of the curse is what persists. In October 2022, fellow Hall of Famer Peyton Manning dedicated an episode of his ESPN series *Peyton's Places* to it. Manning filled a bathtub with whiskey — in place of water, owing to Layne's fondness for a snort or two — along with a cup of salt, at old Ford Field. He and actor Jeff Daniels then performed a chant in an attempt to exorcise the curse.

It didn't work.

In 2024 the Lions set a slew of franchise records, including a gaudy, best-ever 15-2 regular-season record, and hopes were understandably high to end the championship drought, but Detroit was dismantled 45–31 by the underdog Washington Commanders at Ford Field in the divisional round playoff game.

So is the curse fact? Fiction? Fantasy?

What we do know for certain is that as of 2025, the title frustration that Layne is reported to have promised the Lions has stretched to an agonizing 67 years. And counting.

NO. 12 Viewer Discretion Is Advised

The first pro football game to be televised was the clash between the Philadelphia Eagles and the Brooklyn Dodgers on October 22, 1939. Brooklyn won the game 23–14. The crowd at Ebbets Field that day numbered 13,057.

But the main outside interest was in this crazy, new magic box that beamed images out of nowhere into (a few, at least) people's homes. Television was in its infancy.

It was later joked that the viewing audience was approximately 1,000 New Yorkers who owned a TV set at the time. The game was broadcast on NBC, then in its early days as a network.

Allen "Skip" Walz, a former Golden Gloves boxing champion, called the game. There were fewer than 10 crew members for the broadcast, and Walz was reportedly paid $25 to be a part of history.

Recordings of television broadcasts would not begin for another nine years, although some claim that portions of that first game still exist on film. Walz remembered that two cameras were used by NBC.

"I'd sit with my chin on the rail in the mezzanine, and the camera was over my shoulder," he'd later reminisce to the Pro Football Hall of Fame. "I did my own spotting, and when the play moved up and down the field, on punts or kickoffs, I'd point to tell the cameraman what I'd be talking about.

"It was late in October on a cloudy day and when the sun crept behind the stadium there wasn't enough light for the cameras. The picture would get darker and darker and eventually it would be completely blank and we'd revert to a radio broadcast."

Regular TV broadcasts of games began after World War II, with the first NFL championship to be televised being the 1948 match between the Eagles and the Chicago Cardinals. Since then, television and the NFL have, of course, become inseparable bedfellows.

In 2021, the league received a $110-billion, 10-year contract from its broadcasting rightsholders.

THE 1960s

Contents

No. 13 He Came Clean and Said Yes 35

No. 14 The Last of the 60-minute Men 38

No. 15 Breaking Football's Final Color Barrier 39

No. 16 Where the Immortals Live On 41

No. 17 Wrong Way Marshall 43

No. 18 America's Sweethearts 44

No. 19 Here's Mud in Your Eye 45

No. 20 Ode to a Unique Friendship 47

No. 21 Lucky No. 7 48

No. 22 The GOAT Running Back 50

No. 23 The Lost Weekend 52

No. 24 Have a Drink on Him 53

No. 25 Frozen in Time 54

No. 26 Mr. Lombardi Goes to Washington 56

No. 27 Good Drama, Bad Call 57

No. 28 He Had a Crystal Ball 58

No. 29 The Super Bowl Is Born, Officially 60

No. 30 Now That's a Scorekeeper's Nightmare 61

No. 31 Aaaaaand ... Action! 62

He Came Clean and Said Yes

NO. 13

ALVIN RAY "PETE" Rozelle always believed he was the right man at the right time. It only took the NFL's governors' 23 ballots and a week of squabbling to decide he was indeed the right man for the commissioner's job.

What ultimately turned the governors in Rozelle's favor in January 1960 was both his youthful confidence and his life experiences. At 33, he was a Depression-era kid whose father, Ray, tried to run a grocery store in Lynwood, California, but failed. (Ray Rozelle eventually got a job with Alcoa.)

Rozelle attended Compton High School, where he played tennis and basketball and graduated in 1944. That same year, he was drafted by the U.S. Navy and served 18 months on an oil tanker in the Pacific Ocean. Returning to California, he enrolled at Compton Community College and worked as a part-time public relations assistant with the LA Rams. After a slew of P.R. and marketing-related jobs, including one for the 1956 Summer Olympics in Melbourne, Australia, Rozelle was named the Rams' general manager in 1957.

It took just three years for him to transform the team's financial plight into a tangible success, which is what excited the NFL's governors looking for a more permanent successor to commissioner Bert Bell, who had died of a heart attack in 1959. The governors wanted a new-age thinker to improve TV ratings, increase franchise stability and value and expand into markets that the upstart AFL was about to claim. While he waited for the governors to decide his fate, Rozelle occupied a nearby men's room, saying he washed his hands every time someone came in because he didn't want to appear suspicious. When he was finally hired, he joked he came to them with clean hands.

They wouldn't stay that way for long.

Rozelle's first on-the-job crisis had to do with the AFL, a fledgling operation financed by a collection of millionaires who dubbed themselves the Foolish Club. Leading the Foolish was Lamar Hunt, the son of filthy rich H.L. Hunt, who had been ignored in his bids to buy an NFL team.

Pete Rozelle, center, is congratulated on his appointment as NFL commissioner by league owners and executives on January 27, 1960. From left to right: Chicago Bears owner George Halas, Philadelphia Eagles president Frank McNamee, Rozelle, Washington Redskins owner George Preston Marshall and Eagles executive vice president Joe Donoghue.

That sparked a full-on war that saw the two leagues share media markets in New York, Los Angeles, Oakland (San Francisco) and Dallas. The other AFL teams were in Boston, Buffalo, Denver and Houston, none of which had an NFL presence but looked to fill a football void. (There would be some shuffling to that list of teams. Hunt moved his Dallas outfit to Kansas City, and a group of owners wanting an AFL team for Minnesota got their wish by signing up with the NFL.)

In the struggle to make things work, the AFL kept putting the NFL's feet to the fire. Al Davis, the Oakland Raiders' co-owner, was named the AFL's commissioner. It was his stated belief that signing NFL free agents was "a situation that called for some constant pressure to be put on the other side."

An example of that pressure had come a year before Davis rose to the commissioner's chair, when the AFL's New York Jets signed University of Alabama quarterback Joe Namath for a staggering $427,000 over three years.

That pretty much broke the bank. By 1966 the NFL and AFL had spent $7 million on their draft picks. The two leagues, represented by the NFL's Tex Schramm and the AFL's Lamar Hunt, met privately to discuss a potential merger. Rozelle then took control of the negotiations and did the best he could by agreeing to 10 AFL teams entering the NFL. It was also agreed that the winners of the AFL would meet the winners of the NFL in a championship game in 1967. This would later become known as the Super Bowl.

Under Rozelle's authority, the NFL grew quickly. The league would jump to 26 teams by 1970. Rozelle was able to coax more money from the TV networks by playing them off each other. He made sure the revenue was shared, which was good since revenue was going up and fast. In 1967 he sold the broadcast rights to the Super Bowl to CBS and NBC for $9.5 million for four years.

Rozelle wasn't done with TV. It was his desire to take the game into prime time, to see the players shining under the lights and viewership increasing. So it was that *Monday Night Football* came to be, and it may have been Rozelle's greatest accomplishment. It ran for 36 years on ABC. The game with the highest rating was the December 2, 1985, clash between the Chicago Bears and Miami Dolphins. According to the site Pro Football Talk, 29.6 percent of all TVs, on or off, were showing the game. The game was watched by more than 39 million viewers.

Not everything Rozelle touched turned to gold, though. He and the NFL failed to block the Raiders' move from Oakland to LA. There was also the NFL Players Association strike of 1982, which saw the regular season reduced from 16 games to 9. Once resolved, the players received better preseason and postseason pay, along with a career transition program said to be the first of its kind in professional sports. During the rough patches, he was called the "arrogant czar." It was a play on the "boy czar" nickname he was given when he was first hired by the NFL.

But the totality of his work made Rozelle the prototype commissioner, a caretaker who made the game great with his vision for the future while managing the fires of the moment. He retired in November 1989 and the Super Bowl MVP award was named in his honor. He was 70 years old when he passed away from a brain tumor at his home in Rancho Santa Fe, California.

NO. 14

The Last of the 60-minute Men

CHUCK BEDNARIK'S NICKNAME was "Concrete Charlie," and it suited him on and off the field.

In the off-season, he sold concrete in his home state of Pennsylvania. During the football season, he played center on offense and hammered out openings for the Philadelphia Eagles' running backs. Then when the Philly defense went to work, Bednarik switched to linebacker. His reputation was built on ferocity and the way he hit, especially the one that blew up Frank Gifford of the New York Giants. Gifford was running toward the sideline with his head turned away from the incoming 6-foot-3, 233-pound Bednarik. Completely blindsided, Gifford took the hit, then hit the ground, where he lay motionless while Bednarik pranced over him, saying, "This f★★★★★ game is over."

Gifford's teammates and his wife feared he was seriously injured, perhaps even worse. Philadelphia defensive back Tom Brookshier said the impact of the hit "sounded like an axe splitting a piece of wood." Diagnosed with a concussion, Gifford was sidelined for the balance of the 1960 season and for all of 1961.

Concrete Charlie made another epic hit in the 1960 NFL championship game between the Eagles and the Green Bay Packers. With the Packers threatening to score late in the fourth quarter, Bednarik wrapped up fullback Jim Taylor and held him down until the game clock ran out, giving the Eagles a 17–13 win. It gave Bednarik one of his two NFL titles and enhanced his reputation as a guy you didn't want to mess with.

"Everybody reminds me of it and I'm happy they remind me of it," Bednarik once reminisced. "I'm proud and delighted to have played in that game."

He had that same attitude with him when he served as a waist gunner on a B-24 bomber in World War II. (The plane was known as the Flying Coffin because of its single exit located at the rear of the plane, which made it difficult for the crew to leave the plane in an emergency.) Bednarik flew in 30 combat missions over Germany and was awarded the Air Medal with four oak leaf clusters and four battle stars. Following the war, he enrolled at the University of Pennsylvania, where the Eagles made him the first pick in the 1949 draft, ahead of such future stars as Norm Van Brocklin, Doak Walker and George Blanda.

Bednarik spent 14 seasons in the NFL and was named to the NFL's 100th Anniversary Team. In 1967 he was inducted into the Pro Football Hall of Fame.

Concrete Charlie held little regard for the modern players, saying "They suck air after five plays."

"For what my generation did and went through and so forth, and what these glamor boys earn for what little they play, it's a joke," he complained. "Is it football? Are you guys football players? Is that what they call football? It's not iron-man football, where you stay on the field for 60 minutes. Everybody! We were iron men. Not a bunch of pussyfoots."

Bednarik was considered the true two-way warrior, given the positions he mastered. He was the last NFL starter to play regularly on both offense and defense until Deion Sanders, who was both a receiver and a cornerback, did so in 1996.

Not that Concrete Charlie was in the least impressed.

"The positions I played, every play, I was making contact, not like that ... Deion Sanders," Bednarik sniped. "He couldn't tackle my wife. He's back there dancing out there instead of hitting."

Unrepentant to the end, Bednarik was 89 when he died in March 2015. He missed only three games during a 14-year career.

Breaking Football's Final Color Barrier

NO. 15

WASHINGTON REDSKINS' OWNER George Preston Marshall had to be forced to have a Black player on his team by the U.S. government.

Syracuse star running back Ernie Davis was to be the first pick in the 1962 NFL Draft, a selection Marshall couldn't bring himself to make, let alone say Davis' name. He had his coach do that.

Davis had excelled at Syracuse, convinced by Cleveland Browns great Jim Brown to join that program. Nicknamed the "Elmira Express," he was named an All-American two years running and helped the Orangemen win a Cotton Bowl and a national title.

During his collegiate career, he broke Brown's career records in rushing (2,386 yards), all-purpose yardage (3,414), scoring (220 points) and touchdowns (35).

John F. Kennedy was a fan. The president had followed Davis' career and set up a meeting in New York when Davis was there to receive the Heisman Trophy. Later that year, when the town Davis called home, Elmira, New York, celebrated the historic Heisman, Kennedy sent a telegram of congratulation: "Seldom has an athlete been more deserving of such a tribute. Your high standards of performance, on the field and off the field, reflect the finest qualities of competition, sportsmanship and citizenship. The nation has bestowed upon you its highest awards for your athletic achievements. It's a privilege for me to address you tonight as an outstanding American, and as a worthy example of our youth. I salute you."

Davis was an obvious No. 1 selection at the draft. But such was Marshall's anti-integration stance that U.S. Secretary of the Interior Stewart Udall and Attorney General Robert Kennedy forced the issue with an ultimatum: unless Marshall signed a Black player, the government would revoke the Redskins' 30-year lease on D.C. Stadium.

Marshall reluctantly relented, but after being drafted by the Redskins, Davis, understanding he wasn't wanted in the nation's capital, was quickly dealt to the Cleveland Browns — where his mentor and idol, Brown, held sway — for Bobby Mitchell, ironically another Black athlete who went on to have a fine NFL career.

Davis then signed a record rookie contract worth $200,000 for three seasons. But later that year he was diagnosed with leukemia, triggering a rift between Brown, who wanted only the best for his protégé's health, and owner Art Modell, who brought in doctors claiming Davis was well enough to play given that, at the time, the leukemia was in remission.

Davis' only appearance at Cleveland Stadium came at a preseason game on August 18, 1962, when he ran onto the field as a spotlight followed him.

Tragically, Ernie Davis died on May 18, 1963, without ever playing in an NFL game. He was 23. In 1979 he was posthumously enshrined in the College Football Hall of Fame.

Where the Immortals Live On

NO. **16**

CANTON, OHIO, THE county seat of Stark County, lies approximately 60 miles south of Cleveland and 20 miles south of Akron. The population today is a shade over 69,000. Not exactly New York City or Chicago.

For the longest time, Canton was known primarily as the home of William McKinley, the 25th President of the United States. McKinley is buried in Canton and his Presidential Library is located there.

And then, in 1963, the Pro Football Hall of Fame opened its doors in an unexpected location, greatly expanding the city's profile.

Why Canton, exactly? Well, because the NFL was actually founded there in 1920 as the American Professional Football Association, because the long-defunct Canton Bears — led by future Hall of Famer Jim Thorpe — were the game's first repeat champions, and mainly because the community badly wanted it located there, fundraising $400,000 (over $4 million in today's dollars) to help get the original structure built.

The Hall's website reports that the idea was pushed forward to the public in the city as early as late 1959 by the *Canton Repository* newspaper, imploring its readers with this headline: "Pro Football Needs A Hall of Fame and Logical Site is Here."

As of 2024, 378 of the game's greatest coaches, players, administrators and innovators — everyone from Night Train Lane to Bronko Nagurski and Johnny U, Jerry Rice to Jim Brown, Lynn Swann and Sweetness to Butkus, L.T. and Lombardi to Halas and Shula — are enshrined there.

The original Hall covered only two rooms and 19,000 square feet of interior space. Today, the size has mushroomed to 118,000 square feet.

A charter class of 17 members was enshrined on September 7, 1963. Enshrinees are selected by a 50-person committee, largely made up of media members.

A view of the Pro Football Hall of Fame in Canton, Ohio.

The Hall's building was expanded first in 1971, and subsequently in 1978, 1995 and 2012–2013, while other major exhibit gallery renovations were added in 2003, 2008 and 2009. In February 2024, an $80 million expansion project was announced.

A popular tourist destination for Canton since its inception, the Hall welcomed its 10 millionth fan in 2016, and 208,000 fans visited the facility in 2023.

Wrong Way Marshall

NO. **17**

If you watch it on YouTube you can't help but wonder: "What was he thinking?"

There's Jim Marshall, the Minnesota Vikings' athletic defensive end, and there's a fumble by the San Francisco 49ers' Billy Kilmer. In one motion, Marshall picks up the ball and sees nothing but an open field — so he runs full out into all that openness. All the way to the end zone. The Minnesota end zone. This prompts the TV announcer to shriek, "He's going the wrong way. Marshall's going the wrong way; thinks he's scored a touchdown; he has scored a safety." Thus was born the Viking who would forever be known as Wrong Way Marshall, the guy who got all turned around and thought he scored a TD until a San Francisco player came up to him and said thanks for the two points.

"That's when I knew I really messed up this time," Marshall said long after his October 25, 1964, miscue. The irony of that play was that Marshall was one of the best, most reliable defensive linemen of his era. At 6-foot-4 and 248 pounds, he was a bit undersized but made up for that with quickness and agility. His career stats include 130.5 QB sacks stretched out over 282 starts. He also showed he had a nose for the football, recovering a then-record 30 fumbles. It was a big reason why he was twice named to the Pro Bowl and helped Minnesota reach four Super Bowls. Still, it took some time for him to get past his San Francisco faux pas.

"That [fumble] is something I would rather forget, although it's not going to happen," Marshall told *Viking Update* in 2001. "In the years I spent playing football, trying to play the best I could play, to have that all overshadowed by one play … it's not the ideal situation."

The true measure of Marshall's character came through in what happened after the wrong-way run back. Not only did he get right back into the fray, he forced a fumble that linemate Carl Eller recovered and ran the right way into the 49ers' end zone. The Vikings went on to win 27–22.

NO.

18 America's Sweethearts

To refer to Tex Schramm as "an innovator" would be a gross understatement. Among the myriad innovations that the Dallas Cowboys' long-time president and general manager championed in terms of game play and rules are instant replay, computer technology, the 30-second clock and using headsets in a quarterback's helmet for hearing plays. A shrewd promoter and marketer, Schramm was also always on the lookout for ways to get his organization in the news and add to the spice of its game environment.

So when, during a Cowboys and Atlanta Falcons game in 1967, a buxom 20-year-old, short-skirted stripper and film actress named Bubbles Cash elicited an uproar in the stands at the Cotton Bowl, sashaying down a staircase on the 50-yard stripe with a mound of cotton candy in each hand, Schramm was one of the thousands on hand who took notice.

The city of Dallas was besotted, and Bubbles became an instant celebrity who was quickly installed as the Cowboys' "unofficial mascot."

As one of the first to meld sports and the entertainment industry, and with Bubbles Cash in mind, Schramm decided in 1970 to change the team's cheerleading persona — creating an all-female squad and altering the style of the routines from the accustomed acrobatic fare to a more showbiz, dance-oriented flavor.

A choreographer was brought aboard to streamline the routines. Skirts were replaced by the now-trademark hot pants. Tryouts proved to be a publicity blitz.

As their fame began to explode, the cheerleading team produced a poster and soon became so well-known and sought-after that they were featured on popular television shows, had two made-for-TV movies centered around them, made USO tours to entertain troops overseas, produced their own reality TV series, were the subject of a Netflix documentary and have sold all manner of merchandise — from calendars and T-shirts to trading cards.

And just like the team they supported, the cheer squad would go on to become synonymous with the Cowboys brand and tagged with a rather expansive nickname mirroring that of the team they cheered for: America's Sweethearts.

Here's Mud in Your Eye

NO. 19

Chicago Bears rookie running back Gale Sayers scored an astounding six TDs in one game on December 12, 1965, against the San Francisco 49ers.

At Wrigley Field, on mud thick enough to slow a charging elephant, Sayers had a wondrous afternoon, scoring on an 80-yard pass play in the first quarter before scoring on runs of 21, 7, 50 and 1 yard. For good measure, he added an 85-yard punt return before sitting out much of the fourth quarter.

"I can still see the 49ers sloshing around in the mud," Sayers told the *Los Angeles Times* in 1985. "It seemed like everyone was slipping but me."

Sayers had 113 rushing yards and four touchdowns on only nine carries, 89 receiving yards and a touchdown on two catches, and 134 yards and a score on five punt returns.

The final tab was 61–20 for the Bears and 336 all-purpose yards for Sayers.

Teammate Mike Ditka was left awestruck.

"It was really incredible, something to behold," Ditka told the Bears' website in 2015. "Probably the greatest single game, I think, in the history of the game."

The six majors tied the NFL record set by Dub Jones of the Cleveland Browns in 1951. New Orleans Saints running back Alvin Kamara joined the six-TD club in 2020.

Sayers finished the 1965 season with 2,272 all-purpose yards, a rookie record that stood for 23 years until Tim Brown was drafted by the LA Raiders and rang up 2,317. For the season, Sayers also scored 22 touchdowns — 14 by rushing, 6 by receiving and 1 each on a punt and kickoff return. That rookie record still stands.

For his sensational efforts, Sayers was named NFL Rookie of the Year and a First Team All-Pro.

"Give me 18 inches of daylight. That's all I need," Sayers fondly recalled. "I had a lot of moves. I just put everything I could into a run."

But in November of 1968, Sayers tried to make a move on San Francisco defensive back Kermit Alexander only to be cut down by a hard tackle. The

Gale Sayers on a 96-yard touchdown run against the Minnesota Vikings on October 17, 1965.

diagnosis was not good; Sayers had suffered torn ligaments in his right knee and had to miss the balance of the season. Through an arduous amount of rehabilitation, the man known as the "Kansas Comet" was able to win the Comeback Player of the Year award in 1969. But that burst of speed on a change of direction was never the same.

In 1970 he had surgery on his other knee, and managed to play two games in 1971, but just like that, his career was over after just 68 games.

In 1977, at age 34, Sayers — who died in 2020 after suffering from dementia for several years — became, and remains, the youngest player ever inducted into the Pro Football Hall of Fame.

Ode to a Unique Friendship

NO. 20

On November 30, 1971, *Brian's Song* debuted on ABC's Movie of the Week. The biographical film detailed the unlikely friendship between two men of sharply differing temperaments and racial backgrounds playing for the Chicago Bears: star running back Gale Sayers (played by Billy Dee Williams) and undrafted free-agent full back / running back Brian Piccolo (played by James Caan).

Piccolo had died the year before the film's release from embryonal cell carcinoma, an aggressive form of germ cell testicular cancer that had spread. He was only 26 years old.

The emotional tone of the film was set in its opening narration, read by actor Jack Warden, playing Bears coach George Halas: "This is the story about two men, one named Gale Sayers, the other Brian Piccolo. They came from different parts of the country, they competed for the same job. One was white, the other Black. … Our story is about how they came to know each other, fight each other and help each other. Ernest Hemingway said that every true story ends in death. Well, this is a true story."

Players of that era were still segregated by race for hotel-room assignments on road trips. The Bears decided to go against the norm and reassigned roommates by position. Running back was the only position in the 1967 edition with one Black and one white player, respectively.

The moment in the movie that struck a resounding chord with the nation came when Sayers — who had overcome knee surgery the year before to lead the league in rushing — dedicated the 1970 George S. Halas Courage Award to his friend and roommate, then in a hospital fighting for his life.

An emotional Sayers, his voice cracking, said that night in tribute during the awards dinner: "You flatter me by giving me this award, but I'll tell you here and now that I accept it for Brian Piccolo … I accept it tonight, but I'll present it to Brian tomorrow. I love Brian Piccolo. And I'd like all of you to love him, too. And tonight, when you hit your knees, ask God to love him, too."

Piccolo died less than a month later, in the early morning of June 16, 1970. Following his death, the Brian Piccolo Cancer Research Fund was founded, spurred by a group of friends, teammates and family members. Helped by the efforts of the fund, the cancer that took his life now has a 95 percent cure rate, according to the research fund's website.

Based on a part of Sayers' autobiography, *I Am Third*, Brian's Song was watched by 55 million viewers on its first showing — half of the U.S. population that owned televisions at that time. It is widely regarded as one of the finest sports movies ever made, a touchstone for football fans of a generation and an enduring reminder of the unbending power of friendship.

NO. 21 Lucky No. 7

Joe Kapp's throws were rarely tight spirals. He never gripped the ball by its laces and his back-pedaling in the pocket was less than classic.

Told that, he replied, "Classics are for Greeks."

Kapp may have come from Mexican-German-American stock, not Greek, but one Sunday afternoon he offered up a passing classic, doing something that Tom Brady never did. Nor Broadway Joe. Nor Montana, Marino or Johnny U, for that matter.

On September 28, 1969, Kapp tied an NFL record by throwing seven touchdown tosses in a game. What made his showing so stunning was the fact that the Minnesota Vikings' QB was arguably the worst passer in the NFL.

Frills were for others. Kapp was mainly tough as old shoe leather. During the length of his career in both the NFL and CFL, he was all about attitude and team. He was the one to deliver the "40 for 60" slogan to the Vikings, meaning 40 men giving their best for 60 minutes. As a leader, he was formidable. As a passer, not exactly textbook or film room material.

"I figure that I can't scramble like [Fran] Tarkenton, but I've got to move around now and then," he told the *Minneapolis Star* in 1967. "I mean, I may not run with much speed, but I make up for it with a lot of desperation."

Once featured on a *Sports Illustrated* cover with the headline "The Toughest Chicano," Kapp personified the indomitable spirit of the game.

"Success," he once said, "is living up to your potential. That's all. Wake up and go with a smile after life. Live it, enjoy it, taste, smell it, feel it."

That particular afternoon in '69, Joe Kapp enjoyed life immensely, shredding none other than the defending NFL champion Baltimore Colts' defense for 449 yards on 28 completions in 43 attempts. And, of course, those seven TDs.

The Vikings won in a cakewalk, 52–14.

In league history, beginning with Sid Luckman in 1943, eight quarterbacks have tossed seven scoring passes in a single game, the most recent being Drew Brees of the New Orleans Saints in 2015.

But none, it's safe to say, have done it with quite the same unlikely, ungainly panache as the Toughest Chicano.

Quarterbacks Who Have Thrown Seven Touchdowns in One Game

Player	Date	Team	Opponent	Result
Sid Luckman	November 14, 1943	Chicago Bears	New York Giants	W, 56–7
Adrian Burk	October 17, 1954	Philadelphia Eagles	Washington Redskins	W, 49–21
George Blanda	November 19, 1961	Houston Oilers	New York Titans	W, 49–13
Y.A. Tittle	October 28, 1962	New York Giants	Washington Redskins	W, 49–34
Joe Kapp	September 28, 1969	Minnesota Vikings	Baltimore Colts	W, 52–14
Peyton Manning	September 5, 2013	Denver Broncos	Baltimore Ravens	W, 49–27
Nick Foles	November 3, 2013	Philadelphia Eagles	Oakland Raiders	W, 49–20
Drew Brees	November 1, 2015	New Orleans Saints	New York Giants	W, 52–49

NO. 22 The GOAT Running Back

To this day, nearly 60 years after he walked away from the Cleveland Browns, there are football fans and historians who say that of all the outstanding running backs to have performed on the NFL stage, Jim Brown was the greatest.

Absolutely, unequivocally.

Consider this: In 1965, Brown led the league in rushing (one of eight times he'd accomplish the feat) with 1,544 yards. That was 677 *more* than runner-up Gale Sayers of the Bears. He was a punisher and an absolute pile-driver of a runner. "Make sure," Brown once lectured, "[that] when anyone tackles you, he remembers how much it hurts."

Untold defensive players of the era exited the game with that feeling seared into their memory banks and the bruises to prove it.

The Sporting News published a list of football's all-time greats in 2002, and Brown came in at No. 1. Why exactly then did he retire in July of 1966 at the hardly decrepit age of 30? Because his boss, Cleveland Browns' owner, Art Modell, ordered him off a movie set in London, England, where he was filming *The Dirty Dozen*. Modell told Brown he would be fined $1,500 every week (some sources say every day) he was absent from training camp. Brown flexed his considerable will. No one told him what to do. So after nine seasons, 12,312 rushing yards, 106 touchdowns and nine consecutive Pro Bowl selections, he left the NFL knowing he could still play but chose not to. He had other things in mind.

After football, and aside from his budding film career, Brown took a deep interest in civil rights issues. Not only did he voice his concerns over how Black Americans were being mistreated, he convinced two other notable athletes — basketball greats Kareem Abdul-Jabbar and Bill Russell — to meet with heavyweight boxing champ Muhammad Ali at what became known as the Cleveland Summit. The men offered Ali their support and spoke out against the injustice of him being stripped of his title and threatened with jail

Muhammad Ali (right) visits Jim Brown (left) on the set of *The Dirty Dozen* in August 1966.

time for refusing to be drafted into the U.S. Army. Ali's refusal to join the war in Vietnam was based on his religious beliefs. Brown backed Ali even though he had served four years as a member of the U.S. Army Reserve and was discharged with the rank of captain.

A year before the 1967 Cleveland Summit, Brown had launched the Black Economic Union to help promote business opportunities for marches and protesting, and it caught the eye of the FBI, which had tried to discredit the organization and Brown as extremists. Declassified files showed the FBI had gathered evidence in the hope of incriminating Brown.

Arguably, the most incriminating material collected on Brown came from the repeated allegations that he was abusive to women. While the majority of sexual assault charges against him were dropped, one misdemeanor vandalism charge for damaging his wife's car resulted in Brown serving three months in jail after he refused to do his court-ordered counseling and community service.

In one of the few interviews he did about his jail time, Brown insisted that violence against women was never the answer nor justified. He spent his final days in his LA home with his second wife, Monique.

He died May 18, 2023, of natural causes. He was 87 and still adamant he made the right decision to retire from football when he did.

NO. 23

The Lost Weekend

On November 22, 1963, the nation — no, the world — found itself numbed, cloaked in disbelief and grief at the news that President John F. Kennedy had been assassinated in Dallas, Texas. There was no precedent for how to act, how to grieve, how to proceed.

In less than 48 hours, a full slate of games was scheduled on the NFL docket. Then in his fourth season as league commissioner, Pete Rozelle had an extremely delicate decision to make.

In search of a more close-to-the-situation opinion, he called an old classmate from his University of San Francisco years, Kennedy press secretary Pierre Salinger.

Salinger told Rozelle that he believed the president would've wanted the games to go ahead; that the distraction would provide some normalcy to a grief-stricken nation.

Rozelle agreed, and on November 24, with the loss of the president still achingly fresh, the games went ahead. Instead of providing a healthy diversion, the decision to proceed produced a tidal wave backlash of anger. Rozelle would eventually admit — at least publicly — it was his biggest regret as commissioner.

Worsening matters on that surreal afternoon, television screens were naturally blanketed with Kennedy coverage. Then, less than an hour before kick-offs around the country, accused assassin Lee Harvey Oswald was gunned down on live TV, on CBS, by nightclub owner Jack Ruby in Dallas while being arraigned.

What's forgotten is that while the rival AFL decided to cancel its schedule for that weekend, the NBA and NHL went on as scheduled, along with many college football games.

Rozelle's decision, however, did serve as an example of what not to do 38 years later, for then-commissioner Paul Tagliabue, in the aftermath of another unthinkable atrocity — the terrorist attacks on the World Trade Center and the Pentagon on September 11, 2001.

On the Thursday after that tragedy, two days following the attacks, the NFL postponed all Week 2 games.

NO. 24

Have a Drink on Him

THE GREEN BAY Packers won three consecutive NFL titles in 1965, 1966 and 1967. The last two wins came in the first two Super Bowls, before they were officially called the Super Bowl. In the 1966 title game (Super Bowl I), Green Bay rolled over the Kansas City Chiefs.

Packers receiver Max McGee didn't expect to play, so he went out the night before and toasted his team, many times. He stayed out until 6:30 a.m. and bumped into quarterback Bart Starr, who was getting ready for a game-day meeting.

McGee was so hungover he told fellow receiver Boyd Dowler, "Don't get hurt. I'm not in very good shape."

Dowler had a wonky shoulder coming into the Super Bowl and reinjured it during the game. Right on cue, the call went out for McGee, who had left his helmet in the dressing room. Wearing a lineman's helmet until his could be delivered, McGee caught seven passes for 138 yards and two touchdowns in a 35–10 Green Bay victory.

McGee's first TD was the first in Super Bowl history. He summed up his approach to football the same way he navigated his life: "When it's third and 10, you take the milk drinkers and I'll take the whiskey drinkers every time."

His quirky magnetism even managed to bewitch one of the most strait-laced people in the game's annals: Packers coach Vince Lombardi. No one else would've dared breathe — let alone speak — after an irate Lombardi stood at the front of the dressing room following a listless practice one day, held up a ball and announced, dripping with sarcasm, "This, gentlemen, is a football."

"Coach, could you slow down?" came an unmistakable voice from the back. "You're going too fast."

McGee–Lombardi stories have gone into the realm of legend. Another example? A 1968 testimonial banquet honoring the coach.

"I pulled the bread and fish thing on him," McGee recalled gleefully. "Just before the food was served — there were about four or five thousand people there — I brought out this platter and on it were five fishes — little ones — and nine loaves of bread.

"He just about rolled on the floor."

Max McGee always did love to laugh. And to make others laugh, too.

NO.

25 Frozen in Time

THE 1967 NFL championship game was quickly dubbed the "Ice Bowl" when the Green Bay Packers and Dallas Cowboys took to the frozen tundra of Lambeau Field — and discovered it was pretty much a hockey rink.

With the temperature at -13 degrees Fahrenheit, with a wind chill reaching 48 degrees below zero, Lambeau's turf-heating system went on the fritz, leaving behind moisture that froze once the field-sized tarp was rolled back. The troubles didn't end there.

The Wisconsin State University-La Crosse marching band was slated to play at halftime, but that was scrubbed when several of its members were taken to a nearby hospital for hypothermia. As for referee Norm Schachter, he was left bloodied when he had to tear his metal whistle from his frozen lips. For most of the game, the officials had to shout their commands instead of blowing their whistles.

And at one point during the CBS television broadcast, announcer Frank Gifford joked, "I'm going to have to take a bite of my coffee."

All that aside, the Packers leapt to a 14–0 lead with Boyd Dowler on the receiving end of two touchdown passes from QB Bart Starr. But then the Cowboys got hot — or at least lukewarm. Dallas scored 10 points off two Green Bay fumbles, then took a 17–14 advantage on a halfback option toss to Lance Rentzel. "The wind was really whipping us," Packers offensive lineman Jerry Kramer wrote in his book *Instant Replay.*

Starting from his own 32-yard line with less than five minutes in the fourth quarter, Starr engineered what would become a legendary 12-play drive. With less than a minute left on the clock, the Packers were scrimmaging from the Dallas 3-yard line. After two failed lunges by running back Donny Anderson, with 16 seconds remaining, Starr made good on a key block by Kramer — aided by center Ken Bowman — on Dallas defensive lineman Jethro Pugh for the successful quarterback sneak and a 21–17 win.

Prior to the snap, most people, including Dallas head coach Tom Landry, were

With seconds remaining, Green Bay quarterback Bart Starr (No. 15), protected by a block from Jerry Kramer (No. 64), charges his way into the end zone for the 1967 championship win.

sure Starr would elect for a roll-out pass play so the Packers could intentionally stop the clock (they had no timeouts left) with an incomplete pass and get in another play — either a field goal to tie or a pass/run to win — on fourth down.

Should they have failed on a run play, the game clock likely would've expired.

But plotting strategy on the sidelines before a snap that would be forever frozen in time, Starr, who had been sacked eight times during the game attempting to pass, remembered saying this to Lombardi: "Coach, the linemen can get their footing for the wedge, but the backs are slipping. I'm right there, I can just shuffle my feet and lunge in."

Lombardi replied: "Run it, and let's get the hell out of here!"

Caught on film and television, it remains one of the NFL's most iconic images. And certainly remained a touchstone for all involved.

"You play for 12 years and somebody says: 'What's your biggest moment?'" split end Boyd Dowler once reminisced. "There's absolutely no doubt about it. That was it."

In a list of the NFL's Greatest Games, the league itself slotted the Ice Bowl in at No. 3, and ESPN's *SportsCentury* ranked it as No. 6 on its list of the greatest games of the 20th century.

NO. 26

Mr. Lombardi Goes to Washington

After coaching the Packers to a second Super Bowl win in January 1968, Vince Lombardi stepped aside to move upstairs in the press box as the team's general manager, handing the coaching reins to long-time assistant Phil Bengtson.

This was a move that uber-competitive Lombardi would quickly realize was a massive mistake. Because if ever a man was built to prowl a sideline, that man was Vince Lombardi.

"After the third game of (that) season," recalled sports writer Ed Breslin, "[Lombardi] said: 'This is killing me. I just can't stand it.' I told him not to worry. I told him to relax because the season had a long way to go and maybe it would get better.

"He said: 'I know me. It'll get worse.'

"It did."

The next year, Lombardi did the unthinkable — he left Green Bay, agreeing to be part owner, GM and coach of the Redskins. The Lombardi effect was immediate, working its magic on many Redskins players, such as rookie running back Larry Brown.

"He was the first one to notice that I might have a hearing problem," recalled Brown years after retiring. "He got on me but I told him that between learning his system and reading defenses, even Einstein should forget counts sometimes. The coach smiled at that and then he told me to get a hearing test. He'd noticed that I was like 1/50th of a second late coming off my stance. He was right, like always.

"No other coach had ever noticed."

Brown had his helmet fitted with a hearing aid and would go on to fashion an eight-year NFL career, highlighted by a 1,126-yard MVP season in 1972.

The old guard weren't immune to the message, either.

"I walked into his office in Washington not knowing what to expect," conceded quarterback Sonny Jurgensen, known as a something of a free spirit. "After we shook hands, he looked at me and said, 'Sonny, I want you to be yourself. Just be what you are.' What a thing to say! Jeez, right then I felt like running into a wall, anything to let him know I would do whatever he wanted of me.

"I learned to love him. I learned more in my first five days of listening to him than I did in 12 years of listening to other coaches."

That first season in the Nation's Capital, Lombardi steered the Redskins to a 7-5-2 record, the team's first winning season in nearly a decade and a half, since 1955.

Good Drama, Bad Call

NO. 27

NBC television execs made the wrong call November 17, 1968, when they decided to leave the New York Jets–Oakland Raiders game before it was over so the network could show the movie *Heidi* in its entirety.

Oakland scored 14 points in a minute to beat the Jets. People who phoned their NBC affiliate to complain were not impressed. The whole mess was known as the "Heidi Bowl."

It began with a seemingly sound decision: NBC executives gave the much-anticipated Jets–Raiders match-up a three-hour window to do their thing. Both teams were 7-2 and had a history of nastiness. In one of their 1967 meetings, the Raiders had gone after Jets quarterback Joe Namath, hitting him hard and late and breaking his cheek bone in the process. Players from both sides did little to hide their contempt for one another, making their 1968 regular-season meeting a much anticipated event. The game most definitely lived up to that.

In a back-and-forth affair, both teams had the lead only to watch the other mount a ferocious come back. In the fourth quarter, New York's Jim Turner kicked a field goal to build a 29–22 advantage. Raiders QB Daryle Lamonica found receiver Fred Biletnikoff for a 22-yard touchdown completion to tie the game with less than four minutes left. Turner added another field goal, his fourth of the game, to put the Jets back on top with just over a minute showing on the game clock.

At that point in time, NBC officials were in full panic. The network's showing of *Heidi* was locked in for a seven o'clock Eastern start, and the two teams were showing no signs of going away quietly or quickly. A decision was made to show the game to its conclusion. But getting that message to every NBC executive involved proved to be impossible because of the thousands of phone calls pouring in from viewers who wanted to know if the game was going to be shown in its entirety or if *Heidi* would begin as scheduled. (A dedicated phone line dubbed the "Heidi phone" was later installed to inform the necessary executives about programming issues.)

Meanwhile, back at the game, the Raiders moved downfield with running back Charlie Smith scoring a touchdown on a 43-yard scoring strike from Lamonica. That put Oakland on top 36–32. There were still 42 seconds left when the Raiders kicked off to the Jets' Earl Christy, who fumbled the ball. Oakland's Preston Ridlehuber recovered the fumble and ran it in for the clinching touchdown in a 43–32 classic.

Fortunately for the Jets the payback wasn't long in coming. They beat Oakland 27–23 in the AFL championship game, then pulled the upset of all upsets, taking out the NFL champion Baltimore Colts in Super Bowl III.

NO. 28

He Had a Crystal Ball

When Joe Namath guaranteed that his New York Jets would beat the Baltimore Colts for the NFL title on January 12, 1969, the staid old guard of the NFL thought he was off his rocker.

Turned out Broadway Joe was as good a fortune teller as he was a passer.

Namath represented the new age of pro football players. He wasn't as buttoned down as most of his fellow NFL quarterbacks. He didn't wear his hair short or sport those high-top black football cleats. His shoes were low-cut and white. He paraded around in fur coats. And when it came to dealing with the media, he didn't speak in clichés. He left little to the imagination: "I like my Johnnie Walker red and my women blonde." In the 1968 Super Bowl season, he sported a Fu Manchu mustache and received $10,000 (a tidy sum at the time) to shave it off for a Schick razor promotion.

It was hard to imagine the Colts' conservative 35-year-old Johnny Unitas ever saying such a thing. Or, for that matter, growing a Fu Manchu.

The 25-year-old Namath arrived in Miami for Super Bowl III to a chorus of doubters, all claiming the Jets were about to crash land against a Baltimore team that had finished 13-1 for the regular season. They had reached a new level by beating the Minnesota Vikings 24–14 in the first round of the playoffs, then crushing the Cleveland Browns 34–0 in the NFL title game.

According to the oddsmakers, the Jets were 18-point underdogs. Tex Maule of *Sports Illustrated* had the Colts winning by 43 points. Weary of the lack of respect from the media and football fans, days before the game Namath responded to a heckler at a sports banquet in Miami who had yelled, "The Colts are going to kick your ass!" with the line, "We're going to win the game. I guarantee it."

What followed proved to be one of the biggest upsets in professional sports.

With a strong showing from running back Matt Snell, combined with a ravenous defense that produced five turnovers, the Jets fed off Namath's confidence and built a 16–0 lead by the fourth quarter. Namath didn't throw a TD pass, but he was able to keep the Colts at bay with some timely first down completions. Thirty-four-year-old Earl Morrall started for Baltimore but gave way to Unitas, who did produce a touchdown drive but that was it.

In the end, Super Bowl III was more than just a single game, one team beating another; it was a symbolic passing of the torch from one generation of QBs to the next and a moment of legitimacy for the AFL.

Joe Namath looks to pass during Super Bowl III on January 12, 1969.

The kid from Beaver Falls, Pennsylvania, named game MVP, naturally became the first quarterback to start and win a collegiate championship, a major professional league championship and a Super Bowl.

As he ran off the field to the Jets' dressing room, Namath wagged a finger in the air indicating his team was, as he'd guaranteed, No. 1.

This time there were no doubters to be heard.

NO. 29

The Super Bowl Is Born, Officially

THE FIRST FOUR Super Bowls, as they're now called, were known back then as the AFL–NFL world championship.

Some football historians have argued that it wasn't until Super Bowl V that the game earned its highly immodest "super" label.

Kansas City Chiefs owner Lamar Hunt came up with the name after watching his daughter play with the coolest toy of the day, the Wham-O Superball. Whatever the name, Hunt's Chiefs won the fourth AFL–NFL world championship game, Super Bowl IV, by pounding the Minnesota Vikings.

Counting Lessons

In case you wondered, the Super Bowl was given Roman numerals instead of numbers for clarity. Given that the championship finale was played in a different year than the regular season, the league chose not to name it based on the year. The fifth Super Bowl, for example, was played on January 17, 1971, capping the 1970 season. Labeling it Super Bowl V made it easier to identify — until it got to XXXVIII, which incidentally was won by the New England Patriots over the Carolina Panthers by a score of XXXII to XXIX.

Now That's a Scorekeeper's Nightmare

NO. 30

THE HIGHEST-SCORING NFL game in history? The Washington Redskins over the New York Giants, 72–41, on November 27, 1966. That was the kind of score normally reserved for the Harlem Globetrotters and the Washington Generals.

A colossal cavalcade of points. On that November day, a total of 16 touchdowns were scored.

Washington running back A.D. Whitfield scored three times in the first half to put his team up 27–7. But on a day when the Redskins' offense was firing on all cylinders, it was defensive back Brig Owens who stole the spotlight by scoring on a New York fumble he returned for 62 yards, then scoring again on a 60-yard interception return.

Given the 72 points Washington amassed, quarterback Sonny Jurgensen's 10-for-16-for-145 yards stat line seems impossibly modest. But he did toss three TD passes.

Perhaps the Redskins were still smarting from their 1940 wipeout, that 73–0 disaster against the Chicago Bears.

Five Highest-scoring Games in NFL History

Total Points Scored	Final Score	Winning Team	Opponent	Date
113	72-41	Washington Redskins	New York Giants	November 27, 1966
106	58-48	Cincinnati Bengals	Cleveland Browns	November 28, 2004
105	54-51	LA Rams	Kansas City Chiefs	November 19, 2018
101	52-49	New Orleans Saints	New York Giants	November 1, 2015
101	52-49	Oakland Raiders	Houston Oilers	December 22, 1963

NO. 31

Aaaaaand ... Action!

THE FUSION BETWEEN sports and entertainment began to blur long ago.

Whether you remember O.J. Simpson schlepping around the *Naked Gun* movie series as the accident-prone Officer Nordberg, Alex Karras as the ox-riding Mongo ("Mongo only pawn in game of life") in Mel Brooks' *Blazing Saddles* or Bubba Smith in *Police Academy*, the connection is there for all to see.

A handful of footballers-turned-actors have become even more synonymous with their onscreen persona as opposed to on-field exploits. Look at Carl Weathers as Apollo Creed in *Rocky*.

Some performances by retired NFLers on both film and TV have been widely lauded, such as three-time Oakland Raiders Pro Bowler Nnamdi Asomugha, whose performance in *Crescent Heights* wowed the 2017 Sundance Film Festival. Others, such as Rosey Grier in 1972's science fiction comedy *The Thing with Two Heads* (Rosey's head is one of the two, alongside Ray Milland's — you get the picture), are best left to the curious.

The small screen has over the years seen a whole slew of retired NFLers queue up, too — from Merlin Olsen's turn as a farmer for seven years on *Little House on the Prairie* to Ed Marinaro on *Hill Street Blues*, Howie Long on *Malcolm in the Middle,* Fred Dryer in the '80s crime drama *Hunter* or the ever-visible Broadway Joe Namath in a string of cameos (usually as himself) on *The Love Boat*, *Alf*, *The Brady Bunch* and *The A-Team*.

Everyone from Tom Brady to Brett Favre to Dick Butkus has had at least a short go at the acting profession.

The football/athlete–thespian dynamic actually dates all the way back to the early 1930s, when Jim Thorpe displayed his acting chops in such epics as *Battling with Buffalo Bill* and *Always Kicking*. (Thorpe would later be the subject of a movie bio himself, *Jim Thorpe – All American*, starring Burt Lancaster, released in 1951.)

Then, in the 1940s, to earn some extra cash, Woody Strode began doing bit parts in movies before his pro football career — in both the NFL and then the CFL — took off. His first appearance on the big screen was in 1941's *Sundown*, starring Gene Tierney, Bruce Cabot and George Sanders.

After returning to a film and TV career post-football, Strode landed parts in epics such as Cecil B. DeMille's 1956 *The Ten Commandments* (he got $500 a week for five weeks of emoting) and Stanley Kubrick's *Spartacus* (1960), as well as credits for another legendary director, John Ford. His work for Ford, a friend until the director's death in 1973, included classics such as *Sergeant Rutledge* (1960) and *The Man Who Shot Liberty Valance* (1962).

If players such as Thorpe and Strode should rightly be considered trail-blazers, the connection between the NFL and entertainment really sprang to life during the 1960s and '70s, as the profile of players began to explode with the increased fame born of weekly television exposure. Jim Brown spent onscreen time with, among others, Lee Marvin, Telly Savalas, John Cassavetes, et al., in *The Dirty Dozen*; Namath cozied up to Ann-Margret in *C.C. and Company*; Simpson was featured in the mega-hit *The Towering Inferno*, starring, among others, Steve McQueen and Paul Newman; and Fred "The Hammer" Williamson had a small part in *M*A*S*H* with Elliott Gould and Donald Sutherland.

Since then, there has been no end of former grid stars to be found in front of the big and small screens, from Super Bowl champ Terry Bradshaw (retired in 1984) taking roles on *Blossom*, *Malcolm in the Middle*, *King of the Hill* and *Failure to Launch* to Terry Crews segueing from six years in the NFL to a starring role on *Brooklyn Nine-Nine*, among other credits, and Travis Kelce taking his turn with a cameo appearance in Adam Sandler's *Happy Gilmore 2*.

Dwayne "The Rock" Johnson, who may not have played in the NFL but did win a national collegiate grid championship at the University of Miami in 1991, was a short-time CFLer and is now considered one of filmdom's most bankable action stars.

So the direction begun by Thorpe and Strode just keeps growing.

The 1970s

Contents

No. 32 Three in the Booth 65

No. 33 Cue the Orchestra and Strike up the Replays 66

No. 34 The Steelers Draft a Beast at Linebacker 67

No. 35 He Had the Leg for It 69

No. 36 Aging Most Splendidly 71

No. 37 Yeah, *That* John Wayne 72

No. 38 "Perfection" Personified 73

No. 39 What's in a Name? Plenty 75

No. 40 America's Team 77

No. 41 The First 2,000-yard Man 78

No. 42 "After Further Reviews ..." 80

No. 43 Heavenly Intervention 81

No. 44 On a Wing and a Prayer 83

No. 45 The Miracle at the Meadowlands 84

No. 46 A Devastating Blow 85

No. 47 Dressed for Success 87

No. 48 The Passing of a Legend 88

No. 49 A Mean Star Is Born 91

Three in the Booth

NO. 32

MONDAY NIGHT FOOTBALL first lit up the cathode rays on September 21, 1970, with ABC broadcasting the New York Jets versus the Cleveland Browns. Joe Namath was still at the top of his game, which made him the NFL's No. 1 attraction. But on this night, Cleveland got what it wanted — a 31–21 win for the home team. ABC charged advertisers $65,000 per minute.

Calling the game were three announcers who ABC figured would play off one another, challenge and entertain: Keith Jackson was the original play-by-play man, former Dallas Cowboys QB Don Meredith provided the color and singing, and the bombastic Howard Cosell said whatever he wanted.

Each had his strengths. Jackson provided the just-the-facts-ma'am element, Meredith the folksy former-player insight and Humble Howard the outsized swagger ("Arrogant, pompous, obnoxious, vain, cruel, verbose, a showoff," he once said of himself. "I have been called all these things. Of course, I am.").

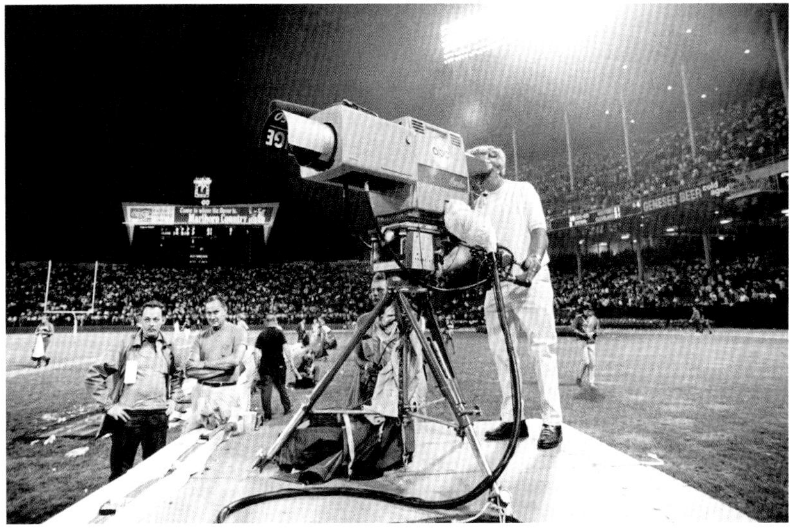

A sidelines scene during the first telecast of *Monday Night Football*. An ABC cameraman shoots the Browns–Jets matchup from Cleveland on September 21, 1970.

When former New York Giants star Frank Gifford replaced Jackson in the second season of the show's existence, proving surprisingly adept at play-by-play, things really took off.

Before long, *Monday Night Football* became a rite of passage for fans, a true phenomenon. From the signature theme music and the interplay between the three men in the booth to Meredith's slightly off-key rendition of Willie Nelson's "The Party's Over" when a game score got out of hand, the show proved to be a ratings bonanza.

Beginning in a three-network television world, *MNF* then went on to become the longest-running prime-time sports program in history.

The show was also innovative in adding an entertainment element to the game coverage. Celebrity guests — ranging from former Vice President Spiro Agnew, singer Plácido Domingo, former Beatle John Lennon, former President Bill Clinton and even Kermit the Frog — have made appearances to expand the broadcast's viewer base.

Over the decades, the broadcast team has changed to include former players and coaches, guest spots with other athletes, artists and comedians.

The rights to *MNF* currently belong to ESPN, which has been working to stop a slide in viewership numbers.

NO. 33 Cue the Orchestra and Strike up the Replays

LONG BEFORE ACTOR James Earl Jones made the "This is CNN" voiceover his own, the NFL had its own distinctive set of pipes.

John Facenda was a Philadelphia radio and TV broadcaster whose authoritative tone was described as "the Voice of God."

His rise to fame began with a chance meeting in a bar. Facenda was watching football footage on TV. He especially liked the slow-motion clips and began calling the plays in true Facenda fashion for fun. Ed Sabol, founder of NFL Films, just happened, by chance, to be in the bar at the time.

Sabol liked what he heard and asked Facenda to do an audition. It was the beginning of a beautiful partnership. The league established a promotions department with the best of its work showing game action in slow motion with symphonic music accompanied by Facenda's commanding voice.

Commissioner Rozelle had negotiated an agreement on behalf of the NFL clubs to purchase Sabol's Blair Motion Pictures, which was then renamed NFL Films. The rest is football history.

Thanks to those distinctive pipes, Facenda also dabbled in voice acting. IMDb lists his credits as *The Burglar* (starring Jayne Mansfield and Dan Duryea), *Middle Age Crazy* (starring Ann-Margret and Bruce Dern) and *The Son of Football Follies.*

Facenda died in 1984, aged 71, still voicing football highlight packages. A full 37 years after his passing, he was posthumously awarded the Pete Rozelle Radio-Television Award by the Pro Football Hall of Fame.

"For nearly 20 years, John Facenda's resonant voice was, and even today still is, synonymous with the power, strength and character of the NFL," Hall of Fame president and CEO David Baker said during a television appearance announcing the honor.

"His narration of the league's history, the legacies of those who played and coached in it and the stories of its greatest moments and memories helped generations of fans fall in love with the game and make it America's passion."

The Steelers Draft a Beast at Linebacker

NO. 34

THE PITTSBURGH STEELERS STOLE the 1974 NFL Draft by taking four future Hall of Fame players: Lynn Swann, Jack Lambert, John Stallworth and Mike Webster. It was sports writer-turned-Steelers-scout Bill Nunn who studied the four players and recommended they be selected, if available. They were available, along with defensive back Donnie Shell, a free-agent signing who went undrafted in 1974 but was good enough to be honored with a spot in the Pro Football Hall of Fame.

That amazing influx of talent quickly helped Pittsburgh become a championship team. Of the four draftees, Lambert best personified the Steelers' ultra-aggressive persona. He looked especially fearsome with his four front

Los Angeles Rams running back Wendell Tyler is taken down by Jack Lambert during Super Bowl XIV, on January 20, 1980.

teeth missing, a carryover from playing high school basketball. The toothless look emphasized his bicuspids and resulted in his nickname "Dracula in Cleats."

The Steelers scouted Lambert and, to the doubts of many, selected him with the 46th overall pick. Although they liked his mobility and attitude, they were cautious about his size (6-foot-4, 220 pounds) and had planned for him to study under veteran Henry Davis at middle linebacker. All that changed when Davis suffered a career-ending neck injury. Thrust into the starting lineup, Lambert displayed his football savvy and called the defensive signals as if he was born into the position. (Oddly enough, Lambert started off as a high school quarterback before switching to linebacker at Kent State.)

Lambert made a sudden impact on the Steelers, winning the Defensive Rookie of the Year award. It was the start to an 11-year run that included such highlights as being named Defensive Player of the Year in 1976 and winning four Super Bowls as captain of Pittsburgh's Steel Curtain.

Former Denver Broncos quarterback John Elway described his first game against Pittsburgh and seeing Lambert in full vampire mode: "He had no teeth and he was slobbering all over himself. I remember thinking, 'You can have your money back. Just get me out of here. Let me go be an accountant.'"

"I can't tell you how badly I wanted out of there," Elway said.

He couldn't have been alone in that feeling.

He Had the Leg for It

BACK AT THE dawn of the 1970s, soccer-style placekicking was just beginning to gain a foothold, so to speak, among the game's booting brigade.

But on November 8, 1970, a journeyman kicker / defensive lineman in the employ of the New Orleans Saints named Tom Dempsey put the old-school, straight-ahead kicker squarely back in the limelight.

That afternoon, Dempsey launched a last-gasp 63-yard field goal against Detroit at Tulane Stadium in the Big Easy to give the Saints a 19–17 victory over the Lions. Not only did it break the existing record held by Bert Rechichar, it obliterated it. By seven full yards.

Further igniting interest in the feat was the fact that Dempsey had been born without toes on his right foot, his kicking foot, as well as without fingers on his right hand.

There was instant talk around the NFL that Dempsey's condition was an unfair advantage because he got to wear a special custom-made shoe — costing $200 (equivalent to $1,000 in today's currency), as reported by *Sports Illustrated* in 2021 — given his clubbed foot. Later, in 1977, the NFL invoked the "Tom Dempsey Rule," citing that "any shoe that is worn by a player with an artificial limb on his kicking leg must have a kicking surface that conforms to that of a normal kicking shoe." Dempsey scoffed at the suggestion that his right foot was unfair.

"I guess if not having any toes is an unfair advantage, I have an advantage," he shot back.

Dempsey would go on to have NFL stints in Philadelphia, LA, Houston and Buffalo after leaving New Orleans the season following his record-setting boot.

Dempsey credited his parents with refusing to let him make excuses for his disability.

"I was very fortunate and my dad had a lot to do with it," Dempsey said, as reported by Pro Football History. "I remember one day I was building

Tom Dempsey moves to kick a then-record 63-yard field goal against the Detroit Lions on November 8, 1970.

something and I said, 'Dammit, I can't get this done.' And he said: 'Boy, you never say can't. You may have to do something differently, but you can do it.'"

Dempsey passed along his father's advice and was the recipient of the 1971 Pro Football Writers Association's George Halas Award, given annually to an NFL player, coach or staff member who overcomes the most adversity to succeed.

After the 63-yarder was tied on three occasions, Denver's Matt Prater broke Dempsey's record with a 64-yarder in 2013, a full 43 years later. Then Justin Tucker of the Baltimore Ravens put his name in the record books with a 66-yard field goal in 2021. Ironically, Tucker's record breaker beat Detroit by a 19–17 score, just as Dempsey's had 51 years earlier.

Suffering from dementia, Dempsey died of complications connected to COVID-19 at 73 years old in 2020. He made only 159 field goals during 11 years in the NFL (career leader Adam Vinatieri has 599), but he won't soon be forgotten.

The famous custom shoe, used in his moment forever frozen in time, now resides in Canton, Ohio, at the Pro Football Hall of Fame.

NO. 36

Aging Most Splendidly

On January 4, 1976, George Blanda, the Slovak-born son of a Pittsburgh coalminer, played his final game for the Oakland Raiders against the rival Pittsburgh Steelers. Blanda spanned 26 seasons of pro football, with time in both the AFL and NFL. That afternoon, he kicked a 41-yard field goal and an extra point for the Raiders during their AFC Championship game against the Steelers. He remains the oldest player ever to participate in an NFL game, at 48 years, 109 days.

In 1970, at 43, Blanda turned back time with a near-miraculous showing over a five-week span. It started against Pittsburgh in the fifth game of the regular schedule, with Blanda taking over for the injured Daryle Lamonica and

The NFL's Oldest Players

Player	Position	Last Season/ Team	Birthdate and Retirement Age
George Blanda	QB-K	1975 Oakland Raiders	September 17, 1927; 48
Morten Andersen	K	2007 Atlanta Falcons	August 19, 1960; 47
Ben Agajanian	K	1964 San Diego Chargers	August 28, 1919; 45
Gary Anderson	K	2004 Tennessee Titans	July 16, 1959; 45
Tom Brady	QB	2022 Tampa Bay Buccaneers	August 3, 1977; 45
John Carney	K	2010 New Orleans Saints	April 20, 1964; 45
Bobby Marshall	E	1925 Duluth Kelleys	March 12, 1880; 45
John Nesser	G-T	1921 Columbus Panhandles	April 25, 1876; 45

throwing three touchdown passes. The following week, he kicked a 48-yard field goal with three seconds remaining to earn a 17–17 tie with the Kansas City Chiefs. The following week, he came off the bench to throw a touchdown pass to tie the Cleveland Browns 20–20 with 1:34 remaining on the game clock before kicking a 53-yard field goal with 0:03 left for a 23–20 win. The following week, Blanda took over for Lamonica in the fourth quarter and threw a TD pass to Fred Biletnikoff with 2:28 left in the game to beat the Denver Broncos, 24–19. The following week, Blanda kicked a 16-yard field goal in the final seconds to defeat the San Diego Chargers.

Blanda's amazing season came to an end in the AFC Championship game against the Baltimore Colts when he rallied the Raiders by passing for 271 yards and two TDs and adding a 48-yard field goal. It wasn't enough to beat the Colts.

Blanda lasted another five seasons before playing in his final game, the 1975 AFC Championship game in Pittsburgh. He kicked a 41-yard field goal and added an extra point in a 16–10 loss to the Steelers. The following August, he was released by the Raiders and retired.

NO. 37 Yeah, *That* John Wayne

The Atlanta Falcons drafted John Wayne, also known as "the Duke." Rooster Cogburn. The Man Who Shot Liberty Valance. The Ringo Kid himself.

With the 1972 NFL Draft set at 17 rounds, every player picked that low had little chance of making the team. Falcons coach Norm Van Brocklin asked his scouts, "Do we want the toughest S.O.B. in the draft?" The Falcons called in their pick to the NFL office as "John Wayne from Fort Apache State."

Okay, so the Duke had played football for the USC Trojans before a broken collarbone ended his athletic career. But, c'mon — in February 1972 Wayne was 64 years old.

Speculation had it NFL Commissioner Pete Rozelle replied with an emphatic "No way, pilgrim."

NO. 38

"Perfection" Personified

Surrealist artist Salvador Dali once said, "Have no fear of perfection — you'll never reach it."

Given that to be literally true, at least, the 1972 Miami Dolphins may not have been perfect, but they were damn fine and, more importantly, unbeaten: 17-0.

In the crazy world of professional football, that's as close as anyone can ever aspire to perfection.

Through that season for the ages, the Don Shula–coached Dolphins outscored their opposition 385–171 over 14 regular-season games, pitching three defensive shutouts in the process.

Perhaps most amazingly, they did much of the winning without their leader, quarterback and future Hall of Fame Bob Griese.

Griese suffered a dislocated ankle and a broken fibula in the fifth game of the season. The injury did not require surgery but confined Griese to a brace for six weeks. He was replaced behind center by veteran Earl Morrall, then 38, who was signed in the offseason as an insurance policy.

It would be a policy that paid amazing dividends: Morrall went 9-0 in the regular season, then started, and won, the team's two AFC playoff games.

"There would not be an undefeated team on the books if it weren't for Earl Morrall," Griese, who would return for Super Bowl VII versus Washington, later acknowledged.

And while that '72 edition of the Dolphins had its share of star offensive players — Larry Csonka, Jim Kiick, Griese and Paul Warfield — the team was best known for its "No-Name Defense," which sent several starters to the Pro Football Hall of Fame.

Players like defensive captain Nick Buoniconti, defensive safeties Dick Anderson and Jake Scott and defensive tackle Manny Fernandez weren't anonymous for long after '72. Seeking redemption for a 24–3 Super Bowl loss the year before at the hands of the Dallas Cowboys, the Dolphins relied

Head coach Don Shula is hoisted up after his Miami Dolphins defended their perfect season with a victory at Super Bowl VII on January 14, 1973.

on that stubborn, if largely undervalued, defensive resistance to suffocate Billy Kilmer and the Redskins' attack in Super Bowl VII. Star Washington running back Larry Brown was limited to just 72 yards on 22 carries. Scott snared two interceptions to be named game MVP.

Washington only found the end zone late, with just over two minutes remaining, thanks to Miami kicker Garo Yepremian's infamous gaffe: Yepremian's kick attempt was blocked, and instead of falling on the loose ball, he picked it up and threw a pass, which was intercepted by Redskins cornerback Mike Bass and returned 49 yards for a touchdown.

The Dolphins held tight for a 14–7 victory, their first Super Bowl title and an unbeaten season.

Since then, teams have occasionally teased at piecing together an unbeaten campaign but have come up short. Most famously, in Super Bowl XLII the New England Patriots had a chance at it only to lose to the New York Giants on a Krazy Glue helmet catch by David Tyree.

Which, over a half-century later, leaves the '72 Dolphins as the one, the only.

Perhaps they were not "perfect" in the most literal sense of the word. But unbeaten, inarguably. And that will do just fine, thanks.

What's in a Name? Plenty

NO. 39

During the 1960s and 1970s, it wasn't enough to have a good defense.

What overtook the NFL was the need to have a clever, hopefully threatening, nickname for that defense.

The LA Rams had the right idea. Their defensive front featured Lamar Lundy, Rosey Grier, Merlin Olsen and Deacon Jones and was known as "the Fearsome Foursome."

That handle for a four-man defensive front was originally conceived in 1957, when the tabloid newspaper *New York Daily News* ran an article about the Giants' defensive line consisting of ends Andy Robustelli and Jim Katcavage and tackles Rosey Grier (more about him later) and Dick Modzelewski with a headline that read, "A Fearsome Foursome."

Front fours in Detroit and San Diego of the AFL were also half-heartedly dubbed "Fearsome."

The legendary group to be tagged with the nickname solidified in Los Angeles when the aforementioned Grier arrived in 1963 via trade from the Giants. It was then that NFL quarterbacks began taking out larger-than-usual insurance policies.

No less an authority on defensive punishment than Dick Butkus would label them "the most dominant line in football history."

The line even battled (albeit good-naturedly) among themselves; Grier and Jones constantly debated over who exactly made the head-slap fashionable. Outlawed today, the slap was a tuning-fork whack upside the helmet to throw an offensive lineman off, before Jones, a sensational combination of size, strength and speed, would steam around the befuddled tackle and make a beeline for the QB.

"(Grier) may have invented it but I popularized and perfected it," the Deacon, never one to miss a chance at self-publicity, boasted to the *LA Times* in 1985.

A tear in his Achilles tendon forced Grier into retirement in 1967, and he was replaced in the Foursome by Roger Brown, acquired from the Detroit Lions. The group didn't miss a beat, surrendering only 196 points during the season of Brown's arrival over the 14-game schedule, or 14 per. That was also the year Jones coined the term "sack" for taking down a quarterback behind the line of scrimmage. He compared it to the sack of a city in wartime.

In '67, Jones would record 26 "sacks."

These were unofficial, of course, as the sack didn't become a recognized league stat until 1982.

By 1969 both Brown and Lundy had been replaced as starters in the front wall, leaving only Jones and Olsen from the original quartet. But the fame of the Fearsome Foursome nickname had taken hold in the imagination of football fans with the dominance of the Jones-Grier-Olsen-Lundy quartet.

Notable Nicknames

The popularity of the "Fearsome Foursome" moniker would lead to other memorable names for defensive units, such as the Purple People Eaters, the Doomsday Defense, the No-Name Defense, the Orange Crush, the Steel Curtain, the Gritz Blitz and the New York Sack Exchange, to name but a few.

America's Team

NO. **40**

LOVE 'EM OR loathe 'em, mention the nickname "America's Team" somewhere in conversation and every football fan knows precisely which franchise you're talking about.

Oh, fans of the Green Bay Packers and New England Patriots might put up a bit of a squawk, but the Dallas Cowboys feel they have an exclusive copyright.

Bob Ryan, now VP and editor-in-chief of NFL Films, actually coined the phrase while planning the Dallas Cowboys' 1978 season recap video.

"I saw all these fans in away stadiums (wearing Cowboys gear)," recalled Ryan. "Hey, they're the most popular team in the country. How can I use that? Why don't we call them 'America's Team?'"

Catchy, right?

Adding to the allure, Dallas was in full swagger at the time, in the midst of an NFL-record 20-seasons-with-a-winning-record streak, appearing in 12 conference championship games and five Super Bowls during that remarkable span.

So, when play-by-play man Pat Summerall introduced the Cowboys with the moniker "America's Team" during the telecast of their 1979 opener versus the St. Louis Cardinals, it stuck in the public consciousness — either a source of pride or disdain, depending on your rooting interests.

And does still, to this day.

Ironically, but unsurprisingly, old-school coach Tom Landry was at first dead-set against the nickname, feeling its rather grandiose implication would provide extra incentive to opponents. But club president Tex Schramm, a shrewd marketer who made sure that his team played in the marquee games such as on Thanksgiving Day and *Monday Night Football*, immediately fell helmet over heels in love with the title.

The stoic Landry, and Cowboys fans everywhere, quickly did, too.

NO.
41

The First 2,000-yard Man

Buffalo Bills offensive center Mike Montler reportedly was the person to tag him with the nickname "the Juice."

On December 16, 1973, Orenthal James Simpson became the first running back to breach the 2,000-yard barrier with a 7-yard carry in the final regular-season game versus the New York Jets.

In the midst of a blizzard at Shea Stadium in New York, he tore the Jets asunder for 200 yards to finish with 2,003 yards on the season, 140 more than legend Jim Brown's record set a decade earlier.

Simpson said later he felt as if he was "floating," that afternoon. "I was in the locker room all by myself right before the game ended," he said back then.

O.J. Simpson runs through the New York Jets line on December 16, 1973. That game, he surpassed the single-season 2,000-yard mark — a gold standard for running backs to this day.

"I started walking around thinking how I couldn't wish to do anything more or be anyone else. I was part of the history of the game. If I did nothing else in my life, I'd made my mark."

Simpson would, of course, go from fame to infamy a couple of decades later. In his highly publicized 1995 murder trial, he was found not guilty of killing his ex-wife Nicole Brown Simpson and Ronald Goldman.

On the field, Simpson was, before injuries hit, a unique blend of speed, elusiveness and power. How explosive was his 1973 showcase? Well, he rushed for over 100 yards in 11 games and averaged an astonishing 143 yards per start. Simpson's O-line that year was dubbed the "Electric Company" for turning on the "Juice."

And it later came out that cracking the 2,000 barrier had been the goal all along.

"We got a 1,000 in the first seven (games)," Simpson told NBC midway through the 1973 campaign. "We'll go for another 1,000 in the next seven."

Eight other men have ascended the 2,000-yard Everest since then, most recently Saquon Barkley of the Philadelphia Eagles in 2024, at 2,005 yards. LA Rams' Eric Dickerson holds the yardage record at 2,105, set in 1984. But the indisputable facts remain: O.J. Simpson was the first and he accomplished the feat in a 14-game season. The others had 16.

The 2,000-yard Club

Player	Season	Team	Yards	Number of Games
O.J. Simpson	1973	Buffalo Bills	2,003	14
Eric Dickerson	1984	LA Rams	2,105	16
Barry Sanders	1997	Detroit Lions	2,053	16
Terrell Davis	1998	Denver Broncos	2,008	16
Jamal Lewis	2003	Baltimore Ravens	2,066	16
Chris Johnson	2009	Tennessee Titans	2,006	16
Adrian Peterson	2012	Minnesota Vikings	2,097	16
Derrick Henry	2020	Tennessee Titans	2,027	16
Saquon Barkley	2024	Philadelphia Eagles	2,005	16

NO. 42

"After Further Reviews ..."

THE NFL TINKERED with using instant replay as far back as 1976. It didn't like it. Too many time delays.

NFL Football Operations reports that the initial replay review involved Art McNally, the then-director of officiating. McNally was curious as to how long a video review would delay a game. So during a *Monday Night Football* clash between the Dallas Cowboys and the Buffalo Bills, McNally brought a video camera and a stopwatch into the press box at Rich Stadium to find out.

He saw a missed call on a play involving Bills' running back O.J. Simpson that could have been corrected via a replay review.

McNally may have been sold on the innovation, but others weren't. Still, the seed had been sown in the minds of the football establishment.

In 1978 the league tried again, this time in preseason games, to see if it was worth the effort and cost of more cameras to cover all the angles. After an eight-game preseason audition in 1985, support increased but the implementation of replay narrowly failed by vote.

Prior to the 1986 season, with growing concern that a bad call could cost a team come playoff time, owners voted 23-4-1 in favor of adopting the limited use of instant replay that year. Twenty-one votes were needed to pass.

After even more fits and restarts, the NFL's governors finally got serious about things in the mid-1990s.

Advancement in technology, changes in equipment and format along with the establishment of the Art McNally GameDay Central in the league's New York headquarters to oversee replay issues have all helped in upgrading the results.

It hasn't by any means been a smooth ride, but numbers calculated by the NFL show that since 1999 41 percent of the replay reviews have overturned the original call on the field.

It's better, more consistent officiating through technology, and it's here to stay.

NO. 43

Heavenly Intervention

THE IMMACULATE RECEPTION. Just mention it in passing and you see the drama play out in your mind's eye yet again. In dreamy slow-motion, of course.

In the dying seconds of the 1972 AFC divisional playoff game, rookie Pittsburgh running back Franco Harris snagged a deflected pass and ran all the way to the Oakland Raiders' end zone, as well as into history.

On fourth-and-10 with 22 seconds remaining and the ball on their own 40-yard line, the Steelers were trailing 7–6. All hope appeared lost for the home team, which was making its first playoff appearance since 1947.

So dire was the outlook that Pittsburgh linebacker Jack Ham had reportedly begun cutting off his tape on the sidelines in submission. Steelers owner Art Rooney had already left his box for the elevator to field level and the inevitable post-playoff-loss sorrow.

Franco Harris dodges a tackle by Oakland Raiders' Jimmy Warren as he runs for a touchdown after catching a deflected pass. The moment was dubbed the "Immaculate Reception."

And then …

It was christened the "Immaculate Reception" by Steelers fan Michael Ord during post-victory revelry at a local bar and elevated into the lexicon by announcer Myron Cope. The Raiders and their fans dubbed it the "Immaculate Deception," insisting the pass had been deflected by Steelers running back John Fuqua to Harris, which would have made it an illegal catch.

However, officials determined the ball glanced off defender Jack Tatum and ricocheted to Harris, who took it 60 yards to the end zone as fans cascaded out of their seats and onto the field.

The Steelers had somehow won, 13–7.

Harris insisted years later that in the huddle prior to the snap he hadn't given up hope.

"I'm saying to myself: Franco, this will probably be the last play of the season," Harris told *The Athletic* in 2022, shortly before his passing at age 72, "Play it to the end. Play it to the end."

Harris, of course, had already become wildly popular during his freshman year in Steeltown, rushing for 1,055 yards and 10 touchdowns (he would later be named NFL Offensive Rookie of the Year). Local fans Al Vento and Tony Stagno had formed "Franco's Italian Army" to cheer on Harris, the son of an African American father and an Italian American mother. Games at Three Rivers Stadium featured the Army outfitted in World War II helmets, drinking Italian wine and feasting on homemade Italian cuisine in the stands.

The Immaculate Reception immediately upgraded Harris' status to legendary among Pittsburgh sports aficionados. One of several can-you-believe-it plays of the decade, this moment would go on to be voted the greatest in NFL history in 2020 during the league's 100th-anniversary season.

Ol' Blue Eyes, singer Frank Sinatra, a fairly famous Italian American himself, was awarded membership as an honorary one-star general in Franco's Italian Army.

On a Wing and a Prayer

NO. **44**

THE DALLAS COWBOYS beat the Minnesota Vikings on a last-play, 50-yard touchdown pass from Roger Staubach to receiver Drew Pearson on December 28, 1975.

Staubach was asked about the play and explained it this way, "I closed my eyes and said a Hail Mary."

A catch phrase was born.

There have been literally dozens of last-play long bombs in the NFL, with mixed results. Some of the most memorable include these moments:

Jacksonville Jaguars quarterback David Garrard staring at 50 yards for the winning touchdown and just three seconds left on the game clock. He lofted a pass into the Houston end zone, where Texans defensive back Glover Quin batted the ball away from the Jags' intended receiver, Mike Sims-Walker — right into the hands of Jacksonville's Mike Thomas at the 1-yard line. Thomas ran it in for a 31–24 celebration on November 14, 2010.

Green Bay QB Aaron Rodgers threw a 61-yard dart into the heart of the Detroit Lions on December 3, 2015. For at least one player it was déjà vu all over again. Glover Quin, once again playing deep, was on the field for the Lions when Rodgers completed his throw to Richard Rodgers II, a former basketball player who used his jump-ball skills to catch the pass. For inspiration, Richard Rodgers may have thought of his father, Rodgers Sr., who had played a key role in "The Play." It happened in the November 20, 1982, game between the University of California, Berkeley Golden Bears and the Stanford Cardinal. On what was the last play of the game, the Bears transformed a kickoff return into a five-lateral act of improbability, with Rodgers Sr. twice handling the ball before Kevin Moen ran it into the Stanford end zone and crashed into a Cardinal marching band trombonist named Gary Tyrrell. (The Stanford band and spectators alike had come onto the field thinking the game was over before Moen's touchdown.)

To this day, that kickoff return is known as "The Play," and Tyrrell's battered trombone is enshrined in the College Football Hall of Fame in Atlanta, Georgia, to commemorate that moment.

NO. 45

The Miracle at the Meadowlands

THE PHILADELPHIA EAGLES' 1978 playoff chances looked ready for a toe tag.

They trailed the home team, the New York Giants, 17–12 with 31 seconds left in the fourth quarter. Giants quarterback Joe Pisarcik should have ended matters by kneeling with the ball and letting the clock wind down to zero.

The Eagles had no more timeouts to call. Instead, Pisarcik botched a handoff to fullback Larry Csonka and then tried to recover his fumble. The ball bounced perfectly to a speeding Herman Edwards, who ran 26 yards for the winning points.

Prior to the play, Edwards noticed Pisarcik and Csonka glancing at one another and guessed something completely unexpected was up. He inched closer to the line of scrimmage.

Herman Edwards (No. 46) pounces on the ball fumbled by New York Giants' Joe Pisarcik (No. 9). The Philadelphia Eagles would go on to win the game 19–17 off of that fumbled play.

Victory Formation

Now, of course, taking a knee is a regular occurrence known as the "victory formation." This type of play became more common after the Miracle at the Meadowlands.

"When I saw the ball being bobbled, my curiosity kinda rose," Edwards explained to *Sports Illustrated*. "Once it hit his hip and I saw the ball getting ready to hit the ground, my thought process was: I've gotta get it on the first bounce.

"You do these drills that the coaches teach you, like fall on the fumble. That was never even a thought. I just thought: Get it on the first bounce and run it in for a touchdown."

Cue a blooper reel highlight moment for all time.

The Eagles were ecstatic; the Giants too stunned to say much of anything. They fired their offensive coordinator, Bob Gibson, the next morning. He wasn't a fan of a QB being surrounded by his teammates, taking the snap and dropping to one knee.

Following the Miracle (or the Debacle, depending on your rooting interests), the Giants dropped three of their final four games to finish 6-10. Head coach John McVay, his entire staff, general manager Andy Robustelli and the rest of his front office joined Gibson in looking for work.

All triggered by one "what-were-you-thinking?" decision. Pisarcik, strangely enough, signed with the Eagles in 1980 and lasted five seasons before retiring.

A Devastating Blow

NO. **46**

For Darryl Stingley, life was on the upswing. The 26-year-old receiver had spent five seasons in the NFL and was becoming a key cog in the New England Patriots' machinery. Awaiting his signature at the team's office was a contract extension that would make him one of the highest-paid pass catchers in the league. It was all there for the likable veteran — and then it was taken away. All of it.

It happened on a routine play in a routine preseason game on August 12, 1978. Stingley burst off the line of scrimmage, then cut to his left for a pass through the heart of the Oakland Raiders' defense. As he leaned forward to catch the ball, a figure dressed in silver and black appeared in an instant with only one thought in mind — to hit his target as hard as possible.

Jack Tatum had a reputation for being a heavy hitter. Conrad Dobler, a former NFL offensive lineman with his own reputation for being a player who ignored the rules, said this about Tatum: "Some defensive backs covered receivers. Jack buried them." Tatum zeroed in on Stingley and rammed his shoulder pads into Stingley's helmet. The collision compressed Stingley's spinal cord, breaking the fourth and fifth cervical vertebrae. The end result was ruinous. Stingley would spend the rest of his life as a quadriplegic.

Technically, there was nothing wrong with Tatum's hit. It was not deemed illegal at the time. But, partly in response to Stingley's injury, the NFL changed its rules to restrict what amounted to a dangerous practice, such as late hits and, later, hits to the head.

What drew even more attention to the Tatum/Stingley incident was Tatum's apparent lack of compassion for leaving his victim sprawled motionless on the ground. Stingley was widely quoted as saying Tatum had never apologized for his actions. In fact, Tatum wrote a book entitled *They Call Me Assassin*, which played up his image as a football player intent on creating mayhem. The closest he came to an apology was admitting, "When the reality of Stingley's injury hit me with its full impact, I was shattered. To think that my tackle broke another man's neck and killed his future." Raiders head coach John Madden would say of Tatum in 2010 that "It was something that ate on him his whole life."

While hospitalized, Stingley was visited by Raiders offensive lineman Gene Upshaw and Madden. Upshaw helped Stingley get his benefits from the NFL Players Association.

A year after the hit, Tatum said, "It's one of those things where you have to keep playing and work it out within yourself, and I think I'm finally playing really good ball for the Raiders." Asked what he'd say to Stingley if given the chance, Tatum answered, "I wish him a full and speedy recovery. I wish him well."

Tatum finished his career with 37 interceptions for 736 return yards and 10 fumble recoveries for an additional 164 yards. Then life played a cruel trick on him, too. He lost all the toes on his left foot in 2003 due to complications from diabetes. He eventually lost his left leg below the knee. To help those fellow sufferers, he established the Jack Tatum Fund for Youthful Diabetes, which financed diabetes research.

Tatum died in Oakland on July 27, 2010, after a heart attack. Stingley died three years earlier from heart disease and pneumonia. Tatum was 61; Stingley was only 55.

Dressed for Success

NO. 47

While the Pro Football Hall of Fame's enshrinement process has been ongoing yearly since 1963, the signature item representing the honor only came along a full decade and a half later.

Since 1978, one of the highlights of any induction ceremony in Canton has been the presentation of the handcrafted, gold-colored, custom-made, one-of-a-kind Hall of Fame blazers, produced since their inception by the Dallas-based Haggar Clothing Co. (Inductees are also presented with a commemorative ring.)

A detailed look at the gold-colored material and insignia of the famous Pro Football Hall of Fame blazers.

The Hall's website details that each jacket takes 90 days just to weave, and the production process, from start to completion, requires two months. In 2019 the actual cost of producing the jacket was reported at $1,500. But to that select number who own them, they're priceless.

In case you're wondering, the jackets feature hopsack wool, sharp lapels and two large waist pockets. Each one's interior features custom lining and a specially printed woven label that includes the enshrinee's name, class year and induction number.

What makes them even more unique is the golden hue of the fabric, a blend so secretive that it hasn't been cataloged with any color registry. So there can be no copies.

The NFL Alumni Association originally suggested the idea of gold, forever marking anyone who owns a jacket as being part of the "gold standard of football." The symbolic color association is along the lines of the much-coveted traditional green jacket presented each year to the Masters golf champion at Augusta, Georgia.

Whoever receives one of the jackets fully understands the select company they've joined. "It's bigger than me," Buffalo Bills wide receiver Andre Reed told the *Canton Repository* upon receiving his jacket at the 2014 enshrinement ceremonies. "It's just not what I did as an athlete, it represents ... all the things that sports is about.

"It's just a piece of cloth, but it's a special piece of cloth that the greatest in the game get to wear. You can't just go to Nordstrom and say, 'Can you duplicate this gold jacket here?'"

NO. 48 The Passing of a Legend

When Vince Lombardi told his family they were leaving New York so he could become head coach of the Green Bay Packers, his daughter, Susan, was flummoxed when the city wasn't even shown on the map she had consulted.

"Don't worry," her father assured her. "When I'm done, it will be on the map."

Truer words have rarely been spoken.

The coming of Lombardi to Green Bay, Wisconsin, proved to be one of the greatest stories in NFL history. A certifiable workaholic with a keen yet often brutal approach to dealing with his players, Lombardi was a complex man, driven by an insatiable need to be the best — and then be better than that.

He drove his players to their physical and emotional limits, and because of that they enjoyed unparalleled success: five NFL championships in seven years, including three in a row, along with two Super Bowls. That amazing run earned Green Bay the moniker "Titletown, USA." It was precisely what the Packers' governors had hoped for when they signed Vincent Thomas Lombardi in 1959.

Lombardi had set his mind on becoming a head coach in the NFL. After a stellar playing career at Fordham University, where he was one of the fabled Seven Blocks of Granite, he served as the team's offensive assistant coach. He moved on to the U.S. Military Academy at West Point and worked with the Army offense. In 1954, he accepted an assistant coach's position with the New York Giants, joining a staff that included Tom Landry, the eventual head coach of the Dallas Cowboys. It was his time with the Giants that helped prepare Lombardi for the Green Bay offer, where he demanded — and got — full autonomy as head coach and general manager.

Green Bay Packers' Gary Knafelc (No. 84), Dan Currie (No. 58), Hank Gremminger (No. 46) and Jerry Kramer (No. 64) give coach Vince Lombardi a victory ride after the Packers defeated the Los Angeles Rams 35–21 on December 17, 1960.

The Packers, talented but young and leaderless, found Lombardi to be a horror show of a taskmaster. He would run some fitness drills until the players were vomiting and passing out. In their first season under him, the Pack won seven of 12 games. In 1960, Green Bay advanced to the NFL title game but lost to the Philadelphia Eagles. It was after that defeat that Lombardi vowed to his players that they would never again lose a championship game. Through the next two seasons, the Packers played the Giants for the league title and won both times, 37–0 in 1961 and 16–7 in 1962.

After a pair of second-place finishes, Green Bay returned to the championship final, beating the Cleveland Browns in 1965, the Dallas Cowboys in 1966 and again in 1967's famed Ice Bowl. In beating the Cowboys, Lombardi then took each of the first two Super Bowls to ensure the NFL's supremacy over the fledgling AFL's Kansas City Chiefs and Oakland Raiders.

At that point in time, Lombardi chose to concentrate on his GM duties and appointed defensive assistant Phil Bengtson as head coach. The move was short-lived for Lombardi, who was released from his Green Bay contract to sign with the Washington Redskins.

Just as he had with the Packers, Lombardi guided the Redskins to a winning record in his first season as coach, 7-5-2.

Lombardi was equally progressive when it came to race and sexual orientation. With the Redskins, he advocated for former receiver Bobby Mitchell to be appointed to the team's front office, making him the first Black executive in the NFL. Lombardi was against all kinds of discrimination and told Washington receiver Jerry Smith that he was not going to be judged on being gay but on what he could do as a player.

By 1970, Lombardi's health began to fail. A proctoscopy found the cancer in him to be terminal. Near the end he told long-time family friend Father Timothy Moore, "Tim, I'm not scared to die. I'm not afraid to meet my God now. But what I do regret is that there is so damn much left to be done here on earth."

Vince Lombardi passed away on September 3, 1970. He was 57. In Green Bay and New Jersey, schools, streets and football fields were named after him, as, later, was the Super Bowl trophy.

He had fulfilled his promise and put Titletown on the map.

A Mean Star Is Born

NO. 49

LEGEND HAS IT that Mean Joe Greene had to drink 18 16-ounce bottles of Coke before he got it right, before he flipped his uniform to the kid who would co-star in arguably the most memorable TV commercial in Super Bowl history.

Aside from selling a lot of Coke, the Mean Joe ad was a 60-second mini-drama that had a young white kid (child actor Tom Okon, then nine years old) giving his Coke to Greene, who was walking down the tunnel dressing-room-bound after sustaining an injury.

Greene then tosses his game-worn No. 75 Pittsburgh Steelers jersey to the kid.

"Wow! Thanks, Mean Joe!" says Okon reverently.

The commercial's working title was "Hey Kid, Catch!" and was part of Coca-Cola's "Have a Coke and a Smile" ad campaign of the late 1970s. It made Greene the first Black man to promote a national brand.

As for Mean Joe, it helped soften his image as a surly D-lineman who'd start fights on the field just because he could. It's worth noting that the commercial actually made its debut during a *Monday Night Football* broadcast after October 1, 1979, but really gained traction after multiple showings nearly four months later, during Super Bowl XIV (featuring Greene and his Pittsburgh Steelers, who defeated the LA Rams 31–19).

The game, of course, was a huge TV draw, garnering an estimated 76.2 million viewers.

The cost of a 30-second commercial was a (then) cool $222,000. "Hey Kid, Catch!" was 60 seconds long. After the torrent of publicity and kudos, Coke undoubtedly felt the cost was more than worthwhile. The ad would go on to win a Clio Award. Greene and Okon reunited for the first time since the filming in 2016 as part of CBS's *Super Bowl's Greatest Commercials* special.

And as for the legend of the 18 Cokes washed down before Greene got it right, it must have been true. When he finished one of his re-takes, he had to burp. So he did.

Repeatedly.

THE 1980s

Contents

No. 50 Forever a Bear 93

No. 51 This, Most Definitely, Is Not for the Squeamish 95

No. 52 Stickum-up 97

No. 53 The Drive, Denver-style 98

No. 54 The Catch 100

No. 55 "An Unspeakable Tragedy" 102

No. 56 Long-distance Delivery 103

No. 57 Chicago's 1985 Bears 105

No. 58 The Iceman Cometh 107

No. 59 The West Coast Offense 108

No. 60 The Drive, San Francisco-style 109

No. 61 When Nothing Made the News 111

No. 62 The New England Snow Job 112

No. 63 Not Good for Business 114

No. 64 The Best, Bar None 115

No. 65 NFL Madden-ess 117

Forever a Bear

NO. 50

IF IT WASN'T for George Halas, Chicago's pro football team might still be named after a corn starch manufacturer, the Chicago Staleys.

Thankfully, the man who spent six decades as owner and 40 of those years as head coach knew what best suited the local sports fan.

"If baseball players are cubs," he said, "then football players are bears."

And with that, the Chicago Bears were born, and George Halas was on his way to earning his *nom de football*, Papa Bear.

Few men in the NFL have been as synonymous with one team and one city as Halas was with the Bears. He did it all — play for them, recruit for them, pick their team colors, coach and manage them. He welcomed those tasks when approached by A.E. Staley, who ran the Decatur Staleys as an independent football team and was looking for someone to take over the operation.

Halas paid the $100 franchise fee to the American Pro Football Association and received $5,000 from Staley to move the team from Decatur, Illinois, to Chicago, where he agreed to keep the Staley team name (though only for a year). The Staleys won the 1921 APFA championship, then switched to being the Bears for the first official season of the NFL. Among the many highlights of Halas' career was the pursuit and signing of Red Grange and Bronko Nagurski, who helped the Bears win the 1932 and 1933 NFL championships. Chicago went on to win four more titles in the 1940s, the most memorable coming in 1940 when the Bears mauled the Washington Redskins, 73–0. The game got so one-sided that the on-field officials asked Chicago to run plays after scoring their touchdowns instead of kicking extra points. Why? Because the officials were running out of footballs.

Halas would go on to coach the Bears to 324 wins, a total that stood as an NFL benchmark for nearly three decades until Don Shula bettered it with his career count of 347. Halas also won six NFL championships, according to his Pro Football Hall of Fame biography.

An Unlikely Ally

The Chicago Bears and Green Bay Packers became natural rivals given the proximity of the cities as well as both being NFL founding members. But when the Packers needed help, they had no better ally than Papa Bear. In 1956 Green Bay held a referendum on whether it should finance a new stadium for its team. Halas went to Green Bay and implored its citizens to vote in favor of supporting a new 32,000-plus-seat facility or else they would lose their team. The vote was overwhelmingly in favor of the project known as Green Bay (New) City Stadium. In 1965 the stadium was renamed Lambeau Field after team founder Curly Lambeau. He named the team the Packers after acquiring $500 in financing from the Indian Packing Company. Within eight years of its opening, Lambeau Field was expanded to accommodate 50,000 spectators.

Chicago-born and reared, he mirrored the city of his birth — tough and indomitable. Even the boos of the fans at stadiums the Bears were visiting amused him.

"San Francisco has always been my favorite booing city," he once mused. "I don't mean the people boo louder or longer, but there is a very special intimacy. When they boo you, you know they mean you. Music, that's what it is to me.

"One time in Kezar Stadium, they gave me a standing boo."

George Halas was one of the first 17 inductees named to the Pro Football Hall of Fame in 1963.

Papa Bear passed away on Halloween in 1983. Where else but in Chicago?

"He *was* the National Football League," lauded NFL commissioner Pete Rozelle. "Its founder, the driving force that sustained it during struggling pioneer years, the owner–coach–innovator whose dynamic Bear teams triggered public acceptance of the NFL and the revered elder statesman whose vision and vitality were pivotal in the league's growth."

Halas was 88 at his passing.

This, Most Definitely, Is Not for the Squeamish

NO. 51

On November 18, 1985, in a game between the New York Giants and the Washington Redskins, a hard-charging Lawrence Taylor took aim at Joe Theismann and came at the Washington quarterback on a full-out blitz.

While being tackled, Theismann's right leg got caught at an awkward angle and snapped under the combined weight of the Giants' star linebacker and teammate Harry Carson. One of his bones pierced the skin under the kneecap.

Taylor took one look at Theismann's compound fracture and began frantically waving for the Redskins' medical staff.

"I knew he was hurt when I heard him under the pile yelling and I

Redskins' athletic trainers and players surround Joe Theismann immediately following his career-ending leg injury.

understood," Taylor wrote in his autobiography *My Giant Life*. "That's why I tried to get everybody off him and get some help for him. I knew when you're sitting on the bottom of the pile — I don't care if it's a toe sprain, or an ankle sprain, I don't care what it is — it seems like forever, like the people on top of you are never going to figure it out. All you want is the people to get off of you and to get some help. And to breathe again."

Replays of the tackle were kept to a minimum. On air, play-by-play man Frank Gifford told his TV audience: "And again, we'll look at it with the reverse angle, one more time, and I suggest, if your stomach is weak, you just don't watch."

On the ambulance ride to the hospital, Theismann was accompanied by his girlfriend at the time, actress Cathy Lee Crosby, who told *People* magazine that to try and keep his spirits up she "joked that his punting game was finished."

Sadly, it was Theismann, the quarterback, who was finished. He'd battled to reach the NFL after a stint in the Canadian Football League and been part of Washington's Super Bowl XVII–winning team.

"I was always told that I was too small, too skinny, too slow, not tough enough," he once reminisced. "I never ever believed what people told me."

Psychologically, as well as physically, the injury proved devastating for the 36-year-old, in his 12th season as a Redskin. That play would be the last of his NFL career, and a compound fracture of the tibia and fibula led to insufficient bone growth, making his right leg shorter than his left.

He tried to launch a comeback in 1986 but failed a physical, after which he segued into broadcasting, a career he'd dabbled in while playing. For a few years he clung to the hope of one day being able to get back out on the field.

So, understandably, he lapsed into a "why me?" state of despair. But after a period, upon reflection, Theismann saw his misfortune as a chance to grow and become a better man.

"That night, that was divine intervention. I was heading down a path where my ego was getting the best of me," Theismann said on the *Pat McAfee Show* in 2023. "I thought I was the [guy] they couldn't be without ... After I got hurt it gave me a chance to be introspective and look at the person I was becoming as opposed to the person I wanted to be. I want to be able to help people.

"I want to be able to help other people achieve success."

And in 2005, after two decades of flat-out refusal, he was finally able to sit down and watch a replay of the incident.

Stickum-up

NO. 52

NFL OFFICIALS TOOK one glance at Oakland Raiders cornerback Lester Hayes and said, "This guy needs to clean up his act."

Hayes covered everything, from his hands to his pants to his socks, with Stickum until it was dripping off him, and he credited it for his success.

Oakland receiver Fred Biletnikoff introduced Hayes to the yellow-colored, glue-like gunk, and it proved to be a magical pairing. In 1980 Hayes made 13 interceptions, one less than the single-season record set by Dick "Night Train" Lane in 1952. But consider this: Hayes had four picks called back due to Oakland penalties. And in the playoffs, he added five more in three games.

Altogether, he could have taken the single-season record of 22 to other worldly heights. Regardless, he was rightfully voted NFL Defensive Player of the Year.

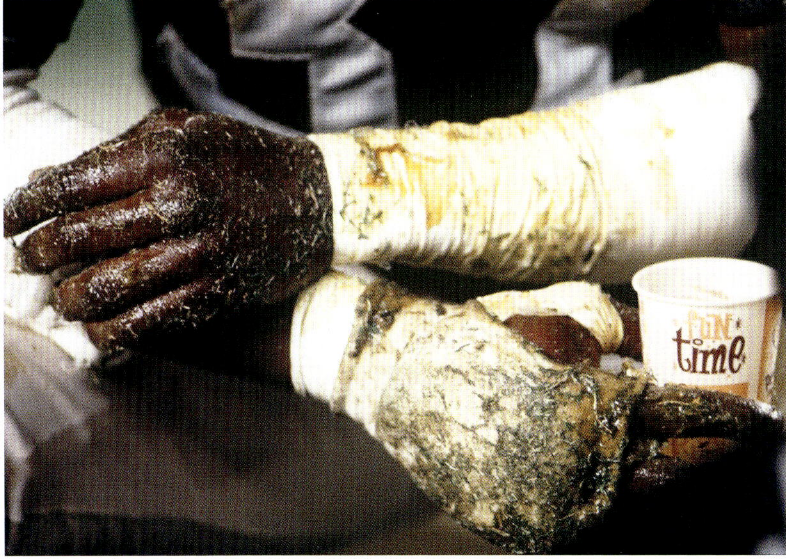

Lester Hayes' hands covered in Stickum as he sits on the sidelines of the Oakland Raiders–San Diego Chargers game on January 11, 1981.

But the NFL was tired of seeing one of its marquee defenders act like a wad of gum stuck to the bottom of a shoe. The Lester Hayes Rule was put into effect in 1981, banning players from using and abusing Stickum, much to Hayes's chagrin. "I could catch a football behind my back on one knee," he said of his pro-Stickum abilities. "It was tremendous stuff."

Former San Francisco 49ers receiver extraordinaire Jerry Rice admitted to defying the league ban by using Stickum during his career. "I just put a little spray, a little Stickum on [my gloves] to make sure that texture is a little sticky," he explained.

Playing without Stickum proved to be as much of a mental adjustment for Hayes as a physical one. In his first four seasons in the NFL, he had 25 interceptions. In the six seasons he played without Stickum, he had 14. In an interview with ESPN, Hayes said: "The sole focus of our team was to win consistently. Whether it was a mental or a physical advantage, we were going to do whatever was necessary to win. Our attitude was that if we could get away with something, we were going to do it."

The drop in interceptions minus Stickum can also be explained by the fact that he saw fewer passes thrown his way. Opposing quarterbacks viewed Hayes' side of the field as a no-go zone. For that, he was named a Second-Team All-Pro four times after 1980.

You could say his reputation as a hard-to-beat cover man stuck with him.

NO. 53 The Drive, Denver-style

In the 1986 AFC Championship game, staged in early January 1987, quarterback John Elway and his fellow Denver Broncos trailed the Cleveland Browns 20–13 with just over five minutes remaining.

The distance to the Cleveland end zone?

Nothing to speak of. A mere trifle.

Only 98 yards. Against a stellar Cleveland defense.

Elway began his transcontinental journey with some running plays and a 22-yard completion to Steve Sewell.

Slowly, the Broncos began to escape the shadow of their own goal posts and make headway.

"Honestly," Denver coach Dan Reeves would say later, "I felt like we had a chance. Any time you have a John Elway as your quarterback you have a chance." Receiver Mark Jackson contributed a 20-yard grab then, as a capper, scored the final TD of the game on another hook-up with Elway on third-and-one from the Cleveland 5-yard line. The crowd of 79,973 at Cleveland Municipal Stadium was left stunned.

Kicker Rich Karlis then forced overtime by making the extra point with 31 seconds left on the clock. "The Drive" had lasted 15 plays and taken five minutes and one second to engineer. Legend has it that once the Broncos' offense huddled up at the 2-yard line to attempt (and, as it turned out, execute) the impossible, offensive guard Keith Bishop announced, "We've got 'em right where we want 'em!"

Turns out, they did.

Brimming with momentum, on the first possession of OT, Elway and the Denver offense then pieced together another superb drive, covering nine plays and 60 yards. Karlis completed the comeback by drilling another field goal through the uprights to propel the Broncos into Super Bowl XXI against the New York Giants.

"It put us on the map," Elway reminisced about The Drive to *The Athletic* in 2020. "The Broncos went to the Super Bowl in '77 and had some good football teams, but The Drive, it gave us a hell of a lot of confidence that we were a darn good football team. The confidence of The Drive carried over."

The Broncos and Elway would lose that title bid 39–20 at the Rose Bowl in Pasadena and subsequently go through another decade-plus of painful door-knocking until finally hitting Super Bowl paydirt. But the legend of The Drive lives on to this day.

The Catch

OFFICIALLY, IT WAS known as "Change Left Slot – Sprint Right Option."

In broader terms, it was San Francisco quarterback Joe Montana rolling to his right and looking for 49ers receiver Freddie Solomon, who was to run a quick out to the sidelines where he could either (a) gain a first down and step out of bounds to stop the clock or (b) score the winning touchdown.

The ball was positioned at the Dallas Cowboys' 6-yard line with less than a minute left in the fourth quarter of the 1981 NFC Championship game. Montana took the snap as Solomon ran his short route and Dwight Clark went to the back of the Dallas end zone, where he suddenly stopped, changed direction and ran to help his quarterback.

Montana was just about out of bounds when he timed his jump-ball pass over the out-stretched arms of 6-foot-9 Dallas defensive end Ed "Too Tall" Jones. The 6-foot-4 Clark snared the ball at its apex to make the score 28–27 for the 49ers as the Candlestick Park faithful roared in jubilation.

Clark later revealed what Jones had said to Montana after what has been forever remembered simply as "The Catch." It was a stunned Jones who said, "You just beat America's team."

To which Montana replied, "Well, you can sit at home with the rest of America and watch the Super Bowl."

Beyond the sheer dynamics of the play, the end result signaled a change in the NFC hierarchy. For San Francisco, the win over Dallas filled the 49ers with confidence, the likes of which resulted in their first Super Bowl win. And they didn't stop there. They won three more Super Bowls in the 1980s, dominating the opposition under the genius of coach Bill Walsh and the play of his QB, Joe Cool Montana. (Montana would set a then-record by being named Super Bowl MVP three times. Tom Brady has five MVP honors.) The fallout for Dallas wasn't so rewarding. The Cowboys were America's Team in the

Wide receiver Dwight Clark celebrates by spiking the football after making "The Catch" in the 1981 NFC Championship game.

1970s, making five trips to the Super Bowl and winning twice. They weren't as fortunate following the loss in San Francisco. In fact, they didn't make it to the Super Bowl even once in the 1980s.

In a television documentary about that seismic shift in power, the fallout from the 1981 drama, Clark admitted: "It's humbling, really. I feel honored people are still talking about it, 25 years later. I am honored to be able to be a part of a play that was kind of the culmination of just this incredible surprise season.

"It's great to give 49er fans that moment that they can relive over and over and over, and I know they do because when I am in San Francisco and a lot of places, people want to talk about that play and how it crushed the Cowboys and sent them into submission for a decade."

NO. 55

"An Unspeakable Tragedy"

THE BOMBASTIC HOWARD Cosell had for a generation become the voice of so many stirring, iconic sporting moments, from Joe Montana comeback drives to Muhammad Ali title fights.

On December 8, 1980, though, he made the call on a moment that ranged far outside his usual spectrum.

That night, as the time ticked down on a game between the New England Patriots and the Miami Dolphins, an uncharacteristically subdued Cosell informed much of America that a true musical icon, former Beatle John Lennon, had been shot outside his Manhattan apartment home, the Dakota.

"Remember, this is just a football game, no matter who wins or loses," Cosell began before breaking the news. "An unspeakable tragedy confirmed to us by ABC News in New York City. John Lennon, outside of his apartment building on the West Side of New York City. The most famous perhaps, of all of the Beatles, shot twice in the back, rushed to Roosevelt Hospital.

"Dead on arrival."

Six years prior to the shooting, Cosell had interviewed Lennon on the *Monday Night Football* telecast of an LA Rams–Washington Redskins clash. The game marked the Liverpool-born Lennon's first in-person experience with American football. Of the atmosphere inside the stadium, Lennon quipped, "It makes rock concerts look like tea parties."

They'd first met when Lennon guested for half an hour on Cosell's radio talk show.

So initially, when informed in the broadcast booth of the shooting, Cosell balked at making the announcement, arguing that a football game wasn't the proper backdrop to break such a significant moment.

Unsure of what to do, he asked for advice from his *MNF* sidekicks. Commentator Frank Gifford urged him of the necessity to deliver the news, the exchange captured by off-air recordings.

"You've got to. If you know it, we've got to do it," Gifford declared.

"Don't hang on it. It's a tragic moment, and this is going to shake up the whole world."

During a Patriots timeout, as New England place kicker John Smith prepared for a field-goal attempt, Gifford pressed the issue. "Three seconds remaining. John Smith is on the line. And I don't care what's on the line, Howard, you have got to say what we know in the booth."

Cosell then did.

Long-distance Delivery

NO. 56

An epic 99-yard touchdown run by Dallas Cowboy Tony Dorsett was the result of a busted play.

Not only that, it came with the Cowboys one man shy on offense.

It was also broadcast coast-to-coast, on a *Monday Night Football* telecast, to boot.

It happened January 3, 1983, with Dallas playing the Minnesota Vikings. The Vikings had opened the fourth quarter by intercepting a pass thrown by Dallas quarterback Danny White and returning it for a touchdown. The Cowboys botched the ensuing kickoff when running back Timmy Newsome fumbled the ball out of bounds at his 1-yard line. White called a running play with Ron Springs to take the ball and plow straight ahead to give the offense some breathing room.

Apparently, something got lost in the translation as Springs stayed on the sidelines thinking the play was for a single running back, not two in an I-formation. That meant the Cowboys were a man short. White took the snap, turned and handed the ball to Dorsett, who filled in as the designated ball carrier. He was past the Minnesota defensive line before it could react. From there, Dorsett cut to his right, then slapped it into high gear, scoring on what will always be the longest run from scrimmage in NFL history.

It was timed as taking 16 seconds from Dorsett taking the handoff to crossing the Vikings' goal line.

Prior to Dorsett's effort, the longest scamper was 97 yards. It was set by Andy Uram in 1939 and equaled by Bob Gage in 1949.

"When I got to the sideline, Gil Brandt [the Cowboys' chief talent scout] told me: 'I think that's an NFL record,'" said Dorsett. "The first thing I thought was I should have kept the football."

Dorsett's shoes from that run can be found in the Pro Football Hall of Fame. More importantly, Dorsett was inducted into the Hall in 1994, making him a member of an even more select group. The University of Pittsburgh alumnus is one of only 10 players who've won the Heisman Trophy as the best player in college football and then made it to the Hall of Fame as a pro.

In early December 2018, Derrick Henry, then of the Tennessee Titans, equaled Dorsett's cross-country run of 99 yards, shredding the Jacksonville Jaguars defense in the second quarter.

And the Other Heisman Trophy-winning Hall of Famers Are ...

O.J. Simpson
1968 Heisman Trophy winner, Pro Football Hall of Fame Class of 1985

Roger Staubach
1963 Heisman Trophy winner, Pro Football Hall of Fame Class of 1985

Paul Hornung
1956 Heisman Trophy winner, Pro Football Hall of Fame Class of 1986

Doak Walker
1948 Heisman Trophy winner, Pro Football Hall of Fame Class of 1986

Earl Campbell
1977 Heisman Trophy winner, Pro Football Hall of Fame Class of 1991

Marcus Allen
1981 Heisman Trophy winner, Pro Football Hall of Fame Class of 2003

Barry Sanders
1988 Heisman Trophy winner, Pro Football Hall of Fame Class of 2004

Tim Brown
1987 Heisman Trophy winner, Pro Football Hall of Fame Class of 2015

Charles Woodson
1997 Heisman Trophy winner, Pro Football Hall of Fame Class of 2021

The record had stood for 35 years. It can, of course, be tied again but never broken.

Dorsett, typical of the man, responded with a laudatory tweet that same day Henry ran wild: "*Congrats to my @HeismanTrophy brother @KingHenry_2 on tying the 99 yard record tonight. That stiff arm! Rumble, young man, rumble!*"

NO. 57

Chicago's 1985 Bears

THERE HAVE BEEN many other outstanding teams over the years, groups of special individuals who combined to win games and championships and send players to the Pro Football Hall of Fame.

But arguably no team ever had as much personality as the Bears did in the non-stop party of a season of '85.

"It was like following the Beatles, quite honestly. It almost had that sort of aura to it," Ken Valdiserri, the team's longtime PR and marketing director, told ESPN. "When I think of it, I think of it fondly and with a lot of adoration to the people that were part of it.

"There's nothing like it, nothing that I think could ever be replicated in professional sports … It just created a hailstorm of publicity. It also brought about the fact that the Bears solidified their position as THE team in town."

They had a coach who personified grit, former Bears tight end Mike Ditka; an offense with a brash quarterback, Jim McMahon, who was not averse to mooning a media helicopter during a team practice; a superstar running back in Walter Payton; and a receiver who could fly named Willie Gault. The defense was chock full of quirky characters and cranks — guys like Steve McMichael, Dan Hampton and Richard Dent. At middle linebacker was the wild-eyed Mike Singletary.

That defensive stronghold was a singularly dangerous crew that obliterated opponents, allowing a combined 10 points in three playoff games — an average of 3.3 points per outing.

On the strength of that pièce de résistance, the Bears went 15-1 during the regular season, their only loss by a 38–24 scoreline in Week 13 at Miami.

New York Giants running back Joe Morris is stopped in his tracks by Chicago's Richard Dent (No. 95) and William "The Refrigerator" Perry (No. 72) in the Bears' 21–0 victory over the Giants on January 5, 1986.

Typical of the team's swagger, players gathered to record "The Super Bowl Shuffle," a Grammy Award–nominated hit that reached No. 41 on Billboard charts rap hit list.

More importantly it delivered over $300,000 to the Chicago Community Trust to assist needy families in Chicago with clothing, shelter and food (hence Payton's lyric during the "Shuffle": "now we're not doing this because we're greedy, the Bears are doing it to feed the needy").

They then pitched back-to-back playoff shutouts, 21–0 over the Giants and 24–0 on the Rams (they're the first team to ever accomplish that feat) before capping off an incredible season by pasting the Patriots 46–10 in Super Bowl XX, staged at the Superdome in the Big Easy.

The Iceman Cometh

NO. **58**

CHICAGO'S WILLIAM "THE Refrigerator" Perry was as big and wide as a stand-up freezer.

At 6-foot-2 and 335 pounds, he was a guy who didn't care if he was tackling or being tackled.

Born in Aiken, South Carolina, the 10th of 12 children, Perry was quoted as saying, "Even when I was little I was big." Legend has it that by sixth grade, he weighed over 200 pounds. Often ridiculed for his size as an adolescent, he took up sports and soon silenced the trash talkers.

Perry's nickname was born in an elevator, of all things, during his freshman year playing for the Clemson Tigers. When teammate Ray Brown could barely squeeze into said elevator beside Perry — both men had their laundry with them to be washed on a different floor — he quipped, "Man, you're about as big as a refrigerator."

The nickname stuck.

By the time Perry reached pro (his Bears teammates actually called him "Biscuit," as in "one biscuit shy of 350 pounds"), he was as unstoppable as thunder, as luminous as lightning. Bears defensive guru Buddy Ryan didn't want to use the 22nd overall selection in the 1985 draft on what he believed was nothing more than a curiosity pick. Head coach Mike Ditka, who had seen Perry play a few times the previous season, disagreed.

When the situation was right, Perry lined up in the offensive backfield, took a handoff and rumbled straight ahead. He got to score on a 1-yard-plunge touchdown in the Super Bowl XX mugging of the New England Patriots. Big men everywhere celebrated. Over the course of a 138-game NFL career, he registered 29.5 sacks and scored three touchdowns.

The Fridge became one of the best-known players in the league. And one of the most liked. In fact, coach Ditka said that if someone didn't like William Perry, "you didn't like anybody."

Those were the glory days. These days, not so much. Perry's recurring health issues, starting with Guillain-Barré syndrome, described as a "chronic inflammatory disorder of the peripheral nerves," put him at risk of paralysis, even death. Making matters worse is his diabetes combined with his addiction to alcohol. Personal and financial issues have also dogged him.

It's not been a pretty picture, considering Perry has been wheelchair-bound and weighs as much as he did when he played, maybe more.

By 2022 it was reported that he was doing much better, even to the point of appearing at events such as Clemson football games.

"Everything is going well. I'm getting back up, moving around and doing things," Perry said at the time. "I'm really enjoying myself."

Here's hoping for the best for a man who was once the toast of not just Chi-town but the entire NFL.

NO. 59 The West Coast Offense

ITS ORIGINS AS an offensive philosophy remain somewhat up for debate.

What's indisputable is that the "West Coast offense" would gain widespread notoriety and be perfected when the innovative Bill Walsh moved on to become head coach of the San Francisco 49ers in 1979 and was then blessed with one of the most intelligent and mobile quarterbacks ever to grace an NFL field: Joe Montana.

The West Coast offense is based on rhythm and timing, relying on precision passing and quick, short-to-intermediate routes to move the ball downfield, and in the process open up the defensive backfield downfield, in direct contrast to the once more favored "vertical" schemes. Aligned with running backs able to catch short passes out of the backfield and turn them into first downs, as well as tight ends willing and able to catch passes as well as just block, the philosophy thrived.

Although Cincinnati could hardly be classified as "West Coast," football scholars have the scheme's origins dating back as far as 1969 when, as offensive coordinator of the expansion Bengals, Walsh worked with his mentor Paul Brown to help work around a shoulder disorder sustained by rookie quarterback Greg Cook. The solution was to alter the passing schemes.

Hailing from the University of Cincinnati, Cook had gone fifth overall in the 1969 AFL/NFL Draft and was considered a hot prospect. He'd led the Bengals to a 3-0 start to the season but in the third game, versus Kansas City, he felt his throwing shoulder give.

Never officially diagnosed with a tear, Cook soldiered on, taking cortisone shots to alleviate the pain, finishing with 1,854 yards passing and being named the AFL's Rookie of the Year. He would go on to throw for only 11 more yards in a career cut short by his damaged shoulder.

When Cook left the picture, Walsh turned to his No. 2, Virgil Carter. Carter didn't possess a strong arm, but he was a very accurate passer. In 1971 Carter led the league in pass completion percentage and was third in overall passing.

When Walsh moved to the 49ers from a head coaching position at Stanford University in 1979, the combination of Montana — drafted as the 82nd pick in the same year out of Notre Dame — and receiver Dwight Clark and, later, Jerry Rice would go on to help the West Coast offense shine. It was Montana, filling the Arturo Toscanini role as conductor, who became the league's passing completion percentage leader in five seasons (1980, 1981, 1985, 1987 and 1989).

The 49ers collected three Super Bowls under Walsh's transformative guidance.

The Drive, San Francisco-style

NO. 60

JOE MONTANA LATER said he was so overwhelmed that he was hyperventilating on the field.

And that's saying something since Montana had the pulse rate of a blue whale. Precious little unnerved him. But this was not a normal game situation.

This one was for Super Bowl XXIII, on January 22, 1989, against the surprisingly resilient Cincinnati Bengals. The Bengals had just taken the lead with a late field goal to make the score 16–13. The 49ers had just over three minutes to either get into field goal range for the tie or, better yet, go the full 92 yards to score a touchdown for the win. And just to tighten the screws a little more, the San Francisco offense came onto the field just as the officials called for a TV timeout. That got to offensive lineman Harris Barton, who started freaking out during the extra time over how far the 49ers had to go.

"We should be beating this team. We're down by three. We have to score a touchdown to win. This is crap," Barton recalled. "Joe said to me, 'Hey, H. Check it out. Look down there at the other end zone … There's John Candy. Yeah, it's John Candy!' And then the official blew the whistle and the play starts."

Montana went to work alternating his passes between running back Roger Craig and receiver Jerry Rice. At one point, Montana felt the pressure and began hyperventilating. He tried calling a timeout but was denied by the coaches, who had no clue about what was happening with their ace QB. It wasn't long before Montana was back under center, his hands as steady as a diamond cutter's. Then came the finishing blow, a 10-yard completion to John Taylor for the 20–16 final. It was Taylor's first catch of the game. It was Bill Walsh's last game as a head coach before retiring from the NFL.

Montana and the 49ers went on to win their fourth Super Bowl a year later in a 55–10 mugging of the Denver Broncos.

Joe Cool threw five touchdown passes in that game. Three went to Jerry Rice.

Joe Montana (No. 16) passes the ball to running back Roger Craig (No. 33, at the edge of the shot) in the 49ers' thrilling 20–16 win at Super Bowl XXIII.

When Nothing Made the News

NO. 61

THE 30-YEAR FEUD between Al Davis and commissioner Pete Rozelle was always simmering, always there waiting for something to set it off.

It's believed the unpleasantries between the two men began when they negotiated the NFL–AFL merger in 1966. Rozelle, all corporate and polished, represented NFL elitism; Davis was the hardscrabble Brooklyn-raised opportunist who had worked his way up from assistant coach to head coach to general manager to AFL commissioner.

And while the two men fought for the best deal they could get for their side, it was Rozelle who came away with the rave reviews for making it happen, much to Davis' annoyance.

But the key battle point between the two protagonists was Davis' antitrust suit filed against the NFL for blocking his attempt to move the Raiders to Los Angeles from Oakland. Rozelle summed up the league's position by saying, "We don't think the antitrust laws were intended to let a team just get up and move after 12 straight years of sellouts and to set up a situation where every team can conduct an auction for its franchise when its lease is up." In 1982, a federal district court ruled in favor of Davis' antitrust claim and allowed the Raiders to move to LA.

Davis didn't do himself any favors when, in 1986, he sided with the United States Football League in its antitrust suit against the NFL. (The NFL lost the suit but was ordered to pay just $1 in damages.) Still smarting from watching the Raiders relocate to the Los Angeles Coliseum from Oakland, the NFL listened to Davis' pitch to move the Raiders to a new stadium to be built in Inglewood, CA. The league agreed to help finance the facility providing the Raiders shared it with a second team.

"All I asked them for was, 'Help me get a stadium.' And I would have stayed. They know it," Davis said in an interview with ESPN Films. "I wouldn't take a second NFL team into Hollywood Park. I just wanted to be alone there."

Instead, in 1995, the Raiders moved back to Oakland.

While all this was going on, the Raiders were winning two Super Bowls. The Oakland team beat the Philadelphia Eagles in 1980, then the Los Angeles version of the Raiders crushed the Washington Redskins 38–9 in 1983. On both occasions, the traditional Super Bowl trophy presentation had the makings of a major showdown. Would Rozelle say something to infuriate Davis? Would the Raiders' kingpin accept the Vince Lombardi Trophy with a caustic brushoff? Both times promised to be required viewing, even if nothing happened — and nothing did.

Raiders head coach Tom Flores said there was a reason for that: "[Both men] loved the game too much to degrade the moment."

As proof of that, when Rozelle and Davis met following Rozelle's announcement that he was retiring after 29 years in office, the two men shook hands and embraced.

They were likely both relieved not to have to deal with one another ever again.

NO. 62 The New England Snow Job

EVERYONE FOLLOWING THE December 1982 New England Patriots–Miami Dolphins matchup knew it was not going to be a high-scoring, well-played clash.

Just one glance at a TV screen, or for the people in the New England area, a glance out the window, confirmed that.

The night before kickoff, a driving rain had deluged Schaefer Stadium in Foxborough, Massachusetts. Then the temperature dropped and the field froze. Then, wouldn't you just know it, snow began pelting down during the game and the wind was whipping it along.

Only 25,716 people even bothered coming to the action. Little did anyone know the star of the afternoon would be a convicted burglar named Mark Henderson.

With the Patriots lining up for a 33-yard field goal with 4:45 remaining

Mark Henderson clears snow using a now-legendary John Deere tractor on December 13, 1982, during a New England Patriots–Miami Dolphins game at Schaefer Stadium in Foxborough, Massachusetts.

in a scoreless game, Henderson drove his snow removal unit onto the field to clear a path for kicker John Smith.

The kick was good and all the Patriots needed to defeat Miami. The Dolphins immediately cried foul, accusing New England of cheating since it was Patriots coach Ron Meyer who ordered Henderson to take a spin.

Henderson said he was out on a weekend work program and was just there to help. And when informed of the Dolphins' ire, Henderson is reported to have quipped, "What are they gonna do, throw me in jail?"

The league issued no penalty against the Patriots or Henderson, who got a game ball from the players for his timely assistance (the actual game ball was awarded to linebacker Steve Nelson). Henderson's souvenir ball had the date, the score — 3–0 — and the words "A Clean Sweep" written on it.

Henderson became an instant, if unlikely, celebrity.

"I was doing time for burglary and was lucky enough to end up on a work-release program from [MCI]-Norfolk," he told the *Boston Globe* in 2010. "My stepfather got me a job with the maintenance crew. We had a meeting before the game, and nobody wanted to run the tractor. I knew I was the low man on the totem pole, obviously, so I volunteered. At the end of the day, everybody wished they had volunteered."

Even though it's still remembered as "The Snowplow Game," the "plow" used by Henderson was actually a John Deere Model 314 tractor with an attached sweeper. It now hangs from the ceiling of an exhibit inside the Patriots' current home, Gillette Stadium.

NO. 63

Not Good for Business

TWICE IN FIVE years, the NFL was hit with major labor disputes. First, the NFL Players Association went on strike in 1982, when its bargaining terms were rejected by the team owners. The players stayed out for 57 days. No games were played during that time, although the NFLPA staged a pair of NFC–AFC All-Star contests that only a few thousand diehards bothered to attend. The strike occurred because the union demanded that a wage scale be implemented based on a percentage of gross revenues. The NFLPA wanted its share to be 55 percent, and according to the *Los Angeles Times*, this demand "dominated the negotiations."

In the end, the players signed off on a five-year agreement that called for an increase in salaries and playoff pay, along with additional bonuses and a severance plan for retired players. The major U.S. television networks were delighted to have the regular NFL players back in action. In its search for alternative viewing, NBC aired four CFL games, all of them one-sided and dramaless.

The NFL responded to the late deal by staging a nine-game regular season followed by a 16-team Super Bowl tournament. The Washington Redskins captured Super Bowl XVII honors by beating the Miami Dolphins 27–17.

During the 1987 strike for a larger share of the overall revenue, the owners used replacement players, whom the fans were quick to rebrand as the "Seattle Sea-scabs," the "Chicago Spare Bears," the "Los Angeles Shams" and, the wittiest of the lot, the "San Francisco Phony-niners." The strike saw its share of established players crossing picket lines until finally the players caved and returned without a signed collective agreement.

The players' resounding defeat in the boardroom forced them to decertify their union and challenge the owners in court. By 1993 the NFL granted free agency to veteran players provided a newly reinstated NFLPA agreed to a "hard salary cap" of no more than 64 percent of the league's gross revenues.

The current collective bargaining agreement runs to 2030.

The Best, Bar None

NO. 64

HE WAS KNOWN, simply, as L.T.

His nickname was as direct as his playing style.

In 1986, in only his sixth NFL season, the New York Giants' Lawrence Taylor became just the second defensive player to win the NFL MVP award, joining Minnesota Vikings defensive lineman Alan Page 15 years earlier.

Taylor one-upped Page, though, by becoming the only unanimous defensive MVP selection in history.

Taylor had 20.5 sacks that season and proved to be a once-in-a-lifetime talent who forced rivals to come up with special plays designed to keep him away from the ballcarrier.

Taylor's rise to prominence certainly came as no surprise to the team that drafted him second overall in 1981. (Running back George Rogers was the No. 1 pick by the New Orleans Saints.) Giants general manager George Young was so smitten by Taylor that he made a bold prediction: "Sure, I saw Dick Butkus play," Young said of the Chicago Bears' defensive great. "There's no doubt in my mind about Taylor [being better]. He's bigger and stronger than Butkus. On the blitz, he's devastating."

Taylor was indeed a devastating freak of nature. In his rookie season he recorded 133 tackles and 9.5 sacks, forced two fumbles, recovered one and had an interception. In 1988, he proved his toughness by playing a game against New Orleans wearing a special harness to protect a torn pectoral muscle in his shoulder. Undaunted, he made seven tackles, three sacks and forced two fumbles in a 13–12 win for the Giants.

Yet in the wake of what should've been his crowning moment — a Super Bowl XXI victory over the Denver Broncos to end the 1986 season — Taylor admitted to feeling let down.

"When the Super Bowl was over ... Everyone was so excited, but by then I felt deflated. I'd won every award, had my best season, finally won the Super Bowl," he told author Steve Serby for his 2004 autobiography, *LT: Over the*

Washington Redskins quarterback Jay Schroeder is sacked by Lawrence Taylor during a game on December 7, 1986 — Taylor's MVP year.

Edge: Tackling Quarterbacks, Drugs, and a World Beyond Football. "I was on top of the world, right? So what could be next? Nothing. The thrill is the chase to get to the top. Every day the excitement builds and builds and builds, and then when you're finally there and the game is over ... And then, nothing."

Taylor and the Giants would win another title four years later, 20–19 over the Buffalo Bills in Tampa, but when taken as a whole, 1986 remains the greatest season by arguably the greatest defensive player of all-time.

As hard-edged as he was as a player, Taylor's off-the-field persona wasn't much different. In a 2003 interview with *60 Minutes*, Taylor admitted to sending prostitutes to the hotel rooms of opposing players to tire them out sexually. He then revealed he had used a teammate's urine sample to pass a league drug test, which would have shown his cocaine use and led to a suspension.

In the end, Taylor walked away from the NFL after a stellar 13-year run that included over 1,000 tackles, over 130 sacks, three NFL Defensive Player of the Year selections, 10 Pro Bowl selections and the two Super Bowl championships.

L.T.'s 1986 Stats

Games Played	Sacks	Total Tackles	Passes Defensed	Forced Fumbles
16	20.5	105	5	2

NFL Madden-ess

NO. 65

JOHN MADDEN HAD quite the public profile by 1988: the instantly recognizable Super Bowl–winning coach of the Oakland Raiders who had walked off the sideline in 1979 at age 42, citing burnout and deteriorating health from an ulcer condition.

During 10 seasons in charge of the Raiders, Madden's teams never had a losing record, compiling a staggering 103-32-7. They reached the playoffs eight times and won Super Bowl XI by beating the Minnesota Vikings 32–14. Madden called being carried off the field by his players following the Super Bowl triumph "the happiest moment of my life."

By 1988 Madden was a popular CBS NFL color man who was partnered with Pat Summerall on Sunday afternoons, idolized for his folksy style and for the tidbits of wisdom he passed along. Here are just two:

"On third down and short yardage, the Raiders don't jump offside. That's discipline, not a coat and tie, not a clean shave," and

"The fewer rules a coach has, the fewer rules there are for the players to break."

And if that weren't enough, Madden became the unlikely star of a string of immensely popular Miller ("Tastes great! Less filling!") Lite beer television commercials in which he virtually jumped through the screen at viewers. He was quite simply blessed with a larger-than-life personality. Why, in the early '80s he even took a turn hosting *Saturday Night Live*.

Who else could turn a fear of flying, brought on by a severe case of claustrophobia, into a way to meet more fans by traveling across the U.S. in a bus brandishing his name on the side of it? Madden even had a sponsor for his motorcoach, the Outback Steakhouse, and averaged 80,000 miles a season. Whenever he had the time, the driver would park the bus so Madden could grab a bite. Inevitably, he'd end up chatting with people.

Oh, John Madden was one popular dude, all right. He made a tradition out of the NFL's Thanksgiving Day games by awarding the winning team a turducken, a delightful hybrid poultry dish featuring multiple drumsticks.

In 1984 Electronic Arts (EA) founder Trip Hawkins conceived and

Coach John Madden is carried off the field by his team after winning Super Bowl XI on January 9, 1977.

designed an NFL video game with Madden's profile and football acumen as the base. Owing to Madden's desire for as realistic a gaming experience as possible, the first edition did not appear for four years.

And then starting in 1988, Madden's profile got a whole lot bigger.

The original version of the game, *John Madden Football*, sold reasonably well, but by 1996 it had become the best-selling sports video game franchise, with more than 8 million units sold.

Madden did okay, too. In 2005 he signed a deal with EA that gave the company perpetual rights to use his identity in football-focused games. This landmark contract was worth a massive $150 million.

To date, the video game in its various formats, long ago re-named *Madden NFL*, has rung up more than $4 billion in total sales.

Madden passed away on December 28, 2021, two days after his 62nd wedding anniversary. He was 85.

THE 1990S

Contents

No. 66 Is There a QB in the House? 120

No. 67 The Comeback 121

No. 68 Gridiron Technology 101 124

No. 69 It's All on the Line 125

No. 70 The Steroid Era (1980s to 1990s and Beyond) 127

No. 71 Sanders Calls It Quits 130

No. 72 They Called Him Sweetness 132

No. 73 Did We Really See That? 135

No. 74 The Fake Spike 137

No. 75 Snakebit at the Super Bowl 138

No. 76 The Trade of the Decade 140

No. 77 Elway Cements His Legacy 142

NO.

66 Is There a QB in the House?

THE NEW YORK Jets' 1999 season opener was like nothing ever seen before.

In the second quarter against the New England Patriots, Jets' starting QB Vinny Testaverde ruptured his Achilles tendon and was done for the year

Jets' coach Bill Parcells had listed Testaverde as the starter and punter Tom Tupa (not actual backup Rick Mirer) as the official No. 2. Needing someone to punt and Tupa's college quarterbacking experience were factors in Parcells making that choice. But when Testaverde went down, that left Mirer on the sidelines because, under the rules of the time, if the coach chose to insert his emergency quarterback (Mirer) before the fourth quarter, Tupa would be ineligible and the Jets would have no one to punt.

Meaning that a guy who hadn't attempted an in-game pass for three years would be taking snaps with the Jets' offense.

The game, by the way, was Tupa's first as a Jet. So, quite the jazzy debut. Especially given the Big Apple setting.

"When [Testaverde] went down, I didn't realize I was going to be playing all that much," Tupa told the team's website in 2019. "I thought I might go in for a few plays until they got the next guy ready, Rick Mirer."

Playing quarterback wasn't completely foreign to the 6-foot-4, 225-pound Tupa. He guided his Brecksville High School team to the Ohio state championship while lettering in basketball and baseball. He went to Ohio State University and took over at QB in 1987, passing for 2,252 yards, 15 touchdowns and 12 interceptions. He was also selected as an All-America punter. That led the Phoenix Cardinals to use their third-round pick to claim Tupa in the 1988 NFL Draft.

In 1989 he started two games at QB and punted, albeit just six times. In 1991 he started in 11 games, throwing six touchdowns to 13 interceptions. He ended up with the Cleveland Browns, where he held the ball for field goals as well as handled the punting chores. He went into the record books as the first player to score a two-point conversion in the NFL. He would score two more in the 1994 season, earning him the nickname "Two-point Tupa."

In the Jets' game against New England, Tupa was outstanding, connecting three times with all-star receiver Keyshawn Johnson. Overall, Tupa completed six of 10 passes for 165 yards and two touchdowns. It was a most unexpected performance, which came to an end when the Jets decided to switch to Mirer, who was eligible when the fourth quarter began.

"Yeah, I ended up going in and things went pretty well there for a while," Tupa said in 2019. "It was a little bit of a shock obviously; I'm not going to lie. But I think overall, it went pretty well."

Mission complete, Tupa returned to his punting duties (averaging over 45 yards per punt, he'd be named a First-Team All-Pro and selected to play in the Pro Bowl that season).

Mirer, meanwhile, didn't fare nearly as well in that game, serving up two interceptions in a 30–28 loss.

Tupa would finish the sporadic passing portion of a 16-year, seven-stop NFL career with 259 completions in 504 attempts for 3,430 yards, 12 touchdowns and 25 picks.

The Comeback

NO. 67

THE 1992 AFC wild-card matchup was tilted in favor of the Houston Oilers even before the opening kickoff was launched.

Due to injuries, the home team Buffalo Bills were without linebacker Cornelius Bennett and starting quarterback Jim Kelly. Compounding matters, Buffalo also lost star running back Thurman Thomas to a hip injury suffered during the game.

Backup passer Frank Reich took over for Kelly and could do nothing throughout the first half. As ineffective as the Bills were, Houston was operating in high gear. QB Warren Moon and his offense scored a touchdown on each of their first four possessions. Moon's numbers at halftime were a commanding 19 completions in 22 attempts for 218 yards and four touchdowns.

Buffalo defensive coordinator Walt Corey had a colorful explanation for what his players were doing wrong: "I was hollering the same things the fans were hollering at me when we left the field," Corey said. "I can't repeat the words, but the more I talked, the louder I got. The thing that bothered me was their approach. To me, they looked timid. They looked like they were going to get in the right spots, but they weren't going to make anything happen afterward. This is an attitude game. Sometimes you start playing and you're afraid to make things happen or afraid to make a mistake."

Presented with the facts, the players were forced to believe they were embarrassing themselves and their fans, too. They committed themselves to a second-half revival — and promptly fell on their facemasks. Less than two minutes into the third quarter, Reich's pass was deflected into the hands of Houston's Bubba McDowell, who ran it back 58 yards for a touchdown and a 35–3 lead over Buffalo.

That could have been Reich's undoing, but instead it lit a fire under him. At halftime, Reich was reminded of the seemingly impossible comeback he had fashioned in November 1984, when he replaced QB Stan Gelbaugh with the University of Maryland trailing 31–0 against the Miami Hurricanes. With deft ball handling and pinpoint passing, Reich made the final score 42–40 in Maryland's favor.

And so it began.

"If we went down, we'd go down fighting," former Bills coach Marv Levy told ESPN in 2021. "I just was immersed in the game itself. What should we do next? And the game isn't over. [New York Yankees catcher] Yogi Berra once said, 'It's not over 'til it's over.' And so, we kept plugging away."

Running back Kenneth Davis capped a 10-play, 50-yard drive with a 1-yard stroll into the Houston end zone. After recovering an onside kick, the Bills scored again, this time on a 38-yard completion from Reich to receiver Don Beebe. That cut Buffalo's deficit to 18 points, 35–17.

On the Bills' next possession, Reich found receiver Andre Reed open for the first of his three second-half TDs, which covered 26, 18 and 17 yards — the last connection gave Buffalo its first lead, 38–35. Moon had one last scoring drive left in him and positioned kicker Al Del Greco for a 26-yard field goal that forced overtime.

Kicker Steve Christie celebrates with quarterback Frank Reich (No. 14) after kicking the 32-yard winning field goal against the Houston Oilers in the AFC wild-card game.

Houston won the coin toss to begin OT but lost the game when Moon's 50th pass attempt of the afternoon was intercepted by Nate Odomes. With a Houston face-masking penalty tacked on, the Bills sent out Steve Christie, who kicked the 32-yard winning field goal to send Buffalo into a state of euphoria. It went into the record books as the greatest playoff comeback in NFL history (it ranked as the largest comeback, period, until the 2022 Minnesota Vikings overcame a 33-point deficit to stun the Indianapolis Colts in Week 15 of that regular season).

In the wake of their dramatic loss, several Houston players admitted they had "choked." The team was quick to fire defensive coordinator Jim Eddy and defensive backs coach Pat Thomas. And for years, the Oilers wore their humbling loss like a scarlet letter.

They relocated to Tennessee in 1997 and became the Titans two years later. (The NFL awarded Houston a new team, the Texans, which began play in 2002.)

And the Bills? They would ride the momentum of that win to further playoff victories over the Pittsburgh Steelers and Miami Dolphins before losing a third-straight Super Bowl, beaten 52–17 by the Dallas Cowboys.

NO. 68 Gridiron Technology 101

THE NFL GAME experience has changed significantly from the days when Paul Brown, coach of the Cleveland Browns, used a shuttle system of offensive linemen to relay plays to his quarterback.

That was back in the 1940s, before the Browns became the first team to install a radio receiver inside the helmet of the quarterback — a stroke of genius that was banned after just four games in 1956. These days, every starting quarterback has a receiver in his helmet and his coach or offensive coordinator in his ears outlining the next play. The call-in lasts just a few seconds. When the offense stalls or scores a touchdown, the quarterback returns to the sidelines and gets to watch the play on a tablet that shows the action from overhead cameras. The Sideline Viewing System app enables coaches to recognize opposition tendencies, make the appropriate response and help the QB visualize what needs to happen next.

That's been the case ever since the NFL approved its helmet technology in 1994. (In 2008, the league allowed one defensive player to receive his coach's instructions. The offensive and defensive contacts are identified by a green dot on the back of their helmets.) But now there's a new development on the rise, one that provides more info for better decision-making. We're talking about the advent of microchips and their placement under a player's shoulder pads. The Radio Frequency Identification (RFID) microchip tags provide real-time analytical data that teams can use, such as how fast a player ran for a touchdown, how fast a ball was thrown, the trajectory of the pass and how hard a player was hit. It all comes from a chip the size of a nickel that weighs just 3.3 grams, just over a tenth of an ounce.

In 2015, the NFL began a relationship with Zebra Technologies to provide the league with RFID tags to track player movements. The tags worked so well that the league began implanting tracking chips in all game balls starting in 2017.

The Canadian Football League tried using microchip-fitted footballs on extra points and field goals, but several kickers complained that the balls didn't feel right.

The league responded by stating "teams will no longer be mandated to use microchip-implanted footballs for kicking plays," said CFL commissioner Randy Ambrosie. For the 2024 season, the CFL allowed kickers to decide before the game which model they would use, a chip ball or a technology-free ball.

The CFL also fined the four kickers who publicly complained about the chip ball.

It's All on the Line

NO. 69

He may not be the most recognizable figure in NFL history, but Stan Honey's contribution to the game cannot be overlooked or underappreciated.

That yellow line you see on the field that appears on your game telecast, the line that indicates how far a team must move the ball for a first down, has become such a broadcasting mainstay it feels as if it has always been there.

That was Honey's doing. He and the broadcast graphics company he cofounded, Sportvision, created the 1st & 10 down line. It was first used in

Stan Honey, inventor of the 1st & 10 down line for football telecasts, holds a football over a computer-generated yellow line.

a September 27, 1998, meeting between the Baltimore Ravens and the Cincinnati Bengals. That game was shown on ESPN with the line playing to rave reviews. Some in the media went so far as to say the onscreen graphic was the biggest advancement in football broadcasts since the inception of instant replay in 1963.

"We knew early on at ESPN that technology could help differentiate our presentation from our competitors. If these powerful new [virtual-graphics] systems could help the viewer understand their sport better, we were all-in," Jed Drake, then-Senior Vice President and Executive Producer of ESPN, told the Sports Broadcasting Hall of Fame's website in 2017. "Stan was, of course, the lead technology person behind all these enhancements. But here's the key: Putting aside his tremendous intellect, he's a great project leader. He speaks the language of production people and engineers equally well. As for Stan and ESPN? Perfect timing. Perfect marriage."

The notion of a special first down marker had been batted around since the late 1970s. But it wasn't until Honey took charge that the idea went from a talking point to reality. The process was explained this way by the *Atlantic*: "The yellow marker system effectively turned the field into a green screen so that the line would appear on top of the grass [but not on top of players when they passed over it] and remain fixed as the camera moved around."

The technology is so good it can even show the yard lines covered by snow in games played under wintry conditions.

It costs networks telecasting NFL games between $20,000 and $30,000 per game to have the first-down line. For his part in the process, Honey received an Emmy Award for his engineering innovations in sports television broadcasts. He has since won two more Emmys as part of a team and was inducted into the Sports Broadcasting Hall of Fame in 2017.

A Hall-of-Fame offshore navigator as well as a tech whiz, Honey holds 31 patents for a variety of navigation systems as well as for a variety of other sporting ventures, including baseball and NASCAR racing.

The technological advances continue. For the 2025 season, Sony's Hawk-Eye technology — used experimentally in the 2024 preseason — will handle first-down spots on the field during games. The standard first-down manual marker system remains as a back-up.

The Steroid Era (1980s to 1990s and Beyond)

NO. 70

PEOPLE ALWAYS SUSPECTED defensive lineman Lyle Alzado was on the juice, to use the colloquialism of the day.

He was bulked up like a cartoon character. His skin was stretched so tight it looked like shrink-wrap. On the field, he was hyper-aggressive, quick to lose his temper. Alzado went on record with *Sports Illustrated* saying he started using "steroids in 1969" and "never stopped." His former teammate Howie Long called him "Three Mile Lyle" after Three Mile Island, the nuclear reactor station that suffered a partial meltdown in 1979, because "you never knew when he was going to blow. He was a nuclear plant. He really was."

At the height of the steroid era, anecdotes from players and articles suggested anywhere from 20 to 50 percent of the players in the NFL were using performance-enhancing drugs. Atlanta Falcons offensive lineman Bill Fralic went before a U.S. congressional hearing in 1989 and estimated that "75 percent of linemen" used 'roids. The NFL began testing for drugs in earnest in

1987. Within two years, the league was increasing the number of random tests and issuing suspensions.

With those checks in place, in 2022 *USA Today* compiled a list of "at least 258" NFL drug-related suspensions since 2001. And there are still players being caught. Houston Texans defensive end Denico Autry was given a six-game suspension in July 2024 for testing positive for a banned substance. San Francisco 49ers defensive back Tashaun Gipson drew a six-game suspension for his failed drug test, also in July 2024, when he was a free agent. In 2022 Arizona Cardinals receiver DeAndre Hopkins was suspended for six games when a banned substance was found in his system. And in 2018 New England Patriots receiver Julian Edelman was suspended for the first four games of the season for using a performance enhancer to help his recovery from a knee injury. He returned to the starting line-up in Week 5 in the Patriots' march to Super Bowl LIII in Atlanta, where he caught 10 passes for 141 yards to be chosen as the game's MVP. That irked some observers who pointed to Major League Baseball, which doesn't allow players with regular-season drug suspensions to compete in the postseason.

As Adam Kilgore wrote in the *Washington Post*: "Baseball drug cheats are met with pitchforks. Football drug cheats are met with shrugs. They aren't even really considered cheats."

The now-defunct Bay Area Laboratory Co-operative (BALCO) found itself at the center of the biggest steroid scandal on record. There were fingers pointed at BALCO founder Victor Conte, a former bass player with the R&B/funk band Tower of Power, whose connections included baseball star Jason Giambi, track and field Olympians Tim Montgomery and Marion Jones, as well as football's Bill Romanowski.

A two-time Pro Bowler and four-time Super Bowl champion, Romanowski used and promoted a Conte product known as ZMA, a zinc supplement that works as a sleep enhancer and can show greater increases in muscle strength.

"I've got about 90 percent of the [Denver] Broncos on ZMA," Romanowski said at the time. "The guys are telling me they sleep better and feel better."

Romanowski's mood swings and uncontrollable rage were tell-tale signs of steroid abuse, and it wasn't restricted to game days. In 2003, during an Oakland Raiders practice, rookie tight end Marcus Williams tried to block an infuriated Romanowski, who ripped Williams' helmet off his head, then punched him in the face, knocking him unconscious and breaking his left eye socket. When Williams came to, Romanowski was standing over him shouting, "Don't you ever f★★★★★★ hold me!" That brought about the end of Williams' pro career, and he filed a civil suit seeking $3.4 million. He was awarded $340,000. Romanowski paid another $75,000 to prevent any further legal action.

Before the Williams attack, Romanowski had a run-in with San Francisco 49ers running back Dexter Carter. It happened before practice when Carter put his sandwich in a dining room microwave oven. Romanowski had already put his sandwich in the microwave and removed Carter's. When Carter put it back again, Romanowski picked up the microwave and threw it at him.

Romanowski admitted he used human growth hormones but had better results with a Conte concoction called "The Clear." It was a designer steroid that was distributed by trainer Greg Anderson, who worked with home run king Barry Bonds. The former San Francisco Giant slugger said he took a substance given to him by Anderson but was told it was a flaxseed oil supplement and a balm for arthritis.

In 2011 it was up to a grand jury to decide if Bonds had perjured himself when he said he never knowingly took performance-enhancing drugs. The perjury charge was dismissed but he was convicted on one count of obstruction of justice. He was sentenced to house arrest for 30 days and placed on two years' probation.

But it was Alzado's tell-all interview in *Sports Illustrated* that provided the most damning commentary on the steroid era.

"We're not born to be 300 pounds or jump 30 feet. But all the time I was taking steroids, I knew they were making me play better … Now look at me," Alzado lamented. "My hair's gone, I wobble when I walk and have to hold on to someone for support, and I have trouble remembering things. My last wish? That no one else ever dies this way."

Alzado died of brain cancer in 1992 at 43 years of age.

NO. 71

Sanders Calls It Quits

THE ANNOUNCER COULD hardly believe what he saw. You could hear the astonishment in his voice. "Through the right side … Roper's got a shot. Singletary's got a shot. Carrier had a shot, he let him go and now you can just forget it."

That was the replay call of an unforgettable 42-yard touchdown run against a Chicago Bears defense left in tatters by a Detroit Lions running back whose illustrious career was built on making tacklers miss. That was Barry Sanders' claim to fame — his ability to mix power with speed to the point where he authored dozens of unforgettable runs.

And then, just as quickly as he had baffled the Bears, he retired following the 1998 regular season. It made no sense at the time. Sanders, after all, was just 30. He was still physically fit. He could have easily padded his statistics, which had him turning 3,062 carries into 15,269 yards and 99 touchdowns. Why he stopped running was a mystery to some. To Sanders, it all came down to winning — and the Lions were far from being big winners during his tenure with them.

With Sanders, the Lions posted a 78-82 win-loss record. They made the playoffs five times, winning only once, a 38–6 drubbing of the Dallas Cowboys in 1991. One week later, Sanders and his teammates were humiliated 41–10 by the Washington Redskins. It wasn't until years later that he elaborated on his decision to leave the game.

"I'm very competitive when it comes to winning and losing and playing well. And I did put up big numbers," he explained. "There were times in 1997 when I could have gone back in to pad my numbers, but I wasn't as competitive with the numbers as I was about winning and losing."

Sanders had both individual and team successes during his collegiate career at Oklahoma State University, where in 1988 as a junior he ran for 2,628 yards and scored 37 touchdowns in only 11 games. That earned him the Heisman Trophy. It was more of the same once Sanders signed with

Detroit. He ran for at least 1,500 yards five times in his NFL career and scored 15 touchdown runs of 50 yards or more. His greatest season saw him gain 2,053 yards in 1997. The fact that he ran as well and hard as he did was made even more impressive by the fact that he measured in at just 5-foot-8, 203 pounds.

Lions fans felt a lot like tacklers trying to pin him down: he was there one moment, then, suddenly, gone the next.

In 2023 Sanders re-affirmed his unwavering reason for retiring so early in an Amazon documentary on his career, explaining, "There was nothing really left to play for. I didn't see us as any kind of a serious Super Bowl contender … I felt like I was making a pretty clear decision. I just felt like, in my mind, this is pretty much it."

That stunning decision was football's loss.

Consider this: The NFL's all-time leading rusher, Emmitt Smith of the Dallas Cowboys, compiled 18,355 yards in 15 seasons. Barry Sanders logged 15,269 in just 10. As durable as he was prolific, Sanders missed only seven games over that span, so do the math.

No wonder, then, that we'll remember Sanders' best for years to come. As well as ponder the further glories that would surely have followed.

NFL's All-time Rushing Yards Leaders

Player	Rushing Yards	Years
Emmitt Smith	18,355	1990–2004
Walter Payton	16,726	1975–1987
Frank Gore	16,000	2005–2020
Barry Sanders	15,269	1989–1998
Adrian Peterson	14,918	2007–2021

NO. 72 They Called Him Sweetness

THIS WAS NOT a debut. It was a debacle. Eight carries, no yards. Just who was this first-round draft pick from Columbia, Mississippi? And how was he going to empower the Chicago Bears' offense when all he could muster was 0 yards on eight carries?

Those had to be the questions racing through Walter Payton's mind in the fall of 1975. Based on his college statistics, Payton had all the makings of a holy terror. While a member of the Jackson State University Tigers, he ran for 3,600 career yards and scored a school-record 65 rushing touchdowns. For that, he was selected the Black College Player of the Year, and he would win the award a second time one year later.

The Bears were so taken by Payton's abilities that they made him the fourth overall pick, behind Atlanta Falcons quarterback Steve Bartkowski, Dallas Cowboys defensive tackle Randy White and Baltimore Colts offensive lineman Ken Huff. But eight carries, no yards. Something had to get better, and quickly.

Happily for Payton and the Bears, they did. After losing their season opener to the Colts, the Bears responded with a hard-fought 15–13 win over the Philadelphia Eagles. And leading the way was Payton, this time with 21 carries for 95 yards rushing and six catches for 36 yards. By the end of the season, Payton had run roughshod over the New Orleans Saints by posting 196 yards of total offense from the line of scrimmage in a 42–17 win.

From then on, the man known affectionately as "Sweetness" was the Bears' most reliable threat, some insisted the greatest player of his era. His career count of 16,726 yards rushing ranks second to Emmitt Smith of the Dallas Cowboys, who gained 18,355 yards on the ground. And Payton proved to be a workhorse. He led the NFL in carries from 1976 to 1979 and was named a First-Team All-Pro five times and a Pro Bowl selection nine times. He could run with power, turn up the speed, catch passes, throw passes and inspire his teammates without so much as bragging.

Walter Payton scopes out some running room during a game on December 4, 1977, against the Tampa Bay Buccaneers.

With Sweetness, it was all about the doing. On a 1977 afternoon game against the Minnesota Vikings, he rushed for a stunning 275 yards en route to being named the NFL MVP. He was 24 years old at the time.

He had won the hearts of Chicagoans, then and forever.

Payton was respected as much as a person as he was as a player. He wasn't one to brag.

"When you're good at something," he once said, "you'll tell everyone. When you're great at something, they'll tell you."

Anyone who loved the game, regardless of rooting interests, never had the slightest difficulty expounding on the multi-faceted greatness of Sweetness.

Former head coach Mike Ditka told the *New York Times* in 1999 that Payton earned the admiration of his teammates by being there for them, for lending a reliable shoulder to lean on when things went sour. And also for never demanding the ball in the huddle.

"He was so good for the team," lauded Ditka. "He was the biggest practical joker and he kept everyone loose. And he led by example on the field. He was the complete player."

Payton's sense of community led him to give back as much as he could.

Walter Payton retired after the 1987 season, as much a Chicago landmark as Millennium Park, Wrigley Field or the Navy Pier.

In retirement, life was treating him well. And then it wasn't.

On February 2, 1999, during an emotional news conference in Chicago, Payton disclosed that he had primary sclerosing cholangitis, a rare condition that causes inflammation and scarring of the bile ducts. He said doctors had told him he would need a liver transplant within two years. A week later, after further tests, doctors told him he needed a transplant by the end of the year. He was said to have been on a waiting list with 12,000 others at the Mayo Clinic.

Payton passed away on November 1, 1999. He was 45.

"If you ask me how I want to be remembered, it is as a winner," he is quoted as saying in his autobiography *Never Die Easy*. "You know what a winner is? A winner is somebody who has given his best effort, who has tried the hardest they possibly can, who has utilized every ounce of energy and strength within them to accomplish something."

He is remembered as a winner, and so much more.

A Mighty Good Man

The Walter Payton Man of the Year Award is given to the player who makes the biggest impact off the field. The award was originally called the NFL Man of the Year Award, of which Payton was a recipient in 1977, but it was renamed in Payton's honor in 1999.

NO. 73

Did We Really See That?

IN THE BEGINNING, there were Carol Channing, Anita Bryant and a parade of marching bands playing such ditties as the theme song from the TV series *Bonanza*. And let's not forget Up with People, although we'd all be better off if we did.

For decades, these and other singers and musicians were billed as stars of the Super Bowl's halftime show.

Good enough, one supposes, if undeniably blasé.

But all that changed in 1993. Recognizing that the premier game's halftime show needed significantly more pop to draw widespread attention and have TV viewers glued to their sets instead of searching for liquid refreshment, the NFL brain trust went in search of star power. Who better, then, to add pop than the King of Pop himself, Michael Jackson?

Radio City Productions, producers of the halftime show, contacted Jackson and his manager Sandy Gallin. Three meetings netted nothing but a $1 million compensation request from the Jackson camp. The league does not actually pay Super Bowl halftime performers, but a compromise was worked out: chip company Frito-Lay and the league would combine to donate $100,000 to Jackson's Heal the World Foundation, as well as provide commercial time during the game for the foundation's Heal Los Angeles campaign, aimed at helping LA youth in the aftermath of the Los Angeles riots the year before.

The biggest TV audience in NFL history tuned in to watch the show — 133.4 million in the U.S. alone and 1.3 billion around the world.

In the span of five songs — "Jam," "Billie Jean," "Black or White," "We Are the World" and "Heal the World" — Jackson forever changed what was still evolving into an American institution. He made the Super Bowl's halftime gig as monumental as the game itself. Suddenly, the show attracted a standalone sponsor willing to pay big time for big-time talent. It turned even non-football fans into ardent Super Bowl watchers. Now that's a true bonanza.

Since Jackson, the line-up of prime-time artists has included Paul

Michael Jackson performing during the Super Bowl XXVII halftime show on January 31, 1993. Jackson's performance forever changed the halftime show into a must-watch event that attracted the biggest musical artists.

McCartney, the Rolling Stones, Prince, Tom Petty and the Heartbreakers, Bruce Springsteen, U2, the Who, Bruno Mars with the Red Hot Chili Peppers, Usher, Madonna, Beyoncé, Katy Perry, Lady Gaga, Shakira and Jennifer Lopez. Not that every Super Bowl show has worked. The Black Eyed Peas were underwhelming, while the teaming of Aerosmith, Britney Spears, NSYNC, Mary J. Blige and Nelly looked like a thrown-together ensemble. (Up With People must have been working another gig that night.)

To this day, the most notorious halftime act involved Janet Jackson, Michael's sister, at Super Bowl XXXVIII. Things were going well with her co-star Justin Timberlake until he reached over and removed a piece of her costume, exposing her right breast to the world. The incident was later described as a "wardrobe malfunction," and representatives for both performers explained that the plan had been for Timberlake to remove the rubber bustier so only a red lace bra would be revealed. But due to a wardrobe malfunction ...

The fallout from that notorious slipup caused the league and broadcaster ABC to impose a five-second delay and an agreed-upon censorship clause on two songs with sexually explicit lyrics being sung by Rolling Stones frontman Mick Jagger for the Super Bowl halftime show two years later.

Janet has yet to make a second Super Bowl appearance. Timberlake, meanwhile, was back as a headliner for Super Bowl LII.

Peekaboo moments. Rappers. Raunchy rock 'n' rollers. Certainly a far cry from the University of Arizona marching band performing "The Liberty Bell March" and "Bury Me Not on the Lone Prairie" during the first halftime show way back in 1967.

The Fake Spike

NO. 74

As he walked up to the line of scrimmage, Dan Marino had every intention of spiking the football and stopping the clock with 25 seconds left in the game.

It was first and goal for Marino's Miami Dolphins at the New York Jets' 8-yard line, and everyone was expecting him to spike the ball to give his offense time to plan its next few moves.

But a funny thing happened on Marino's way to lining up behind his center. He looked at receiver Mark Ingram, who had already made eight catches for 109 yards and three touchdowns, and figured he'd be good for one more.

"I was going to try to stop the clock, and I saw Mark had man coverage," Marino said afterward. "I gave him a signal and he ran a quick take-off."

The fake spike was made convincing by Marino gesturing that he was going to turf the ball. Adding to the subterfuge, he hollered, "Clock! Clock! Clock!"

It caught the Jets and their homefield faithful off guard. It was a plan that was perfectly orchestrated by the Dolphins, who knew exactly what they were doing.

"We've been working on that play a long time," said Ingram, who beat Jets rookie cornerback Aaron Glenn in the end zone. Ingram's four-touchdown showing tied a franchise record set by receiver Paul Warfield in 1973.

Marino added that the idea had come from teammate and backup quarterback Bernie Kosar, who had previously played for the Cleveland Browns and the University of Miami. "I give Bernie Kosar credit. He brought the spike play to us from Cleveland, and he actually mentioned in my ear: 'Think about the clock play, think about the clock play.' It was perfect and we did it."

The November 27, 1994, clock play capped a wicked comeback by the Dolphins, who were trailing 24–6 in the final minute of the third quarter. With some crucial work by their defense — a fumble recovery along with some timely interceptions off Jets QB Boomer Esiason — Marino was able to make his last drive count. He completed seven of eight passes for 84 yards for a 28–24 win. It was the 27th fourth-quarter, come-from-behind win in Marino's career and his fifth against the Jets.

The victory placed Miami alone atop the AFC East Division. In the wake of the drama, Jets coach Pete Carroll called the loss "staggering."

New York would not win another game that season.

NO. 75

Snakebit at the Super Bowl

Bud Grant and Marv Levy, two of the finest coaches in NFL history, are both enshrined in the Pro Football Hall of Fame — Grant was so honored in 1994 and Levy in 2001.

They also coached in the Canadian Football League and won the Grey Cup, with Grant's Winnipeg Blue Bombers taking it four times and Levy's Montreal Alouettes twice.

And yet, the two men were a combined 0-8 in the Super Bowl. Grant's Minnesota Vikings lost in all four of their Super Bowl appearances, while

Levy's Buffalo Bills went one level worse. They lost in four *consecutive* Super Bowls. The best opportunity the Bills had at an NFL championship was their first Super Bowl, in the 1990 season, when Scott Norwood's 47-yard game-winning field goal attempt sailed wide right. The final score was 20–19 for the New York Giants.

From then on, the Bills couldn't catch a break. They came up short in all four of their Big Game appearances by a combined score of 139–73. The Vikings lost theirs by a 95–34 count.

His teammates and coach Levy made a point of telling Norwood that if only they had done this or done that, the outcome would have been different. He appreciated their support, but it did little to soothe his despair.

"Look, a lot of things happened out there," Norwood told *Sports Illustrated* 13 years after the kick. "A lot of other players didn't make plays, but that doesn't excuse me. I'm a player and I'm paid to perform, and I failed in that instance."

That was the curse, the lingering feeling that he let everyone down and how quickly he could be carried back to that moment, no matter how many teammates or fans wished him well.

Quarterback Fran Tarkenton made the Pro Football Hall of Fame because of his mind-altering scrambles and over-the-top passing numbers, all of which were record setting when he retired. In his second stint with Minnesota, following his time with the New York Giants, Tarkenton was able to take the Vikings to three Super Bowls in a four-year stretch, only to lose them all — each to a different team (Miami, Pittsburgh and Oakland). Two losses came in back-to-back seasons (1973 and 1974). In none of those losses was Tarkenton at his finest. His three-game account reads as follows: 489 yards passing, one touchdown toss, six interceptions — all bad enough for a QB rating of 47.3.

Yet in a video memorial Tarkenton made for his former Vikings boss, he expressed how fortunate he was to have had the understated Grant as his coach.

"In all my life I've never had a coach like [Grant]," said Tarkenton. "He never raised his voice to me or any of [my] teammates, but he knew how to lead.... Whenever someone asked me, 'what's it like to play for Bud?' I've told them the same thing: If you can't play for Bud Grant, you can't play."

NO. 76

The Trade of the Decade

TOGETHER, THEY MADE for an eye-catching couple. The groom wore a bow tie, a black tux and a pensive look. The bride wore a veil, a white dress and carried a blushing-pink bouquet. Only this was not your typical wedding photo. It wasn't your typical anything.

Pictured as the groom was New Orleans Saints coach Mike Ditka; his partner was Heisman Trophy–winning running back Ricky Williams. Their gridiron nuptials were featured on the cover of *ESPN The Magazine* with the headline "For Better or Worse." It was a most-fitting photo and caption, given the Saints' full-out pursuit of Williams. After all, it isn't every day an NFL team trades all its picks in a single draft, and then some more the following year, for the chance to select an NCAA record-setting rusher.

But that's what the Saints did. They dealt their first-round pick in the 1999 NFL Draft and their third-, fourth-, fifth-, sixth- and seventh-round picks, as well as their first-round and third-round picks for the 2000 draft. That grand total of eight picks went to the Washington Redskins for the fifth overall pick, which is where Williams was expected to go. It was, to put it mildly, the most extravagant, high-risk maneuver ever attempted by an NFL team.

And it was the awestruck Ditka who pushed for it to happen. As the man who coached the 1985 Chicago Bears to the Super Bowl, Ditka was keen to add a running back who could do for the Saints what Walter Payton did for the Bears. By all accounts, Williams was that back. In his senior year at the University of Texas, he scored six touchdowns in one game twice, then added a five-touchdown showing against Iowa State in a game in which he ran for 350 yards. He was so successful he set records for setting records.

And that made him the man for the Saints, specifically Ditka, whose record after two years in New Orleans was a failing 12-20. But the couple would last just one year together. In his rookie season, Williams ran for 884 yards and scored two TDs in 12 games. By season's end, Ditka was gone after posting a paltry 3-13 record. Williams would run for 1,000 yards and eight TDs in 10 games in his second season and then 1,245 yards in his third. But that would mark the end for Williams, too. He was traded in the off-season to the Miami Dolphins for — what else? — three draft picks, two of them first-rounders.

Running back Ricky Williams of the New Orleans Saints fends off Chicago Bears safety Tony Parrish on October 8, 2000, during his second season with the Saints. That game, Williams rushed for 128 yards on 30 carries as the Saints won 31–10.

It was with the Dolphins that Williams found himself then almost fumbled it away. In 2002, he ran for an NFL-leading 1,853 yards; in 2004, away from the field, he tested positive for marijuana and was given a four-game suspension and fined $650,000. It was the first of four violations of league policy, the last of which cost him the entire 2006 season. That didn't mean he was done with football, though. With the Dolphins' approval, Williams signed with the Toronto Argonauts of the CFL, which didn't have a drug policy at the time. The lone provision was that Williams would return to Miami for the 2007 NFL season. After signing a one-year, $340,000 contract, making him the CFL's highest-paid running back, Williams didn't come close to tearing up the CFL — lugging the rock 109 times for 526 yards and scoring two touchdowns in 11 starts for the Argonauts — but he did enjoy the city, the league and the overall experience of life in Canada.

Williams' second run with the Dolphins proved more effective than his time north of the border. In 2009 he gained 1,121 yards, setting a record for the longest time span between 1,000-yard seasons — six years in all.

He was 32 when he did it.

In the summer of 2011, Williams left Miami for Baltimore after agreeing to a two-year, $2.5-million contract with the Ravens. He announced his retirement after one season in Baltimore, on February 7, 2012.

Over the duration of his career, Williams ran for 10,009 yards, to go along with 74 touchdowns.

NO. 77

Elway Cements His Legacy

FOR THE LONGEST time, Denver Broncos quarterback John Elway was thought of as this wonderfully talented athlete who couldn't win the Lombardi Trophy to save his reputation.

The proof was in the pounding.

Yeah, he'd fashioned The Drive to push the Broncos to a Super Bowl XXI appearance back in the 1986 season, but since then, with Elway as the starter, Denver had lost two further Super Bowls, including one by the preposterous score of 55–10 — that public spanking being conducted by the San Francisco 49ers and Joe Montana.

It took nearly 10 more years, but things finally changed. The voodoo curse on the Broncos was lifted, and they went on to win back-to-back Super Bowls in the late 1990s.

By then, Elway had become a superstar to rally around — someone only needing a championship to verify his legendary status.

"I don't know if I like being the sentimental favorite," he confessed to reporters prior to kickoff against the Packers at Qualcomm Stadium in 1998. "There are a lot of people who might not get another chance to win a Super Bowl. Not just me."

This time, there would be no stopping him. On one play, Elway took off with the ball and was headed to the Green Bay end zone with the score tied 17–17 when he was hit by three Packers — LeRoy Butler, Mike Prior and Brian Williams. The first two Packers slammed into Elway, giving him lift-off as the third Packer spun him around in the air with a well-timed hit. Elway hung onto the ball, gained a first down and was able to lead his team to its first Super Bowl title.

It had been a long time coming.

A second ring arrived only a year later against the Atlanta Falcons. On that Super Sunday evening in Miami, Elway threw 18 completions on 29 attempts for 336 yards and a TD and was named MVP.

John Elway hoists the Vince Lombardi Trophy after winning Super Bowl XXXII on January 28, 1998.

On that happy note, he retired as a two-time champion at the age of 38. At the time Elway ranked second all-time in three of the game's most significant passing categories: passing yards (51,475), attempts (7,250) and completions (4,123).

Upon retirement, he joined the Broncos' front office, where he would help the only franchise he ever played for to a third championship.

In 2004 Elway ascended to pass through the gates of football's Olympus, located in Canton, Ohio.

"I think probably the thing that I am most proud of," Elway said then, "is that I was able to hang in there long enough to win a couple of Super Bowls."

THE 2000s

Contents

No. 78 Another Crazy Trade 145

No. 79 The Music City Miracle 146

No. 80 One Yard Short 148

No. 81 Laying Down the Law 149

No. 82 Death of a Quarterback 151

No. 83 A Heady Decision 152

No. 84 What the Tuck?! 155

No. 85 Corp. Pat Tillman and the Battle for Truth 156

No. 86 The NFL Network Is on the Air 159

No. 87 A Super Turnabout 160

No. 88 The River City Relay 162

No. 89 The Unstoppable Dante Hall 163

No. 90 Rebirth of a City and Its Team 165

No. 91 Fortune Favors the Bold 166

No. 92 Spygate 168

No. 93 Bountygate 170

No. 94 Overseas Investments 172

No. 95 The Incredible Rise and Fall of Michael Vick 174

Another Crazy Trade

NO. 78

HEAD COACH JON Gruden was a man in high demand in early 2002.

He was still under contract with the Oakland Raiders, but that didn't prevent the Tampa Bay Buccaneers from asking for permission to negotiate with him. Raiders boss Al Davis figured he had a lot to gain, so he asked for Tampa's first- and second-round picks in 2002, a first-round pick in 2003 and a second-round pick in 2004.

Oh, and one more thing: the Raiders asked for $8 million.

"Tampa Bay came to me and they said they wanted Gruden ... I felt that I put the price tag so high that they wouldn't agree to it. And they did [agree]," said Davis. "Gruden is no longer our coach."

Gruden and the Bucs did get a measure of payback in Super Bowl XXXVII when they ransacked Oakland 48–21. The victory made the 39-year-old Gruden the youngest head coach to win the title.

That bit of high-profile karma earned Gruden a second engagement with the Raiders in January 2018, when he signed a 10-year, $100-million contract that included a no-trade clause.

Which should have led to a happy reunion. But an NFL investigation into the Washington Football Team for workplace misconduct found incriminating emails sent to Washington GM Bruce Allen from Gruden. In a series of communiqués, Gruden used racist, misogynistic and homophobic slurs. He not only criticized NFL commissioner Roger Goodell, he slagged former U.S. President Barack Obama and Vice President Joe Biden. There were also emails between Gruden and Washington Football Team staff that contained photos of topless women, including the team's cheerleaders.

Gruden resigned as Raiders coach on October 11, 2021, and he was removed from the Buccaneers' Ring of Honor over the email scandal.

NO.
79

The Music City Miracle

The Buffalo Bills had just kicked a field goal for a 16–15 lead with a mere 16 seconds remaining in their game against the Tennessee Titans on January 8, 2000.

All that was left in this 1999 AFC wild-card playoff game was a deep kick and some special teams tackling, and the Bills would be moving on in the postseason.

But little did the Bills know that Tennessee had called for the "Home Run Throwback," a specially designed play for their kickoff return team. The origin of the Throwback dated back to the early 1980s, when Alan Lowry, then a member of the Dallas Cowboys' coaching staff, watched Southern Methodist University beat Texas Tech on a lateral pass off a kickoff return. Lowry took that return idea with him when he became the Titans' special teams coach in 1999. In fact, Lowry had his players practice it weekly during the regular season.

Against Buffalo, however, there were a couple of unexpected problems. For starters, the Titans' best kickoff returner, Derrick Mason, was unavailable after being hurt earlier in the game. Back-up returner Anthony Dorsett was sidelined with cramps. It was decided that receiver Kevin Dyson would have to catch the lateral pass, only he had never practiced the play. The coaches explained it to him before he took to the field.

Buffalo's Steve Christie kicked the ball to the Titans' Lorenzo Neal, who then handed it to tight end Frank Wycheck. He fired a pass across the field to Dyson.

From there, Dyson raced untouched 75 yards into the Buffalo end zone.

"Well, Jeff Fisher, I mean, he was a detail-oriented coach," Wycheck, who died in 2023 of head injuries sustained during a fall at home, told *The Tennessean* in 2020. "And we, like any team should, you go over every possible situation that can come up in a game and you do that with your two-minute drill, your four-minute drill, how to run out games and even practice the victory

Wide receiver Kevin Dyson (No. 87) races 75 yards for the game-winning touchdown during the 1999 AFC wild-card playoff game.

formation … We hoped we'd never get in that situation, but it proved to be very successful because we were all prepared."

The original plan had been for Dyson to step out of bounds and stop the clock when close enough for a field goal attempt, but the Buffalo sea had parted and he just kept running.

"When Christie went down, everything just went silent," Dyson recalled. "I can remember thinking: 'Should I get out of bounds?' But then I was like: 'This is it!' And it was smooth sailing."

The play was shown from several TV angles. It proved to be a parallel pass and not a forward pass, which would have been illegal.

To this day, it remains one of the most dramatic game-ending scores in NFL history.

NO.

80 One Yard Short

Tennessee receiver Kevin Dyson, the man who capped the Music City Miracle with his last-second touchdown run, had one more call to glory.

In Super Bowl XXXIV, on January 30, 2000, the Titans found themselves trailing the St. Louis Rams 23–16 with time running out in the fourth quarter. Tennessee quarterback Steve McNair moved his offense from the Titans' 12-yard line to the Rams' 10-yard line with only six seconds left on the clock. Dyson ran his pattern — a quick slant over the middle — and caught the ball, then was tackled by Rams linebacker Mike Jones. Dyson, hog-tied by Jones, stretched out as far as he could but was 1 yard shy of the end zone. There were actually two seconds left on the clock when Dyson touched down on the turf, but the Titans couldn't call a timeout because they were out of them. The game was over.

"That team, we were built for comebacks," Dyson said years later about how quickly the Titans moved downfield as the final seconds ticked down. Off a scramble by McNair, Dyson took a pass at the Rams' 11-yard line. On the ensuing play, he ran an inside route to gain an inside position on the linebacker.

"[Jones] spotted me a little quicker than he would have had we been at the 20-yard line," recalled Dyson. "All I remember was how yellow and vivid that end zone looked … It was so close. I felt I was there."

"You can tell when a receiver is going to get the ball. The eyes get a little bigger. They prepare to catch the ball. Little things like that," said Jones. "So when I'm looking at Kevin I'm thinking this guy doesn't see me. I got a great chance of getting a kill shot.

"That tackle was the greatest play of my life."

In a game that also capped the emergence of St. Louis quarterback Kurt Warner, rising from back-up obscurity to Super Bowl MVP, the "One-Yard Short" play managed to command center stage.

And what of Dyson and Jones? Well, the two men are now locked together for NFL eternity in historical league highlight packages.

Jones went on to become a head coach at Lincoln University before being hired as a high school coach in St. Louis. Dyson earned two master's degrees and a PhD in education in leadership and professional practice. In 2021 he was named the principal at Centennial High School in Franklin, Tennessee.

Laying Down the Law

NO. **81**

NFL COMMISSIONER ROGER Goodell has shown he isn't one to shy away from a confrontation. He's had spats with Patriots owner Robert Kraft. He's fined players and coaches and even suspended the likes of Tom Brady. For Bountygate, the money-for-knockouts pay system run by the New Orleans Saints, Goodell KO'd head coach Sean Payton with a one-season suspension. He locked out the officiating crews in hopes of getting a better collective agreement for the league. (That one backfired when the replacement officials proved to be a disaster.)

Goodell also agreed to a $765-million settlement that would pay former players who suffered head trauma during their careers. And to prevent another episode like San Francisco 49ers quarterback Colin Kaepernick not standing for the U.S. national anthem, Goodell made it NFL law that everyone has to stand for the anthem. Protesters can stay off the field until the anthem is done.

Such is Goodell's body of work since September 2006, when he took over from the retiring Paul Tagliabue.

He certainly isn't shy about mixing it up with whoever, over whatever. Goodell, when asked to describe his style, has said, "I have to make a lot of decisions that aren't in the best interests of individuals, whether they be owners, club executives, players."

He added, "No one is above the game or the rules that govern it. Respect for the game and the people who participate in it will not be compromised."

Goodell's ascension to the NFL's highest position began with an

Roger Goodell (left) and retiring NFL commissioner Paul Tagliabue at an owners' meeting in August 2006.

introductory letter he sent to the league and all its 28 teams at the time in the hopes of landing a job. The Jamestown, New York, native was a former high school star in basketball, baseball and football who gave up the gridiron game in college due to injuries.

NFL commissioner Pete Rozelle was impressed with Goodell's letter-writing initiative and offered him an administrative internship. After spending a year with the New York Jets, Goodell returned to the league office as a public relations assistant. (Rozelle had gotten his first taste of the NFL toiling in the PR department of the Los Angeles Rams in the late 1940s and early 1950s.)

By 1987, Goodell was appointed assistant to Lamar Hunt, the president of the NFL's American Football Conference. That was the launch pad that carried Goodell to a new stratosphere. Working diligently in both business and football matters, he was promoted to executive vice president and chief operating officer in December 2001.

From there on, his handling of negotiations with the NFL Players Association for a new collective agreement, dealing with expansion, formulating the NFL Network and a myriad of other issues helped enhance his role as a future commissioner in training. Former New York Giants general manager Ernie Accorsi said of Goodell: "Those of us who have been around a long time were rooting for someone from inside the [NFL] family. He's always been aggressive and always had a presence about him. He couldn't be more qualified for this job."

Goodell has fully embraced the change in media platforms, agreeing to eye-popping deals with NBCUniversal, Paramount+, Fox, ESPN and Amazon in 2021 worth more than $110 billion, with an eye toward streaming services.

"The technology is changing. The platforms are changing. The economy is changing. We have to be ahead of that strategy at all times so that we are where our fans are, on the platforms they want to be on," Goodell explained to *The Hollywood Reporter* of those rights agreements.

Goodell's various public battles have alienated him on many fronts, but he remains true to the men who hired him. And why wouldn't he?

His compensation for the 2019–20 season, as well as for 2020–21, was reported to be a staggering $63.9 million. That, according to talksport.com, was more than what Joe Burrow and Patrick Mahomes made in their deals as star quarterbacks.

Death of a Quarterback

NO. 82

THE NEWS HIT hard in Nashville, as across Tennessee: longtime Titans star quarterback Steve McNair had been murdered by his 20-year-old girlfriend.

Sahel "Jenni" Kazemi was a 19-year-old waitress working at the local Dave and Buster's restaurant, where many Titans players frequented, when she first met McNair.

"Air McNair," as he'd been christened, had enjoyed a prolific NFL career, winning league co-MVP (with Peyton Manning) in 2003 and throwing for 31,304 yards for two franchises, Tennessee and Baltimore, over 13 seasons.

Retired for only a year in 2009, then 36, he quickly became a familiar face at the restaurant just so he could see Kazemi on a regular basis. McNair was clearly smitten.

He helped her buy a black Escalade for her 20th birthday, and everything seemed fine. The two took trips across the country together. But on July 4, 2009, something went tragically wrong. Kazemi either picked up one of McNair's guns or brandished one she herself had purchased, then shot McNair four times, twice in the head, twice in the chest. She then shot herself.

McNair was married with two kids and had two sons from a previous relationship. It was later reported that he had told Kazemi he was getting a divorce, though he still lived at home with his wife of 12 years, Mechelle, and their children. Kazemi allegedly also had suspicions that McNair was secretly seeing another woman.

Whatever the reasons, it all came to a tragic head that July 4.

Afterward, McNair's wife said she had no inkling of the affair with Kazemi, nor were there any discussions with her husband about a possible divorce.

"I didn't know about her at all," Mechelle McNair told ESPN. "You're going to have people who say, 'Oh, she knew.' Did I know about some other people and some other things? Yes. But did I know about her? No, I did not."

McNair's death sent a shock wave through the football world.

"The whole Black quarterback thing, it's like a fraternity," said former NFL QB Jason Campbell. "Guys who played before you pass the torch down to younger guys ... Losing a guy like [McNair] from our fraternity ... it hurts because of how much you looked up to him. He's definitely one of the guys I looked up to."

Authorities ruled the deaths as a murder-suicide.

NO. 83 A Heady Decision

WAY BACK IN the day, NFL players wore only leather helmets, which offered all the protection of a baseball cap.

In 1943 the league made it mandatory for all players to wear more protective plastic headgear. From the 1990s onward, bigger, faster players capable of inflicting all means of damage pushed helmet safety to a higher level of concern.

Scientists have developed better testing to measure how much damage is done by repetitive hits to the head. There have also been changes to the playing rules. Players who commit helmet-to-helmet hits are penalized, fined or suspended.

But the danger is real, and it remains.

An ever-increasing number of concerned former players have come forward in recent years to talk about their mental health issues. Many were so confused and depressed they took their own lives. The autopsies of Mike Webster, Dave Duerson, Ray Easterling, Junior Seau and Aaron Hernandez have underlined just how dangerous concussions can be. The current belief is that repetitive head trauma contributes to chronic traumatic encephalopathy (CTE), a neurodegenerative disease that may result in dementia. Other medical experts have stated there is no definitive scientific connection between concussions and CTE and that more studies are needed.

Andrew Luck didn't need any conclusive evidence to convince him he was playing with fire. It took the 29-year-old former No. 1 draft pick two years to find his rhythm and adjust to NFL defenses. But once he did, he bettered the passing standards set by John Elway during his early seasons with the Denver Broncos. And Luck was able to lift his Indianapolis Colts into the playoffs — a sign of good things to come.

Then the shoulder injuries became a problem, as did the concussions. The Colts, as talented as they were on offense, couldn't protect Luck. The punishment had taken a toll that could not be ignored. He'd been sacked 174 times in 86 games. As Luck would have it, that was enough. He announced his retirement to a stunned NFL two weeks prior to the 2019 season, saying the health issues had "taken my joy of this game away."

"It's been four years of this injury-pain rehab cycle," Luck explained at a career-ending media conference. "I can't live the life I want to live moving forward ... I feel quite exhausted and quite tired. I know I am unable to pour my heart and soul into this position ... and it's sad, but I also have a lot of clarity in this.

"I've been stuck in this process. I haven't been able to live the life I want to live."

Luck, who graduated from Stanford with a bachelor's degree in architectural design in 2012, has since rediscovered that joy he spoke of by coaching a junior varsity high school football team in Palo Alto, California.

He is far from alone in the difficulty of dealing with serious head injuries.

More than 4,500 former players were behind a class-action suit against the league, claiming it downplayed the growing evidence that CTE was more dangerous than the NFL let on. The league settled for $765 million and promised to help players suffering from brain-related disorders. But an investigation by the *Washington Post* showed that qualifying for financial assistance has proven to be most difficult, and that has saved the league money.

As proof of its ongoing concern for its players, the NFL has pointed to some of its new initiatives. For example, there has been better cooperation

Tampa Bay Buccaneers OT Luke Goedeke (No. 67) blocks Chauncey Golston (99) of the Dallas Cowboys in a December 2024 game. As of the 2024 season, Goedeke is one of a handful of players to use the Guardian Cap in regular-season play.

with the Players Association, with both sides working together to reduce the risk of concussions. There has been more testing done using artificial intelligence and the latest technology to design safer helmets.

In 2023, the NFL mandated the use of the Guardian Cap during training camp and practices. The cap fits over the helmet and adds another protective layer to absorb hits. According to the NFL, there was a 50 percent drop in concussions from 2022 training camps to 2023.

That paved the way for the caps to be used in games. Only five players wore them at the start of the 2024 regular season.

At this point, there isn't any helmet that can prevent concussions. And as Vince Lombardi succinctly, and aptly, explained it, "Football isn't a contact sport; it's a collision sport."

What the Tuck?!

NO. **84**

Slightly over two decades after the fact, in 2022, Tom Brady finally came clean.

Well, sort of …

Via a social media video post, the legendary quarterback confessed that the (in)famous play in the Tuck Rule Game "might have been a fumble."

He then backtracked quicker than a member of the quarterbacking fraternity with Mean Joe Greene in hot pursuit.

"I said might. Such a tough call. No choice but to respect the officials probably correct decision."

Trigger a long-smoldering outpouring of angst and fury from Raiders Nation.

January 19, 2002. Foxborough, Massachusetts. AFC Divisional playoff game. Heavy snowstorm. A chilly 19 degrees Fahrenheit at kickoff. A minute and 50 seconds left in the fourth quarter, the homesteading Patriots trailing 13–10 to the Oakland Raiders.

Brady — in his first year at the helm following an early-season injury to Drew Bledsoe — drops back to pass. He's hit on the blind side by college teammate Charles Woodson. The ball pops loose. Raiders linebacker Greg Biekert falls on it.

Raiders possession. Game over.

Wait, not so fast …

Three years earlier, a new rule had been established that read as follows:

> NFL Rule 3, Section 22, Article 2, Note 2. When (an offensive) player is holding the ball to pass it forward, any intentional forward movement of his arm starts a forward pass, even if the player loses possession of the ball as he is attempting to tuck it back toward his body. Also, if the player has tucked the ball into his body and then loses possession, it is a fumble.

The play was reviewed. After a lengthy replay check, referee Walt Coleman reversed the initial call, declaring the play an incomplete forward pass, ruling Brady's arm had been moving forward when the hit occurred and handing possession back to New England.

The Patriots made the most of their good fortune, with Brady subsequently driving his offense to tie the game 13–13 on a clutch 45-yard field goal by Adam Vinatieri. New England won the game in overtime via another field goal, this time from 23 yards.

The Patriots went on to defeat the Pittsburgh Steelers 24–17 in the AFC Championship and the St. Louis Rams 20–17 at Super Bowl XXXVI in New Orleans, igniting the Tom Brady–Bill Belichick title dynasty.

The Tuck Rule Game remains one of the most talked-about refereeing decisions in league history. So hotly debated, in fact, that ESPN's excellent *30 for 30* documentary series produced a film on the play itself and the subsequent controversy.

The Tuck Rule was abolished on March 20, 2013, by a 29–1 vote of current teams.

That, along with Brady's two-decades-later, well-um-sorta social media confession, was of pitifully small solace to the Raiders and their partisans.

NO. 85 Corp. Pat Tillman and the Battle for Truth

The money was real, and it was good — $9 million over five years to sign with the St. Louis Rams. But Pat Tillman turned it down out of loyalty to the NFL team that drafted him, the Arizona Cardinals.

And when he was offered $3.6 million for a three-year extension with the Cards, despite that loyalty, he turned it down, too — out of loyalty to a higher calling, his country.

Watching the September 11 terrorist attacks on the World Trade Center shook Tillman to the point where he vowed to do something about it, something drastic. He and his brother Kevin chose to enlist in the U.S. Army in May

Pat Tillman of the Arizona Cardinals on the field before a game on November 8, 1998.

2002. They were assigned to the 2nd Ranger Battalion in Fort Lewis, Washington, and not long after their basic training was done, they were assigned to a forward operating base in Iraq. It was during an April 22, 2004, attack that Tillman and another soldier were reportedly shot at and killed by enemy forces. It turned out Tillman had been misidentified and felled by friendly fire. Thus began a murky tale of misleading statements, military and government investigations and much hand-wringing over the fact that Tillman was more than just another casualty and that his death was likely preventable.

As a linebacker, the former Arizona State standout had developed into a take-charge leader who would go on to be named the team's MVP. With the Cardinals, he had a breakout season in 2000, when he totaled 118 solo tackles, 1.5 sacks, 2 forced fumbles, 2 fumble recoveries, 9 pass deflections and 1 interception for 30 yards. That a talented NFL player would give it all up — fame, fortune and family, at the age of 26 — only to die in such a haphazard manner did not look good for the Army. In fact, Tillman's mother, Mary, said she was certain their family had been fed lies to protect the Army's image. Patrick Tillman Sr. added, "They purposely interfered with the investigation, they covered it up. I think they thought they could control it, and they realized that their recruiting efforts were going to go to hell in a handbasket if the truth about his death got out. They blew up their poster boy."

As if to pacify the Tillmans, the Army posthumously decorated their son with the Silver Star and the Purple Heart. He was also promoted to the rank of corporal.

In the 20-plus years that have passed since Tillman's death, his family has organized enough charitable events to keep his memory alive. The Pat Tillman Foundation supports Tillman Scholars, who are, according to the foundation's website, "military service members, veterans and spouses with a high potential for impact as demonstrated through a proven track record of leadership, the continued pursuit of education and the commitment of their resources to service beyond self." A non-profit organization, the Foundation collaborates with a host of corporate sponsors, grant, foundation and estate partners, strategic partners and universities. Thanks to the generosity of these partners and individual donations, the Foundation has raised over $37 million to help over 900 military veterans and their spouses achieve their potential through education and leadership skills.

In addition, an annual Pat's Run is held in Tempe, Arizona, regularly drawing over 30,000 participants for a 4.2-mile walk-run that helps fund scholarships and other initiatives for Tillman Scholars.

This quote from Tillman is the inspiration behind the entire enterprise: "Somewhere inside, we hear a voice. It leads us in the direction of the person we wish to become. But it is up to us whether or not to follow."

The NFL Network Is on the Air

NO. **86**

TELEVISION, THEY KNEW, is where the profits and profile lie.

So to supplement its ties with various traditional networks of the day, the NFL officially started its own network on November 4, 2003 — all things NFL, every day, all day. Today the NFL Network is part of a blanket NFL Media, which also includes NFL.com, NFL Films, NFL Mobile, NFL Now and NFL RedZone. The network broadcasts non-NFL football as well, including college-level postseason games and games for other pro leagues, such as the Arena Football League, the Alliance of American Football and the Canadian Football League. The NFL did its best to ensure the network would draw customers to its pay package.

The original NFL Network was housed in Culver City, California, and $100 million was sunk into its formation and operation. Eight months before its launch, the owners of the league's 32 teams had voted unanimously to approve its establishment.

Its ties with NFL Films provided a cornucopia of material. Former NFL Films president Steve Sabol said his company has tens of thousands of canisters and roughly 100 million feet of film in its archives, dating back to a football game between Princeton and Rutgers played in 1894.

The network began broadcasting Thursday primetime live games in 2006, branded as *Thursday Night Football*. In 2021 NFL Network, along with all NFL media properties, relocated to a 200,000-square-foot space in Inglewood, California.

NO.

87 A Super Turnabout

IN FOOTBALL, THINGS can change quickly.

In life, too.

In less than one year, Baltimore Ravens' star linebacker Ray Lewis went from murder suspect to Super Bowl champion.

On January 31, 2000, Lewis, then a four-year NFLer, and his friends were celebrating at a Super Bowl XXXIV party — following the Rams' victory over the Titans — and then left to continue their revelry at the Cobalt Club, a well-known nightspot in the Buckhead Village area of Atlanta.

There, one of Lewis' entourage was struck in the head by a champagne bottle outside the club, triggering a melee. Two men from the rival group, 21-year-old Jacinth Baker and 24-year-old Richard Lollar, died of stab wounds en route to the hospital.

Lewis was one of three men indicted for murder and aggravated assault.

The trial lasted four weeks.

Lewis claimed to have tried to stop the fight. While witnesses said he threw punches, they also testified that he was not seen carrying a knife. Lewis had his murder charge dropped after agreeing to testify against his co-defendants.

On June 5, 2000, the 24-year-old was handed a 12-month probation order and was later fined $250,000 by the NFL for entering a guilty plea for obstructing justice. He admitted to telling defendants Reginald Oakley and Joseph Sweeting to "keep your mouth shut" and acknowledged not providing complete statements to the police.

Oakley and Sweeting maintained that they had acted in self-defense, and a jury acquitted them of all charges.

Lewis eventually reached undisclosed settlements with the families of both young men who died.

From the trial, flash forward several months, to January 28, 2001, and Super Bowl XXXV, where the Ravens crushed the New York Giants 34–7 at Raymond James Stadium in Tampa, Florida.

Ray Lewis celebrates the Baltimore Ravens' Super Bowl XXXV victory. Lewis was named game MVP in the 34–7 win over the New York Giants.

As the MVP of the game, only the second linebacker to be so honored, Lewis was supposed to deliver the then-standard "I'm going to Disney World!" promo plug before heading off to the Florida incarnation of the "Happiest Place on Earth."

But instead, because of the recent murder trial, Baltimore QB Trent Dilfer was given the line. And the trip.

Lewis retired in 2013 after 17 seasons, all with the Ravens, having won a second Super Bowl ring in his final NFL start. He is a 12-time Pro Bowler, a Hall of Famer and universally acknowledged as one of the greatest linebackers in the annals of football.

NO.

88 The River City Relay

OH, THE PAIN of it all. To have done the near impossible only to lose it all on a play so automatic it often gets overlooked.

That had to crawl under the skin of the New Orleans Saints like a 10-pound tick.

Here's how it happened: The Saints needed a win to keep their ultra-slim playoff chances alive, beginning with their December 21, 2003, date in Jacksonville against the Jaguars. The Saints got the ball on their 25-yard line, trailing on the scoreboard 20–13 with seven seconds remaining. Quarterback Aaron Brooks found receiver Donté Stallworth for a 25-yard gain. Stallworth then lateraled the ball to Michael Lewis, who reached the Jags' 34-yard line before lateraling it to running back Deuce McAllister, who did the same to Jerome Pathon, who crossed the goal line with no time left on the Alltel Stadium clock.

After a lengthy officiating delay to go over the legitimacy of the play, it was ruled legal, making the score 20–19 and giving the Saints an option. They could go for a two-point conversion and the win, or they could rely on the reliable right foot of kicker John Carney to send things into overtime.

Carney was next to automatic when it came to kicking extra points. When he retired after playing for eight teams over four decades, his extra point percentage stood at 98.4.

New Orleans head coach Jim Haslett had said earlier in the year that he trusted Carney with his life, so Haslett sent his kicker out to force OT. And off a seemingly good snap and hold, Carney missed the kick, triggering the oft-replayed incredulity of Saints' play-by-play radio announcer Jim Henderson: "NOOOO! He missed the extra point wide right! Oh my God, how could he do that?"

The gaffe also left Carney's coach reconsidering what he had said about trusting his kicker with his life.

"Then I'd probably be dead right now," Haslett quipped. "He's one of the great all-time kickers. I never would have guessed this would happen."

At that point in NFL history, it was the first three-play lateral covering 75 yards.

The play was tagged the "River City Relay" given the location of Jacksonville's stadium, next to the St. Johns River.

The Unstoppable Dante Hall

NO. 89

The nicknames don't begin to do the reality justice.

"Anything that is unexpected," said Dante Hall, "is the X-Factor" — referencing one of his two sobriquets that have stuck.

The other? The "Human Joystick."

Over an astounding four-consecutive-game run in 2003, the 5-foot-8, 187-pound keg of gunpowder scored touchdowns on either a punt or kickoff return under the employ of the Kansas City Chiefs. No returner had ever been able to string together that degree of consistent sizzle before.

When deployed in the offense, Hall was an edge-of-your-seat exciting wide receiver, as well.

Given a bit of space, the man seemed capable of dematerializing at will, of changing direction on a whim. As agile as a Cirque du Soleil performer, he was about as easy to pin down as a shadow in sunshine. When hit, he resembled a pinball arcade ball bouncing off one of the bumpers. Forget X-Factor, he should've been called an X-File. The man was alien-good. Even given the special coverages that were soon designed to stop him, Hall excelled.

The 2003 four-game run cemented his place in the history books — two touchdowns came via punts, and two on kickoffs.

"Everything," said Hall, "is instincts when returning kicks."

Of that magical month, a 93-yard classic stands out, with Hall reversing the field twice to leave the Denver Broncos' cover team utterly discombobulated.

Hall would go on to claim four-straight AFC Special Teams Player of the Week awards during that remarkable span.

"Free advice," sports columnist Bernie Lincicome wrote of the phenomenon, referencing singer-songwriter Jim Croce's mega-hit "Bad, Bad Leroy Brown." "Don't kick the ball to No. 82. You don't tug on Superman's cape. You don't spit in the wind. And you don't dare Hall of the Kansas City Chiefs to beat you."

Hall's performance transformed him into a star. In KC and beyond his popularity went through the roof.

Dante Hall sprints to the end zone during his memorable 93-yard punt-return touchdown against the Denver Broncos on October 5, 2003.

"If I had the hand strength to sign autographs for everybody in Kansas City, I would," he said of that magical time. "But it's just impossible to get to everyone."

Why, he even made an appearance on the *Late Show with David Letterman*.

Not bad for a guy drafted without much fanfare in the fifth round, 153rd overall, in the 2000 draft out of Texas A&M (the same year a certain Tom Brady was selected 46 spots lower by the New England Patriots).

Hall spent the years 2000 through 2006 in KC before being dealt with a third-round draft pick to the St. Louis Rams for their third- and fifth-round draft picks in the 2007 NFL Draft.

He retired after two seasons in St. Louis, but the memory of his incredible ability to escape defenders, especially in that once-in-a-lifetime month of incandescent dazzle, lives on.

Rebirth of a City and Its Team

NO. 90

THE AFTERMATH WAS nothing short of catastrophic.

Over 1,800 people had died. Some 53 breaches to various flood protection structures in and around New Orleans caused havoc and destruction. It was calculated that $150 billion would be needed to fix all the property and economic damage caused by the flooding.

But the famous undying spirit of New Orleans served it well at a time of such crisis as Hurricane Katrina. "You can live in any city in America," it's been said of the Big Easy, "but New Orleans is the only city that lives in you."

So it proved to be. And the New Orleans Saints did their part to help with the healing in the wake of the disaster that hit on August 29, 2005. Players got involved, quickly deploying to hand out supplies to those who needed it since there were so many left homeless and using the Superdome — itself battered by the elements — as a shelter. The team relocated its preseason offices to San Antonio and practiced at a sports complex next to a local high school. The Saints split their home games between Louisiana State University's Tiger Stadium and San Antonio's Alamodome. That fueled speculation that Saints owner Tom Benson wanted out of the Superdome and New Orleans and was eyeing a deal with San Antonio officials.

The NFL was against such a move, and on September 25, 2006, after $185 million in repairs to the Superdome, the Saints came marching in to host the Atlanta Falcons, 21 months since their last regular-season or playoff home game.

The football team provided something familiar for the citizens to rally around. The Goo Goo Dolls, Green Day and U2 performed that Monday. Former President George W. Bush performed the coin toss.

"I think it symbolized not only maybe the resurgence of our football team," said Saints quarterback Drew Brees, "but the resurgence of the city and the recovery and the rebirth."

On the ESPN television broadcast before kickoff, sportscaster Stuart Scott predicted, "It is going to be as an emotional night as you will ever see for a football game."

And it was. During those emotional few hours, New Orleans defensive back Steve Gleason blocked a punt that was recovered in the end zone for a Saints touchdown. That play came to symbolize the fighting spirit of New Orleans. A statue of Gleason's block, named *Rebirth*, was placed outside the stadium.

The Saints won 23–3. The team presented the city of New Orleans with the game ball.

Gleason's Journey

As for Steve Gleason, he spent eight seasons with the team before retiring in 2008. Three years later, he revealed he had amyotrophic lateral sclerosis, better known as ALS or Lou Gehrig's disease.

His struggle and inspirational fight against the disease were featured in a 2016 documentary entitled *Gleason*. Three years later, in 2019, he was awarded a Congressional Gold Medal for his contributions to ALS awareness.

NO. 91 Fortune Favors the Bold

LESS THAN FIVE years later, with the memory of Hurricane Katrina still etched in the minds of the city, the long-time doormat New Orleans Saints reached the Big Dance.

Super Bowl XLIV pitted the underdog Saints against quarterback Peyton Manning and his 14-2 Indianapolis Colts.

The game turned on one bold move, orchestrated by head coach Sean Payton.

It was Payton's belief that the Saints, down 10–6 at halftime, needed an emotional jolt of some kind. Something unexpected and, hopefully,

Saints safety Chris Reis (No. 39) recovers an onside kick that bounced off Colts receiver Hank Baskett during the second half of Super Bowl XLIV. This play marked a turning for the Saints, who went on to win the game 31–17.

momentum changing. So, kicker Thomas Morstead opened the second half with a perfectly delivered onside kick. The Colts were caught completely flat-footed. The ball bounced off the facemask of Colts wide receiver Hank Baskett and was pounced on by a number of Saints. Linebacker Jonathan Casillas was officially credited with the recovery on the Indy 42-yard line, but safety Chris Reis actually emerged with the treasure. QB Drew Brees then pieced together a precision drive for New Orleans to score a touchdown that put the Saints ahead 13–10. New Orleans players would later refer to the onside stunner as "the Ambush."

The Colts never really recovered from the shock, with the Saints rolling to a 31–17 final. It marked their first NFL championship.

Back in New Orleans, fans hugged, kissed and spilled out into the streets to celebrate the victory. In the famous French Quarter district, "When the Saints Go Marching In" blared well into the early morning. A town known for partying hard had found another gear and partied harder.

For the resilience displayed since the horror of 2005, they'd more than earned the right.

Meanwhile, back in Miami at Sun Life Stadium, when handed the Vince Lombardi Trophy, Saints owner Tom Benson, obviously thinking back on the previous five years of courage and rebuilding, said, "New Orleans is back."

NO. 92 Spygate

THE NEW ENGLAND Patriots were swept up in more controversy on September 9, 2007, in a regular-season game against the New York Jets.

The wrongdoing had to do with videotaping their opponents' coaches from an "unauthorized location." The Jets' head coach at the time, Eric Mangini, a former Patriots assistant who had worked alongside Bill Belichick in both New York and New England, was the one to alert NFL security.

A 26-year-old New England video assistant named Matt Estrella was the one videotaping the Jets' coaches' hand signals. Those signals were cues for their defensive strategies. The Patriots cataloged the formations and pass coverages and used that information in their offensive play selection.

Videotaping opposition coaches is not strictly illegal in the NFL, but it is only permitted in authorized areas; doing so from their own sideline during a game is prohibited.

The Patriots admitted to the wrongdoing later in the week.

Commissioner Roger Goodell ordered the Patriots to turn over their notes and tapes. He had the tapes and notes destroyed, a decision that was widely criticized because they may have revealed how extensive and ongoing the spying had been.

U.S. Senator Arlen Specter was so critical of how Spygate was handled that

New England Patriots Head coach Bill Belichick (left) shakes hands with New York Jets head coach Eric Mangini (right) after the game on September 9, 2007. That game, Mangini had informed security about unauthorized videotaping by Patriots staff.

he summoned Goodell before the Senate Judiciary Committee to discuss the destruction of evidence. Specter said Goodell told him the Patriots believed the taping was legal and that Belichick had been doing it since 2000. As punishment, Goodell fined the Patriots $250,000 and took away their first-round pick, No. 31, in the 2008 NFL Draft. Belichick was fined $500,000, the maximum amount allowed and a record at the time.

Echoes of Spygate surfaced a dozen years later, with the Patriots admitting that a three-person crew of theirs producing a web series titled *Do Your Job* had "inappropriately filmed the field from the press box" during a Cleveland Browns–Cincinnati Bengals game in Cleveland as part of a feature on New England's scouting department. The Patriots explained that the filming was to show fans how pregame scouting worked.

They did acknowledge that it took place "without specific knowledge of league rules."

Belichick maintained that neither he nor any of his coaching staff watched any of the video footage shot by the production team.

NO.

93 Bountygate

It was a heinous chapter in NFL history, a pay-for-pain practice that was fittingly administered by a man nicknamed "Dr. Heat."

Known for unleashing an aggressive defense with all-out blitzes, New Orleans Saints' defensive coordinator Gregg Williams was caught on audio tape instructing his players on how to take out key opponents with explicit instructions: "Kill the head and the body will die."

The NFL had been informed of a bounty program operating in New Orleans but was unable to act on it without proof of its existence. Sean Pamphilon provided that. The ESPN film director, who at the time was working on a different story involving the Saints, sat in on a defensive team meeting and taped Williams' instructions for the next day's playoff game against the San Francisco 49ers. Pamphilon turned his 12-minute recording over to the NFL. It shone a spotlight on what was happening in New Orleans, and what it illuminated was the dark underbelly of the NFL.

According to a statement released on March 2, 2012, the NFL had indicted Saints coaches and 22 to 27 players for participating in a bounty system between 2009 and 2011. Players were offered $1,500 for knockout hits and $1,000 for having a player carted off the field. There were other smaller payouts for landing a big hit ($400) or forcing a mental mistake ($100). The money came from New Orleans players and coaches —Williams included — and would carry over to the following week if no one collected.

One of those targeted for a postseason beating was Arizona Cardinals' QB Kurt Warner, who was crushed in a vicious blind-side hit by lineman Bobby McCray on January 16, 2010. Warner was helped to the dressing room and returned to the game in the second half, but it was his last game in the NFL.

Minnesota Vikings QB Brett Favre was next on the hit list. It was alleged that Saints' linebacker Jonathan Vilma put a $10,000 price on Favre's head prior to the 2009 NFC Championship game on January 24, 2010. Vilma has denied ever doing that. Nevertheless, the Saints' defense went after Favre like a pack of wild dogs. Favre took hit after hit over the course of the game. In addition to an ankle injury in the third quarter, Favre later claimed in 2018 that he played through the game despite having a concussion. The Saints won 31–28 in overtime and advanced to Super Bowl XLIV against the Indianapolis Colts.

Williams was in full form for his pep talk leading up to the 2011 NFC Championship game between the Saints and the San Francisco 49ers. Several 49ers were singled out for extra punishment, including Michael Crabtree. Williams had this to say about the San Francisco receiver: "He becomes human when we f****** take out that outside ACL [anterior cruciate ligament in the knee]."

Williams also reminded his defense that 49ers running back Frank Gore could be slowed down with a few headshots: "Beat Frank Gore's head. We want him running sideways. We want his head sideways."

Following the investigation of the Saints' bounty system, NFL commissioner Roger Goodell drew up a hit list of his own and issued some of the most stringent penalties on record, suspending Williams indefinitely, suspending Vilma for the 2012 season and suspending head coach Sean Payton for the 2012 season for his part in covering up the whole affair. Additional players, assistant coach Joe Vitt and general manager Mickey Loomis were suspended for four to eight games, while the organization was fined $500,000 and had two second-round draft picks taken away. Former NFL commissioner Paul Tagliabue, who had been brought in by Goodell to handle a second round of player appeals, reviewed the matter and lifted the suspensions of four players issued by his successor, Goodell.

On February 7, 2013, Williams' suspension was revoked. He was hired as a defensive coordinator for the Tennessee Titans. After stints with other NFL franchises and the United Football League's DC Defenders, he was hired as a defensive coordinator by Tennessee State in March 2025.

"It was a terrible mistake, and we knew it was wrong when we were doing it … I am truly sorry," Williams said in a statement. "I have learned a hard lesson and I guarantee you that I will never participate in or allow this kind of activity to take place again."

NO.

94 Overseas Investments

On June 23, 2007, the NFL Europa League's first (and only) championship game, known officially as the Yello Strom World Bowl XV, was contested at Commerzbank-Arena in Frankfurt, Germany. The defending champions, the Frankfurt Galaxy, were pitted that afternoon against the Hamburg Sea Devils.

The game was financially backed by EnBW Energie Baden-Württemberg AG, a publicly traded energy company headquartered in Karlsruhe, Germany. Meat Loaf headlined the pregame entertainment. A capacity crowd of 48,125 attended. On the field, the Sea Devils defeated Frankfurt 37–28.

Hamburg quarterback Casey Bramlet, who spent brief spells with Cincinnati, Washington, Atlanta, Miami, San Diego and Baltimore in the NFL and one season in Winnipeg as a part of the CFL's Blue Bombers, was named game MVP for a 347-yard, championship-game-record four-TD-pass performance.

Less than a week later the league folded, sunk by losses reported at $30 million that year and finally ending a quest that had taken hold decades earlier.

Not the end of an era, actually; more the end of a protracted experiment.

The NFL's overseas developmental-league initiative had begun in earnest in 1991 with the launch of the World League of American Football (WLAF); followed by the World League (WL), first in 1992 and then resurrected from 1995 through '97; and, finally in 2007 the Europa League.

A handful of franchises in these various leagues flourished, for brief periods, particularly in the UK and Germany. But in the final analysis, the NFL superstar luster was lacking, the odor of "minor-league" quality stuck and the inability of teams to secure European TV deals or gain much traction with North American football fans spelled doom after doom after doom.

The original idea of an overseas NFL-aligned league can be traced all the way back to 1974.

Envisioned as a transatlantic pathfinder, the Intercontinental Football League (IFL) was the brainchild of Bob Kap, a Yugoslav-Canadian soccer and American football coach credited with pioneering soccer-style kicking in North American football.

Hamburg Sea Devils players celebrate after winning Yello Strom World Bowl XV on June 23, 2007.

For all the planning, the IFL never even broke the huddle. Still, the idea of tapping into football's surging popularity overseas, like Walter Payton toting the rock on fourth-and-goal from the 1-yard line, just wouldn't go down. Various league incarnations included stops in Germany, the Netherlands, Spain and the UK as well as, much closer to home, Canada.

A handful of alumni used their experiences abroad to develop their skills, rise from obscurity and carve out outstanding NFL careers, including, most famously, quarterback Kurt Warner (Amsterdam Admirals). Other notables include QBs Jon Kitna (Barcelona Dragons), Brad Johnson (London Monarchs) and Jake Delhomme (Amsterdam Admirals/Frankfurt Galaxy), receiver/returner Dante "The Human Joystick" Hall (Scottish Claymores), linebacker James Harrison (Rhein Fire), punter Brian Moorman (Berlin Thunder) and place kicker Adam Vinatieri (Amsterdam Admirals).

The WLAF also witnessed the brief one-year comeback attempt of an oddball legend, former Chicago Bears D-lineman William "The Refrigerator" Perry, who spent 1996 with the London Monarchs before officially retiring.

Although the formation of developmental offshoots based abroad certainly didn't catch hold, the appeal of the official NFL brand in Europe continues to be strong.

The league continues to visit large international markets successfully, with 2024 regular-season games staged in São Paulo, Brazil, Munich, Germany, and three in London, UK.

NO. 95 The Incredible Rise and Fall of Michael Vick

HE WAS BILLED as a generational talent, the next great quarterback who could run and pass with equal dominance.

In 2006 he became the first QB to rush for more than 1,000 yards in a single season. And yet all that promise was undone by Michael Vick's involvement in a dogfighting ring for gamblers. For that, he was sentenced to 23 months in a federal prison and jettisoned by the Atlanta Falcons shortly before his release.

Author Jim Gorant detailed Vick's story by writing about what happened to the 51 dogs who survived both the fighting and the planned euthanasia that generated a public outcry. A court order led to Vick paying almost $1 million in "restitution" to the dogs, 22 of whom were assessed by the Best Friends Animal Sanctuary in Utah and ended up in stable, loving homes.

Vick had grown up in a violent neighborhood in Newport News, Virginia. He has retold the story on many occasions of how he avoided the perils of drugs, gangs and drive-by shootings by going fishing and hanging out at the Boys and Girls Club.

Vick also had football, a sport he excelled at from high school to Virginia Tech to his time in the NFL.

In two seasons at Virginia Tech, he passed for 3,279 yards and 21 touchdowns and rushed for 1,216 yards and 17 touchdowns. He was featured on a *Sports Illustrated* cover as "Mr. Electric: Why Michael Vick of Virginia Tech has sparked a revolution at quarterback." At his NFL Pro Day workout, he clocked in with a 40-yard dash time of 4.33 seconds. He also stunned scouts with a previous 4.25 showing, which was the fastest ever for a QB. Such potential made Vick the first overall pick in the 2001 NFL Draft — a historic selection for Black quarterbacks.

There was enough growth in Vick's play as a rookie to move him into the starter's role. By 2004, he had improved to the point where the Falcons signed him to a nine-year, $130-million contract extension. The deal included a $37-million signing bonus.

Three years later, Vick pleaded guilty to federal charges involving the Bad Newz Kennels dogfighting ring. He had used a portion of his signing bonus to fund the operation, which forced the Falcons to seek a $19.7-million payback. An arbitrator ruled Vick had to repay that amount since it was used to start up the dogfighting kennels.

"I had $13 million in the bank when I was 25," Vick said. "I didn't know what to do with it … I grew up seeing [dog fights]. I still had the 'hood in me. Nobody went to prison [for it], though." Vick went to a county jail for his first 60 days. He remembers thinking it would be little more than a 24-hour stay — a few days, tops. Then someone would come and post his bail. But when locked in his cell for hours on end, the uncertainty proved almost unbearable.

"It didn't get real until they slammed that door and they locked it … My first day in there they kept coming to check on me," to examine his mental condition. "I cried two weeks straight … I went into my sentence not expecting to get two years."

Vick was eventually transferred to the Leavenworth federal penitentiary in Kansas and, despite being a first-time offender of the NFL's player conduct policy, he was given the most severe punishment on record — an indefinite suspension without pay.

"If I had known better, I would have done better, I promise," Vick admitted. Once he was released, the Philadelphia Eagles signed Vick to a two-year deal with no guarantees. He ended up replacing starting QB Donovan McNabb, who was traded in 2010. Against the Washington Redskins, Vick passed for three touchdowns and ran for two more in the first half, something that had never been done before. The Pro Football Hall of Fame has Vick's jersey from that game on display.

After his release, Vick had to deal with the legalities stemming from his bankruptcy due to a series of bad investments and worse decisions. To his credit, Vick was able to pay back all those he owed.

He also lobbied for the Animal Fighting Spectator Prohibition Act. The goal was to establish federal misdemeanor penalties for spectators of illegal animal fighting and to make it a felony for adults to bring children to fights. The act became law in 2012.

THE 2010S

Contents

No. 96 Deflategate 177

No. 97 Game Changers 179

No. 98 The First Super Bowl OT 180

No. 99 The Super Bore 182

No. 100 It's Up, and He's Good 184

No. 101 Super-ville USA 185

No. 102 Worst. Missed. Penalty. Ever. 186

No. 103 The Magic Mahomes 187

No. 104 Who Really Did What? 190

No. 105 Take a Knee, Lose a Job 191

No. 106 Michael Sam, I Am 194

No. 107 Another Off-field Demise 195

No. 108 Bringing It On 197

No. 109 Everybody Dance Now 198

No. 110 The Top Twosome 200

Deflategate

NO. **96**

SCENE OF THE alleged crime: Gillette Stadium, the site of the New England Patriots' home playoff fixture against the Indianapolis Colts.

Date: January 18, 2015.

Witnesses: More than 68,000 fans in attendance.

Accused: The New England Patriots and their star quarterback, Tom Brady.

The charge: Knowingly tampering with footballs, deflating them so Brady could get a better grip to throw the ball on a frosty, frigid afternoon in Foxborough, Massachusetts.

League rules require footballs to be inflated to a gauge pressure of between 12.5 and 13.5 pounds per square inch. Those rules do not, however, specify the temperature at which such measurement is to be made.

The "Deflategate" controversy was triggered by a first-half interception by Indianapolis linebacker D'Qwell Jackson. Following the pick, Jackson handed the ball to the Colts equipment manager to be kept as a souvenir. A check of the ball and the Colts thought they smelled a deflated rat, informing officials.

Linebacker D'Qwell Jackson (No. 52) intercepts Tom Brady's pass to Rob Gronkowski (No. 87) on January 18, 2015. This would be the starting point of the Deflategate controversy.

At halftime, the footballs were inspected, and former NFL referee Gerry Austin initially stated that 11 of the 12 balls used by the Patriots were measured to be more than two pounds per square inch below the minimum requirement.

Memories of the 2007 Spygate incident — in which the Patriots were sanctioned for positioning a video camera in an unapproved location to film an opponent's defensive signals — were still fresh in people's minds.

From there, the controversy immediately caught fire. The NFL investigated, fining the Patriots $1 million, suspending Brady for four games and taking away their first-round pick in the 2016 NFL Draft plus a fourth-round pick in 2017.

"I feel like I've always played within the rules. … I would never do anything to break the rules," Brady maintained at a media gathering in the fallout of the cheating accusations. "I don't think anyone knew there was an issue with the balls.

"I'm very disappointed we have to be having a press conference like this. I wish I could give you more answers or the answers that you were looking for."

Brady successfully appealed the initial suspension in the U.S. District Court of Appeals for the Southern District of New York. But the U.S. Court of Appeals for the Second Circuit restored the four-game sit down.

On July 28, 2015, Commissioner Roger Goodell announced he had upheld the four-game suspension, citing Brady's destruction of his cell phone as a critical factor: "On or shortly before March 6, the day that Tom Brady met with independent investigator Ted Wells and his colleagues, Brady directed that the cell phone he had used for the prior four months be destroyed," according to a league statement. "He did so even though he was aware that the investigators requested access to text messages and other electronic information that had been stored on that phone.

"During the four months that the cell phone was in use, Brady had exchanged nearly 10,000 text messages, none of which can now be retrieved from that device." Brady's representatives offered to provide a spreadsheet identifying all the people he had been in contact with. That fell on deaf ears.

Brady wound up serving a four-game suspension. The wrangling and legalese continued to go back and forth.

The NFL, finally weary of the chase, shut down the Deflategate melodrama after spending two years and $22 million on the investigation.

Game Changers

NO. 97

SOME OF THEM were all-stars; others were specialists who played just enough to earn their notoriety. All of them were game changers.

Men who altered their sport or their position by having rules implemented to take away their special brand of mayhem. As noted in an earlier story, LA Rams defensive end Deacon Jones modified the head slap to be a devastating blow. He hit offensive linemen on the side of their helmets so hard they lost their concentration and couldn't block Jones. The NFL ultimately banned the slap.

Before Jones there was defensive back Dick "Night Train" Lane. His trademark was the horse-collar tackle mixed with a straight arm, all of it targeting the head. Lane was so notorious his act had its own name: the Night Train Necktie.

Other rule changes were made for specific jobs. Back in 2009, for instance, the NFL banned three or more players from forming a blocking wedge for the ball carrier on kickoff returns. By doing that, it eliminated one of the most potentially dangerous positions in the game — the wedge buster. He was the guy who would sacrifice himself against those three or more blockers to expose the return man.

Josh Mallard (No. 98), Ryan Harris (No. 74) and Larry Birdine (No. 77) of the Denver Broncos form a blocking line, or wedge, during a kick off return in a preseason game against the Green Bay Packers on August 22, 2008. Larry Birdine was shaken up on the play.

NO.

98 The First Super Bowl OT

AT THE TIME, it looked as if the Atlanta Falcons were already posing with their Super Bowl LI rings, and who could blame them?

There they were, up by 25 points against a lackluster bunch of New England Patriots. In the third quarter, no less. And sure, Pats QB Tom Brady was good. But was he resourceful enough to stage the biggest comeback in Super Bowl history?

The 2016 regular season opened with Brady sitting out a four-game suspension for his part in Deflategate. When he resumed the starter's job, the team was 3-1 and kept on rolling all the way to the AFC playoffs. To qualify for their seventh Super Bowl appearance in a 16-year span, the Patriots dispensed with the Houston Texans by 18 points and the Pittsburgh Steelers by 19.

Meanwhile, the Falcons had their way with the Seattle Seahawks and Green Bay Packers to reach their second Super Bowl in franchise history. Both Atlanta and New England arrived in Houston keen to keep their momentum going. The Falcons struck first, converting a New England fumble into a 5-yard TD run by Devonta Freeman. The Falcons scored again on their ensuing possession, then went up 21–0 when defensive back Robert Alford returned a Brady interception 82 yards for a touchdown. The Patriots kicked a field goal to close out their wretched first half.

The third quarter looked like more of the same, with another TD pass from Atlanta QB Matt Ryan. That made the score 28–3 and it seemed as if the Falcons had an answer for whatever question the Patriots posed. Finally, the real Tom Brady showed up and went to work, eating into the Atlanta lead. He threw a 5-yard TD pass to tailback James White, then threw a 6-yard scoring completion to Danny Amendola. White added a two-point conversion and two TD runs, including the winner in OT, which bumped him to 20 points scored.

Brady's numbers were, quite simply, off the charts: 43 completions in 62 attempts for 466 yards, two TD tosses and that one pick-6. The 466 yards

Tom Brady celebrates winning Super Bowl LI at NRG Stadium in Houston, Texas.

eased by the 414 record set by Kurt Warner in Super Bowl XXXIV. Brady's second-half performance proved to be every bit as eye-popping as Lady Gaga's halftime set.

The victory earned him a fourth MVP nod. He became the first quarterback to win five Super Bowl rings, in seven tries, and just the second player at any position — tying defensive lineman/linebacker Charles Haley for the most victories on the game's ultimate stage.

"I'm tired, man," confessed Brady postgame. "That was exactly the way we didn't plan it. That was everything we didn't want to do in the first half. It was better in the second half, so. Just a hell of a football game."

More than 30 existing game records were either broken or tied that day at NRG Stadium — many of them courtesy of New England's No. 12.

Not long after Super Bowl LI, the NFL chose to alter its OT format, making the rules more equitable. Now, for the playoffs, both teams will have an opportunity to possess the ball in overtime. The game will take as many 10-minute periods as needed to declare a winner. There will be a two-minute intermission between periods and each team will get three timeouts per half.

NO. 99 The Super Bore

SLEEP-INDUCING? UNWATCHABLE? DEPENDS entirely on who you talk to.

"Last time I checked," countered Los Angeles Rams tailback C.J. Anderson postgame to the avalanche of complaints, "defense wins championships." Well, it certainly did on February 3, 2019.

The New England Patriots trimmed the Rams in Super Bowl LIII that evening at Mercedes-Benz Stadium in Atlanta. The final score, 13–3, made it then, as it remains today, the lowest-scoring Super Bowl ever. Hardly the definition of "edge-of-your-seat" stuff anticipated of the occasion. This, from two teams that had averaged in excess of 60 points per game combined during the regular season.

New England running back Sony Michel scored the game's only

touchdown, eight minutes into the fourth quarter, tying the lowest TD output in a Super Bowl game by a conquering team — equaling the Joe Namath–led New York Jets in their 16–7 Super Bowl III triumph in January 1969 versus Baltimore. The score was actually knotted 3–3 at three-quarter time, the lowest aggregate 45-minute scoring output in the history of the big game. One of only a handful of offensive standouts on either team was New England receiver Julian Edelman. He snared 10 passes for 141 yards and, in doing so, claimed game MVP honors.

"It just matters that we won," Edelman confessed gratefully afterward. "It was a crazy year. We had a resilient bunch of guys." The victory gave the Patriots their sixth Super Bowl championship, tying them with the Pittsburgh Steelers. The five-time champs are the San Francisco 49ers and the Dallas Cowboys.

No one canvased the over 70,000 ticket buyers to see what they thought of the "action," but TV viewers obviously weren't enthralled by the suffocating defenses. The broadcast on CBS, whose turn it was to televise in the rotation format of the day with rivals ABC and NBC, along with the halftime show featuring Maroon 5, drew the smallest Super Bowl audience in a decade.

Given its low-scoring nature and both teams' offensive struggles, the game has been regarded since as one of the dullest Super Bowls ever contested.

Brady — with 21 pass completions in 35 attempts for 261 yards and an interception — could not, quite frankly, have cared less.

"You know, it was an unbelievable year," he said in a postgame interview. "We just fought through it more so than anything. It's unbelievable to win this game. They played so well, the Rams' defense … played their butts off. What a great defense, they had a great plan. They made it tough on every play. We just kept fighting and finally got a touchdown.

"The (New England) defense played the best game of the year." In hindsight, the most meaningful aspect of the Patriots' triumph that day was that it marked the final championship hookup for the Bill Belichick–Tom Brady coach–QB tandem.

Considering that this would be their title swan song together, there was a nice symmetry about the opponent — a rematch of Super Bowl XXXVI, the first championship won by the two men and the launch of the New England dynasty.

They were also the oldest head coach–quarterback combo to win a Super Bowl. Belichick was 66 years old, and Brady 41.

Truly, the end of an era.

NO.

100 It's Up, and He's Good

AFTER A 24-YEAR career in the NFL, Adam Vinatieri holds a number of kicking records, from most points scored (2,673) to most field goals made (599) to most overtime field goals made (12). But of all the clutch kicks in all manner of weather conditions, two stand out among those almost 600. The first was a 48-yarder on the final play of the game against the St. Louis Rams. The other was a 41-yarder with four seconds left in the fourth quarter against the Carolina Panthers. Both kicks were Super Bowl winners for the New England Patriots. Also earning a special mention was the 2001 AFC Divisional playoff game against the Oakland Raiders. Vinatieri nailed a 45-yard kick in a blustery snowstorm to send the outcome into overtime. He then added a 23-yarder to make it a 16–13 New England final.

"I'm happy it happened that way," Vinatieri said of his 45-yarder in the snow. "But I never want to do it again ... I look back and say [there was a] two percent chance of making it."

Vinatieri signed with the Patriots in 1996, joining the team as an undrafted free agent from South Dakota State. Along with the 10 seasons he spent with New England, Vinatieri played another

Kicker Adam Vinatieri kicks a field goal against the Oakland Raiders on January 19, 2002. His 45-yarder would send the game into overtime, leading to a 16–13 win for New England.

14 with the Indianapolis Colts. He helped the Colts to a 29–17 Super Bowl win to earn his fourth NFL championship.

Vinatieri's kicking records include scoring more than 1,000 points with two teams and becoming the first kicker to hoof 50 career field goals in the playoffs. He accomplished this by ringing up three or more field goals in four consecutive postseason games, another record.

He retired in 2019 at the age of 47 and was eligible for induction into the Pro Football Hall of Fame in 2025, with yards to spare, of course.

Hall of Fame Kickers

Currently, there are four field goal kickers in the Hall: Morten Andersen (Class of 2017), Jan Stenerud (Class of 1991), George Blanda (Class of 1981) and Lou Groza (Class of 1974). The Hall has inducted just one punter, Ray Guy (Class of 2014).

Super-ville USA

NO. 101

THERE HAVE BEEN 16 cities in the U.S. — from Minneapolis to San Diego, from Detroit to Houston — that have hosted the Super Bowl since 1967. Topping the list are Miami and New Orleans, each having staged the Big Game 11 times.

Both places boast a special connection with the NFL championship game. Florida, as a state, has held it a record 17 times. That includes Miami's 11 count plus five in Tampa and one in Jacksonville. (California ranks second overall and will host its 14th Super Bowl with the 2026 game, slated for Santa Clara.)

New Orleans' special distinction came from Super Bowl LIX being held for the eighth time indoors at the now-labeled Caesars Superdome, the most of any one NFL stadium. That's rather fitting, considering the first indoor Super Bowl was held inside the Louisiana Superdome in January 1978. (The other three Super Bowls in New Orleans were held at the since-demolished Tulane Stadium.)

Just how large an influx of cash is generated by hosting a Super Bowl remains up for debate. The NFL and its organizing committees have estimated the profit to be between $300 million and $400 million for cities and surrounding areas hosting the game — in terms of hotel bookings, car rentals, increased traffic to restaurants and local attractions and so on, along with the future benefits of such publicity.

Others openly question the estimated large profit numbers, pointing out the additional expenses to taxpayers in the form of stadium upgrades, event security and the like.

What remains indisputable is the massive, continually growing interest in the game — wherever, whenever. Super Bowl LVIII between the Kansas City Chiefs and the San Francisco 49ers, for instance, averaged 123.4 million domestic viewers across all platforms, making it the most-watched American event since the moon landing.

NO. 102 Worst. Missed. Penalty. Ever.

OFFICIALS IN EVERY sport at all levels take their share of the stick. Sometimes justly. Other times, unfairly.

All part of the job description.

At the 2018 NFC Championship game, though, there wasn't much doubt over what was a hellacious non-call. For the New Orleans Saints and their partisans, it was the wrong call that was then exacerbated by its disastrous consequences.

With the game tied 20–20, on a third-and-10 possession for the Saints inside the LA Rams' 13-yard line, with less than two minutes left in the game, New Orleans QB Drew Brees dropped back to throw what by any standards should have been a completion. Instead, receiver Tommylee Lewis was given literally no chance to make the catch after being crunched helmet-to-helmet by Rams cornerback Nickell Robey-Coleman well before the ball arrived near the 6-yard line. Quite rightly, the Saints and their fans screamed for a penalty, but there was nary a flag to be found on the field.

The Saints argued they would have scored a TD given a penalty call in their favor — meaning the correct call. They would have been granted a first down on the Rams' 6-yard line with 1:45 left in the game and, hypothetically, got the win.

What's been lost in the ensuing furor is that New Orleans did manage a field goal following the egregious non-call — down judge Patrick Turner, side judge Gary Cavaletto and back judge Todd Prukop all having a good view of the transgression — to take a 23–20 lead with 1:41 left, but then surrendered a game-tying field goal with 15 seconds left and would lose 26–23 in overtime.

Still, that non-call — the chance to perhaps salt the game away and cement a trip to Super Bowl LIII — understandably stuck in the Saints' craw.

Further igniting the ire, even Robey-Coleman admitted he'd gotten away with one. "Hell yeah, that was a PI [pass interference]," he confessed to reporters post-game. "I did my part. Referee made the call.

"We respect it."

The Rams may have respected it. The Saints ... not so much. Livid New Orleans fans went so far as to hire a lawyer to try and force the NFL to replay the game.

The Saints disagreed and (probably grudgingly) sided with the NFL in not wanting to open the floodgates for more suits to be filed.

The Magic Mahomes

NO. 103

TODAY, PATRICK MAHOMES is as much a symbol of Kansas City as the sweeping Swope Park or the city's rich history of jazz and blues music.

His, it's universally understood, is a generational talent.

Back in the middle of the decade, though, before Patrick Mahomes was a household name across America, the young collegian was championed by KC's coordinator of player personnel, Brett Veach. Veach had begun raving about the strong-armed Texas Tech QB as far back as 2014.

Fast forward three years, and Mahomes has declared for the 2017 NFL

Draft. The Chiefs held the 27th selection, but it was clear that their target would be a top-10 lock who would be taken by then. Mahomes' stock had improved to the point that heading into the draft he'd been ranked second among available quarterbacks by *Sports Illustrated*, third by ESPN and fourth by NFLDraftScout.com.

So Kansas City orchestrated one of those aim-for-the-stars trades that occasionally pay off like the Colorado mother lode. They sent their first-round pick and a third-round pick that year, and their 2018 first-rounder to the Buffalo Bills in exchange for selection 10. They got him.

No coincidence that Veach, the one to first recognize and unabashedly promote Mahomes' talent, was named general manager roughly three months later, after the firing of John Dorsey.

Following a season spent backing up incumbent QB Alex Smith, Mahomes enjoyed a superstar-making turn in his first year as a starter, throwing for an astonishing 50 touchdowns.

Smith had been dealt to Washington in the offseason, paving the way for Mahomes, the new generation.

In the doing, Mahomes made the position seem ludicrously easy. No-look passes à la basketball legend Magic Johnson. Though a right-handed QB, he'd toss the ball with his left hand, or underhanded, if the situation called for it. He was exciting, dynamic, uber-confident and unpredictable — a veritable football incarnation of *An Evening at the Improv*.

The dream season earned him league MVP honors, but it also ended in disappointment: Kansas City was beaten in overtime in the AFC Championship game by the New England Patriots.

To show his first season wasn't a hoax of some sort, Mahomes opened 2019 by throwing for 378 yards and three TDs in a beating of the Jacksonville Jaguars. Despite some injury issues, he led the Chiefs to a second consecutive 12-4 season.

Unlike 2018, though, this time the Andy Reid–steered Chiefs finished in a blaze of glory, coming from behind at Super Bowl LIV by erasing a 20–10 deficit, peeling off 21-straight points to trim the San Francisco 49ers 31–20. Mahomes was named game MVP, throwing for 286 yards and two touchdowns while running for another major.

"We kept believing," Mahomes said afterward. "That's what we did all post-season. I felt like if we were down by 10, we weren't playing our best

Patrick Mahomes runs for a gain during the fourth quarter of Super Bowl LIV on February 2, 2020.

football. The guys really stepped up. They believed in me. I was making a lot of mistakes out there early. We found a way to win it in the end."

The scoreline made Mahomes the youngest player to win both a league MVP award and a Super Bowl title. He also joined Ben Roethlisberger and Tom Brady as the only quarterbacks to hoist a Lombardi Trophy before turning 25.

Only a couple of months later, the undisputed brightest star in the NFL sky put pen to paper on a 10-year contract extension worth $477 million (the deal would be restructured in 2023 to pay him $210.6 million over four years and be reviewed again following the 2026 season).

Oh, there'd be a bump or two going forward for Mahomes and the team he now symbolized, but the good times, they were just starting to roll. A dynasty was well and truly in the making.

NO. 104 Who Really Did What?

IT REMAINS SOMETHING of a mystery.

Who exactly was responsible for what would go down in Super Bowl history as the most boneheaded, mismanaged, misunderstood play ever called?

Was it Seattle Seahawks head coach Pete Carroll? Was it offensive coordinator Darrell Bevell? Was it quarterback Russell Wilson in partnership with Bevell? Was it receiver Ricardo Lockette for not running an aggressive enough pass pattern? To this day, the last 26 seconds in Super Bowl XLIX have been scrutinized to the max. What people want to know is who ultimately decided not to run the beastly Marshawn Lynch for a game-winning, 1-yard touchdown but instead throw a pass that was intercepted by New England to secure a 28–24 final for the Patriots.

Carroll, as the buck-stops-here head coach, has always said the blame falls on him. Bevell has acknowledged sending the play in to Wilson, who liked the call and decided to pass the ball to Lockette only to see it picked off by Patriots defensive back Malcolm Butler.

Plenty of former NFL players, from Deion Sanders to Emmitt Smith, were critical of the call, labeling it the worst in the history of the game.

The decision not to run Lynch on that second down was part of a game plan sequence, said Carroll.

Lynch had carried the ball the previous play, gaining four yards from the 5-yard line. Lynch had totaled 102 yards rushing on the day and added 31 yards on a pass play. He had also scored a touchdown in the second quarter.

But the play sequence, which was devised by the offensive coordinator, approved by the head coach and delivered by the quarterback, called for a pass.

"We don't ever call a play thinking we might throw an interception," Carroll explained. Maybe not, but on this occasion a little flexibility would have gone a long way, or at least a yard. Instead, the script called for a pass, so it was damn the consequences and let's toss the pigskin.

"Making the call we made was just part of the sequence. We were very confident in the sequence. We had a very clear thought about what was going on," Carroll said. "We thought about our personnel who were coming into the game after the first play when we came up short, with three wide receivers in the game [on second down]. We had thought about throwing the ball there. That was part of the reason we sent that group in. When [the Patriots] sent their goal-line guys in, I [knew we had] the advantage on the match-ups in the passing game.

"One of those downs we were likely to throw the ball," Carroll added, "depending on how we had to save the clock to get all of our plays in. It wasn't just 'run the ball.' That wasn't what the thought was."

The Seahawks had only one timeout left when they scrimmaged from the one. An incomplete pass would have stopped the clock and allowed for Lynch to get his shot at the end zone. Postgame, Lynch stormed out of the dressing room rather than talk to the media. (That wasn't a complete surprise since Lynch had given the media the cold shoulder for most of Super Bowl week.) Carroll lasted nine more seasons in Seattle before leaving the organization. His Seahawks won Super Bowl XLVIII the previous year by crushing the Denver Broncos 43–8. Wilson was traded to Denver in March 2022 before signing with the Pittsburgh Steelers. Bevell became the passing game coordinator and quarterbacks coach for the Miami Dolphins, while Lockette retired in 2016.

Marshawn Lynch retired in 2019 after his second go with the Seahawks. In his last regular-season game, he rushed for only 34 yards on 12 carries against the San Francisco 49ers.

He also scored on a 1-yard run.

Take a Knee, Lose a Job

NO. 105

When San Francisco 49ers quarterback Colin Kaepernick chose to kneel during the playing of the U.S. national anthem, the controversy started. And its fallout continues to this day.

The gesture was his way of protesting racism and police brutality against African Americans in the U.S. Kaepernick was first noticed sitting on the

Safety Eric Reid and quarterback Colin Kaepernick of the San Francisco 49ers kneel on the sideline during the national anthem on September 1, 2016.

bench rather than standing for the anthem by reporters at a preseason game on August 26, 2016, and the protest shifted to kneeling on the sideline at the start of a September 1 game in San Diego. He was joined by safety Eric Reid.

The two men would repeat it for the rest of the season, and it mushroomed into a polarizing lightning rod. Among Kaepernick's supporters was President Barack Obama, who told a news conference at the G20 Summit in China, "he's exercising his constitutional right to make a statement."

Obama's successor, Donald Trump, would be much less gracious in his assessment.

The controversy took a new turn in March 2017, when Kaepernick opted out of his 49ers contract but only after the team made it clear he wasn't in their plans moving forward.

He was suddenly very much persona non grata across the league.

Not one franchise offered so much as a tryout to a QB who had played a pivotal role in taking San Francisco to Super Bowl XLVII against the Baltimore Ravens.

In that game, Kaepernick passed for 302 yards and a touchdown and scored one himself. San Francisco lost 34–31.

As a collegiate player, Kaepernick had attracted his share of attention, with the 49ers trading up to select him in the second round, 36th overall, of the 2011 NFL Draft. He had put up some incredible numbers at the University of Nevada, Las Vegas, passing for 10,098 yards and 82 TDs and running for 4,112 yards and 59 majors. He replaced the 49ers' No. 1 QB, Alex Smith, who had suffered a concussion, and in his first playoff start Kaepernick ran for an NFL quarterback-record 181 yards against the Green Bay Packers.

But none of that seemed to matter as word circulated that Kaepernick now wasn't good enough, fast enough or consistent enough to be a starter. He was marketable enough to sell shoes, though. Nike used Kaepernick in a "Just Do It" ad campaign and followed his advice for its planned "Betsy Ross Flag" model. The shoe was decorated with 13 stars and 13 stripes, which made it emblematic of the time when Black people were sold and used as slaves. Kaepernick told Nike that particular shoe was not a good idea. They scrubbed it.

"I'm going to speak the truth when I'm asked about it," said a defiant Kaepernick. "This isn't for publicity or anything like that. This is for people who don't have a voice." In 2017 he filed a grievance against the NFL, claiming the team owners had conspired to keep him from returning to the league. When an arbitrator ruled against the NFL's motion to have the case dismissed, the league reached a confidential settlement with Kaepernick.

In the summer of 2024, Kaepernick had reportedly received an offer to join Jim Harbaugh's coaching staff with the Los Angeles Chargers. The two men had developed a mutual respect during their time together in San Francisco.

But on an early October episode of *The Tonight Show Starring Jimmy Fallon*, Kaepernick, who was a guest on the program, set the record straight.

"It's not true," he told Fallon. "I found out the same way everyone else did — on social media. I was like, 'Oh, I got a coaching offer.' No, no offer."

As of spring 2025, Kaepernick was still receiving no NFL interest.

NO.

106 Michael Sam, I Am

On August 14, 2015, Michael Sam said he was giving up on football.

The game's first openly gay player had tryouts in both the NFL and the Canadian Football League. Drafted by the St. Louis Rams in 2014, released, signed by the Dallas Cowboys, then released again, Sam turned to the CFL.

He left the Montreal Alouettes after one regular-season game, saying he was going to step away from the game for mental health reasons. He later did a radio interview, saying he wished he had never been drafted.

Retired from football, Sam now works as a motivational speaker.

"To anyone out there especially young people feeling like they don't fit in and will never be accepted," said Sam of his decision to be honest about his sexuality, "please know this, great things can happen when you have the courage to be yourself."

While Sam was the first player to acknowledge that while still active, he wasn't the first gay player in the NFL. Running back David Kopay came out after finishing his career and wrote a book about his experiences in the macho world of football. Jerry Smith, Kopay's teammate on the Washington Redskins, confided to family and friends that he, too, was gay but never said so publicly. He did speak out about having AIDS, saying, "I want people to know what I've been through and how terrible this disease is. Maybe it will help people understand.

"Maybe it will help with development in research. Maybe something positive will come out of this."

Smith had been a pioneering player in the NFL, helping change the tight end position from primarily a blocking role to a pass-catching one. In 1967, he caught 67 passes for 849 yards and 12 touchdowns.

He retired with 421 catches and 60 touchdowns — a record that stood for 27 years. And yet, he has been ignored by the Pro Football Hall of Fame.

Smith died of AIDS on October 15, 1986, at the age of 43.

Another Off-field Demise

NO. **107**

Former New England Patriot Aaron Hernandez was found dead in his cell on April 19, 2017, at the Souza-Baranowski Correctional Center in Lancaster, Massachusetts.

It had already been four years since the murder of Odin Lloyd, a linebacker with the semi-pro Boston Bandits. But the prospect of serving life in prison for Lloyd's death — with no chance for parole — proved too much for Hernandez to endure.

Like so many other professional athletes of the day, Hernandez, just 27, appeared to have a dream life — a career with one of the NFL's most renowned franchises, a fiancée who said he could never commit a murder, adoring fans who loved watching him play, a fellow tight end in Rob Gronkowski to catch passes or throw hellacious blocks, and let's not forget the five-year $40-million contract extension he received, capped off with a $12.5-million signing bonus.

The facts, however, began to tell a different story as soon as investigators identified Odin Lloyd as the body found on June 17, 2013, in an industrial park not far from Hernandez's home.

Prosecutors stated that Lloyd and Hernandez were in contact just hours before his death, concerning a bag of marijuana. (Lloyd was dating the sister of Hernandez's fiancée.) It was believed that Lloyd had done something to spike Hernandez's rage. Footprints at the crime scene matched the shoes found at Hernandez's home. DNA evidence was located on a shell casing and inside the rental car signed out by Hernandez. When police conducted a search of Hernandez's house, they found that his home security system had been smashed, along with the cell phone handed over to police. On the same day Lloyd's body was discovered, Hernandez allegedly hired a "team of house cleaners."

He was arrested at his home on June 26, 2013. The Patriots issued a statement 90 minutes later, saying he had been released, and head coach Bill Belichick advised his players to never again mention Hernandez's name in the locker room.

Over the next two days, two of Hernandez's associates, Ernest Wallace and Carlos Ortiz, were also arrested. Wallace was convicted of being an accessory to murder after the fact and was sentenced to up to seven years. Ortiz pleaded guilty to the same charge and was given the same sentence.

There were several tell-tale moments in Hernandez's young life, all of them serving as potential warning signs for what lay ahead.

As a kid, he was physically abused by his father, who took out his frustrations by beating his wife and two sons. An investigative report by the *Boston Globe* also revealed that Hernandez was molested as a young boy. He also suffered from ADHD and struggled in school. Despite that, he excelled in football and was actively pursued by the University of Florida as a 17-year-old tight end.

He failed a drug test in his sophomore year and never stopped indulging in marijuana. He later said he was high every time he took to the field. It led him to the wrong crowd and deepened Hernandez's view of himself as a guy you wouldn't want to cross. His fiancée, Shayanna Jenkins, maintained his innocence by insisting he was not the violent man portrayed in the media. "I want Aaron to be known as innocent because he was," she told Dr. Phil on his television show.

"He was full of life, so sweet, very lovable, would do anything for anyone ... I want him to be known for what he is instead of what people are speculating. They want to make him out to be this monster and he's not."

On April 19, 2017, Hernandez was found hanging in his cell. He had used the sheets from his bed to make a noose. He had used ink to write the biblical passage 3:16 on his forehead and on the walls of his cell he had drawn a pyramid with an eye at the top of it and the word "Illuminati" underneath it. There were reports that he had been smoking a large amount of K2, a synthetic cannabinoid that can have a variety of negative side effects, ranging from confusion and seizures to paranoia and intense anxiety.

After his death, Hernandez's family had his brain sent to researchers at Boston University, who said he had the brain of a 67-year-old man. There are many who believe the damage came from the repetitive head trauma he endured while playing football, which would explain some of his strange behavior.

NO. **108**

Bringing It On

THE NFL HAS been in legal spats with its players and former players, has been locked in tense sessions with its on-field officials and has even been confronted by a group of fans from New Orleans, who are still miffed about the missed penalty call that could have helped send the Saints to Super Bowl LIII.

So, who's joined the litigation party? Over the years, cheerleaders from an expanding list of NFL franchises have filed lawsuits against the league's teams claiming unfair pay, sexual harassment and gender-based discrimination.

The money issue is a serious point of contention. While each team compensates its cheerleaders differently, many of the cheerleaders who have come forward about the pay issue over the years allege they were paid anywhere between $2.85 an hour and $150 a game. Pay information is usually safely guarded by the teams, but glimpses into the issue sometimes emerge with the lawsuits.

There have been some small strides in resolving the fair pay issue. In 2014 about 90 Oakland Raiders cheerleaders settled a class-action suit for $1.25 million. A lawsuit against the Dallas Cowboys settled in 2019 saw increases in the hourly rate and per-game fee for America's Sweethearts. But many complainants and members of the public who have been watching these lawsuits feel not enough movement has happened in the last decade. The league maintains that the employment conditions for the cheer squads are each team's responsibility, and according to a statement from NFL spokesperson Brian McCarthy, the "league advises clubs that have cheerleading squads to comply with all applicable state and federal workplace policies." There is no mandate from the NFL requiring teams to abide by its minimum payment standard.

NO. 109 Everybody Dance Now

THERE WAS DANCING in the '60s, disco finger pointing à la John Travolta in the 1970s and mosh pits in the early 1990s.

And let's not forget the high-fiving and chest-bumping galore as the decades rolled along. But there was nothing quite like the choreographed end zone celebrations that overtook the NFL in the late 1980s and early 1990s.

More and more players showed off their signature moves: Ickey Woods and the Ickey Shuffle, Deion Sanders' two-steppin' stride, the Atlanta Falcons' Dirty Bird, and Ray Lewis' foot drag.

Then there were the over-the-top celebrations: the scoring team sitting in the end zone and pretending to race in canoes, Terrell Owens scoring a touchdown and hiding a Sharpie in his sock so he could sign the ball and give it to a fan.

The best act yet? On November 5, 2017, three Kansas City Chiefs, including tight end Travis Kelce, lined up for a 100-yard dash only to break into a potato sack race.

In 2016, the NFL sent a letter to all the teams saying to cease and desist such premeditated practices, forcing some to label the NFL as the "No Fun League."

"The (competition) committee looks at this every year," Commissioner Roger Goodell told the *Washington Post* at the time. "I don't think there's been a year where we didn't look at this issue. It comes down to balancing a lot of issues, the professional standards you want to uphold. We believe our players are role models. So that's important to hold that standard up."

In endeavoring to find a balance between appearing too over-the-top while still allowing a sense of excitement surrounding big plays, and following numerous complaints about flags being criticized as unnecessary, rules were relaxed a year later to allow the use of the football as a prop after a touchdown, celebrating on the turf and doing group demonstrations.

That balance Goodell spoke of — the line of what should, and should not, be allowed — remains an ongoing issue.

Deion Sanders of the San Francisco 49ers dances in the end zone after a 90-yard interception return in a 1994 game.

NO.
110 The Top Twosome

IN THE MINDS of most, they are forever fused. Two men who, together, joined to make history.

New England Patriots QB Tom Brady and head coach Bill Belichick were the NFL's dynamic duo, posting a mind-boggling record of 249-75 and winning six Super Bowls, prompting the question: which man needed the other more — the coach who built the team and devised the offense, or the quarterback who made it all work? The argument ended when Brady, set to become a free agent, went public with the news that he had signed as a free agent with the Tampa Bay Buccaneers in March 2020. He pocketed a guaranteed $50 million and, at 43 years old, promptly delivered a Super Bowl championship to Florida via a 31–9 drubbing of the game's new great quarterback, Patrick Mahomes, and his Kansas City Chiefs.

The only thing Brady bungled was his retirement. He quit early in 2022 and then unretired 40 days later. A year later, he made good on his second attempt at hanging up his shoulder pads, at the age of 45.

He eventually spoke about his relationship with Belichick, saying: "I wasn't going to sign another contract [in New England] even if I wanted to play until [I was] 50. Based on how things had gone, I was not going to sign up for more of it."

That said, Brady revealed Belichick was one of the first people to text him offering congratulations after Tampa Bay won its Super Bowl.

"Were there times where you know it wasn't always eye to eye? Very few and far between, actually," Brady said. "I still envision our relationship as positive and always will."

Belichick coached the 2023 season before stepping away from the Patriots. After being interviewed by a few NFL teams, in January of 2025 he officially signed a five-year deal — the first three years guaranteed — to coach the University of North Carolina Tar Heels at $10 million a year plus performance incentive bonuses.

Brady, meanwhile, signed a 10-year contract worth $375 million to work as a commentator on FOX Sports' football broadcasts, including for future Super Bowls.

THE 2020s

Contents

No. 111 The Pro Bowl: Visual Sominex 202

No. 112 The Resurrection of Damar Hamlin 204

No. 113 Man on Fire 206

No. 114 All Hail the Mighty Tight Ends 207

No. 115 Big-time Stadiums 210

No. 116 Big-money Men 211

No. 117 The End Run 213

No. 118 Jayden Daniels and the Year of the Young Guns 214

No. 119 Kicking Them When They're Up and Down 217

No. 120 Rodgers, Over and Out ... of the Playoffs (Again) 219

No. 121 The Brett Favre Saga 221

No. 122 The T and T Watch 223

No. 123 The Trouble with Tua 225

No. 124 Running to Glory 227

No. 125 Where Eagles Dare 230

NO. 111

The Pro Bowl: Visual Sominex

LET'S FACE IT: football played without emotion is like watching someone fall asleep.

Commissioner Roger Goodell has seen that and remarked if the players didn't put any more emotion and competitiveness into the Pro Bowl then why play it?

No one seems to care much anymore, the participants or the fans.

Oh sure, there may be a little prestige-bump in being selected to play, but the only real reason some players enjoy what is little more than an exhibition game is that it's played in warm climes, like Honolulu. They could bring their family and have a nice vacation afterward. Other than that, there just isn't much to get excited about.

The idea that would evolve into the Pro Bowl began back in 1939 as a standard league champion versus all-stars format.

In 1950 commissioner Bert Bell, in search of new ways to publicize the NFL, established the longtime Pro Bowl model, with the first 22 games of the era being staged in Los Angeles. That inaugural Pro Bowl day, the American Conference edged the National Conference 28–27, with Otto Graham of the Cleveland Browns named game MVP.

Since that first Pro Bowl, different gimmicks, such as fans selecting players, have been tried and discarded in an attempt to drum up lagging interest.

The main concern in such a game, of course, is potential player injuries. Teams and players aren't overly thrilled with the possibility of lavishly paid top-end talent risking injury in such a game.

And therein lies the quandary: Teams and players want the game to be little more than a walk-through, while fans have become increasingly turned off by being subjected to something *sort of* resembling an actual football game.

The 2012 edition, for instance, was blasted by the Associated Press as two teams "hitting each other as though they were having a pillow fight."

The growing malaise among fans and injury fears among players saw an increasing number of those chosen for the game opting to skip it in exchange for a welcome bit of R 'n' R. That led to the NFL trying a new Pro Bowl

AFC and NFC players battle at tug-of-war during the NFL Pro Bowl Games on February 2, 2025.

Games format in 2023, which saw the league's top AFC and NFC players taking on one another in a novel non-contact format that featured 7-on-7 flag football matchups. In addition to that, players strutted their talents in a skills competition before engaging in a tug-of-war. Having added a little golf to the proceedings, the league announced it was trading in the closest-to-the-pin accuracy event for a longest drive competition. Plus, it was making the John Madden NFL video game — once an exhibition contest — part of the official skills competition.

Only in the NFL.

Matt Verderame of *SI* labeled the 2024 game as one "that rivals the level of competition you'd expect from playing shuffleboard." Unsurprisingly, it suffered through its lowest TV ratings in 18 years.

Well, at least until a year later, that is.

In 2025, the NFL announced that for a third year the event would feature competitions and a non-contact flag football game of four 12-minute quarters played on a 50-yard field with 10-yard end zones. In case anyone missed it (and many did), the NFC, coached by Eli Manning, defeated the AFC, coached by Peyton Manning, by an aggregate score of 76–63 at Camping World Stadium in Orlando, Florida.

In 2025, Front Office Sports reported an average of only 4.7 million views on ABC, ESPN and Disney XD, an 18 percent decline from the previous year and nearly 30 percent from the year before that.

NO.
112

The Resurrection of Damar Hamlin

JANUARY 8, 2023. It was their first game back at their home field since the near-death of 24-year-old safety Damar Hamlin. His heart had stopped mid-game nearly a week before, and the Buffalo Bills wanted to pay tribute to their recovering teammate.

Someone came up with the idea of sewing a special patch onto the Bills' jerseys. The patch bore the number 3, Hamlin's number. It was a nice gesture, certainly, but not nearly as dramatic as what transpired in their raucous Highmark Stadium.

As if it had all been scripted by Steven Spielberg, running back Nyheim Hines grabbed the opening kickoff and returned it a remarkable 96 yards for a 7–0 lead over the New England Patriots. That sent the Bills and their fans into delirium. TV cameras captured Buffalo quarterback Josh Allen standing on the sidelines with his hands over his helmet, smiling.

From his hospital bed at the University of Cincinnati Medical Center, where he had been sedated for several days, Hamlin texted his reaction to what had happened: "OMFG!!!!!!!!!!!!!"

That he was still alive was a miracle unto itself. In a game against the Cincinnati Bengals on January 2, Hamlin went to make a tackle and took the full impact of the ball carrier on his chest. He got to his feet, then seconds later collapsed from cardiac arrest. He lay there for more than 10 minutes and was given CPR by Bills assistant trainer Denny Kellington. On the field the Bills knelt around their fallen teammate, painfully aware of the magnitude of his injury. An ambulance came and took him to the nearest medical center.

The two head coaches decided not to continue with the game, after which the league postponed it and then outright canceled it three days later.

Hamlin remained in an intensive care unit for days but was eventually able to breathe on his own. His recovery was slow but steady. He thanked those who had treated him on the field. Without their immediate action he would have died. The outpouring of support and love for Hamlin was, in part,

Damar Hamlin intercepts a pass during a game against the Jacksonville Jaguars on September 23, 2024.

a recognition of the hours he had spent in his community working with sick and disadvantaged kids.

But the touchdown tribute in the Bills' first home game since Hamlin last played wasn't done after Hines and his opening kickoff return for a TD. Hines had a third-quarter encore, a 101-yard kickoff return for a second major en route to a win over New England. You had to pinch yourself to ensure you weren't dreaming.

Three days later, Hamlin was discharged from the hospital and would soon watch another Bills game, this time at Highmark Stadium. Less than two years after his near-death experience, he completed an improbable comeback by becoming a starter on the Bills' defense. On September 23, 2024, during his third game of the season, he made the first interception of his career, which came against the Jacksonville Jaguars. His second pick came weeks later in a 34–10 beating of the Tennessee Titans.

"It's special," he said of the reaction he received from his teammates. "They were a big part of me being able to make a comeback like this. They gave me love. They gave me grace. They gave me everything I needed on this journey."

NO. 113

Man on Fire

IN A LEAGUE that prides itself on grit, toughness is a relative thing. Almost every player in the NFL has confronted pain and adversity at some point in their career.

But few, if any, have ever endured what David Njoku experienced in the autumn of 2023.

At his Cleveland home, the veteran tight end, whose 6-foot-4, 246-pound physique has made him a force to be reckoned with in the Browns' offense, experienced a trauma born of fire. It happened when Njoku discovered he had run out of the liquid lighter fluid he used to start his outdoor fire pit. Instead, he used a spray. It proved to be a serious miscalculation.

"I sprayed it down and waited a little bit, and I guess the lighter fluids were still in the air," he recalled. "So when I lit it up, it just exploded. I saw the fire come from my wrists and blow up in my face. I didn't really feel the pain because it just happened so fast."

Perhaps not then but soon, and lots of it.

Njoku's right hand and face were seared. The attending physician who treated Njoku described the damage "as about a 17 to 18 percent of the total body surface area burn of a second-degree partial thickness, probably the most painful burn you can have."

"My recommendation," assessed Dr. Joseph Khouri, "was not to play."

Njoku rejected the advice and prepared for the upcoming game against the division rival Baltimore Ravens. He arrived at the Cleveland Browns' stadium wearing a plastic mask that looked like a prop from a horror movie. He had his face wrapped and wore a ski mask under his helmet. The burns were exceedingly uncomfortable but not enough to sideline a determined Njoku, who would catch six passes for 46 yards on the day.

"Every single play, whether I got the ball or not, my helmet hitting my face, I felt it every single time. When I wasn't even doing anything, just the sweat dripping … it was intense."

Although Njoku was reluctant to show his face before and after the game, he made a point of exposing his burn marks to fans on social media on October 11, 12 days after the accident. It was a cathartic moment, one that freed Njoku from his inhibitions, which in turn helped other burn victims overcome theirs.

That led to an outpouring of direct messages and phone calls from people afraid of showing how they looked and worried about how their burns would affect their future. It wasn't long before Njoku, who was born in Cedar Grove, New Jersey, and is the son of Nigerian immigrants, got involved with the American Burn Association. As part of the NFL's My Cause, My Cleats initiative aimed at supporting noble causes, Njoku helped raise awareness and funding for those scarred by fire.

"Things happen; you put your best foot forward," he said. "I got to make them feel a little bit better about themselves."

And for the record: Njoku finished the 2023 season with 81 catches for 882 yards and 6 touchdowns. All three statistics were career highs.

All Hail the Mighty Tight Ends

NO. 114

FROM EAST TO west, from north to south, the long-neglected appreciation of one position started off as a trickle of an idea before becoming a mighty gusher of yards and touchdowns. All of them coming on the same day. All of them from different players at the same position.

More than ever, to be a tight end in today's NFL means being half-lineman, half-receiver, all-purpose. And today's tight ends proved their worth on the fourth weekend of October 2024, when the league celebrated — what else, but — National Tight Ends Day (NTED), an ongoing celebration that has fast become a fan favorite.

There was plenty of skill on display as the league announced that 14 players at the position on 12 different teams caught a total of 177 passes for 16 touchdowns. The number of catches was a record for tight ends in a single day.

To recap the onslaught: Kyle Pitts of the Atlanta Falcons had four catches for 91 yards and two TDs, and Tampa Bay Buccaneer Cade Otton had nine catches for 81 yards and scored twice. Single-touchdown scorers were David Njoku of the Cleveland Browns, Dalton Kincaid of the Buffalo Bills, Sam LaPorta and Brock Wright of the Detroit Lions, Nate Adkins and Adam Trautman of the Denver Broncos, Tyler Conklin of the New York Jets, Mark Andrews of the Baltimore Ravens, Tucker Kraft of the Green Bay Packers, Evan Engram of the Jacksonville Jaguars, Travis Kelce of the Kansas City Chiefs and George Kittle of the San Francisco 49ers.

Kelce had the most catches (10) to lead the charge, while Kittle gained the most yards (128).

It was the garrulous Kittle who helped originate NTED before the NFL endorsed the concept and threw its full marketing support behind it. According to the 49ers website, the idea was born in the second week of the 2018 season after Kittle and quarterback Jimmy Garoppolo had watched tight end Garrett Celek carry two Detroit defenders with him into the Lions' end zone. Garoppolo joined his teammates in celebration and quipped, "What is it, National Tight Ends Day?" To which, Kittle replied, "Yeah, it's National Tight Ends Day. It's a holiday. Tight ends all over the league are scoring touchdowns." Later, Garoppolo would muse, "That's how it came to be. We just kind of rolled with it."

Doubtless, past greats at the largely unheralded position, from Charlie Sanders to Ozzie Newsome to Dave Casper to John Mackey to The Gronk, would approve.

Kittle is one of the best of the new generation of tight ends. Near the midway point of the 2024 season, he recorded his 500th career catch while surpassing the 6,500-yard and 40 touchdown marks. He finished the season at 7,380 for his career, exceeding the total of Hall of Famer Kellen Winslow. Plus, at 6-foot-4, 250 pounds, Kittle can block as effectively as he can get open and latch onto a deep ball from 49ers quarterback Brock Purdy.

"It's almost annoying the way he's on the field and he laughs and smiles when he's blocking somebody," kidded Minnesota Vikings tight end Josh Oliver, one of several players who spoke glowingly of the 49ers veteran, who was selected by his peers as the NFL's 14th best player of 2024. "It's like, 'Yeah, bro, we all know you're a good blocker.'"

Kittle plays his position with a certain *joie de vivre*, which is why the

Tight end George Kittle of the San Francisco 49ers runs during the October 27, 2024, game against the Dallas Cowboys. Kittle recorded his 500th career catch on that day, which just so happened to be National Tight Ends Day.

cameras follow him and why he's mic'd up so often during games. He provides a running commentary whether he's on the field or on the sidelines.

"He's a charismatic killer," Pittsburgh Steelers defensive tackle Cameron Heyward told NFL.com. "He plays with a lot of energy. He's usually doing some celebration, making sure he knows his presence is being felt."

Houston Texans defensive end Danielle Hunter agreed with that assessment and added this about Kittle: "He's not [just] a tight end. It's like he has some [offensive] tackle DNA in him."

Kittle has accomplished much in his eight seasons in the NFL — reaching the 1,000-yard plateau four times and twice being named a First Team All-Pro and three times a Second Team All-Pro. In the mind of Arizona Cardinals safety Budda Baker, that makes Kittle "The No. 1 tight end in the game. And he's only getting better."

And yet, Kittle's lasting legacy could very well be the national day he helped establish for the men who play his position and play it beyond its limits.

"I want to see tight ends scoring touchdowns," he said. "I want to see them blocking guys, pancaking guys, breaking tackles … I like seeing it all. And so, a day that you can recognize all the great tight ends across the league is a great day."

Indeed.

NO. 115 Big-time Stadiums

If money is no object, and it rarely is among NFL owners, then you get to build a Taj Mahal of a stadium for your team. You spare no expense. You handle every cost overrun. You charge for every on-site service available. You secure a name sponsor for your state-of-the-moment facility. And then you marvel at its luxury.

That's what Stan Kroenke did for his Los Angeles Rams. He built them the grandest open-air stadium the NFL has ever seen, a multi-acre home called SoFi Stadium. Located in Inglewood, California, on the site of the former Hollywood Park racetrack, right next to the Kia Forum, the facility opened in 2020 as the home field for the Rams and LA Chargers. The 70,240-seat stadium, which hosted Super Bowl LVI, won by the Rams, cost more than $5 billion and is said to be one of the most energy-efficient sports facilities ever constructed. It uses solar panels to help augment its power demands and has its own water recycling system. And did we mention the enormous dual-sided videoboard that runs 120 yards in length and features more than 250 speakers? It's called the Infinity Screen by Samsung, and it's part of Kroenke's plan to build a global sports destination in the heart of Los Angeles.

"Inglewood is going to be the epicenter of sports," NFL commissioner Roger Goodell told the *Los Angeles Times*. "And we're right in the middle of that." The NFL is also in the middle of what many would say is the epicenter of sports and entertainment, and gambling, too.

The Raiders' move to Las Vegas' Allegiant Stadium in 2020 gave the football team what it wanted most — a new facility with more than 120 executive suites. The original budget was $1.8 billion but came in with a $175 million overrun.

Since 2011 the Raiders have chosen to honor their founding figure Al Davis in a fiery fashion. Before every home game, the team and fans pay tribute to Davis with a ceremonial torch lighting. The original gas-fed torch, which was routinely lit outside the Oakland Coliseum, was relocated to the Raiders' headquarters in Henderson, Nevada. Former Raiders coach John Madden was the first person to light the torch in 2011.

The 93-foot Al Davis Memorial Torch, which sits inside the Las Vegas Raiders' Allegiant Stadium.

When the Raiders unveiled Allegiant Stadium, they also unveiled the new Al Davis Memorial Torch. Located inside the stadium, the 93-foot statue is, as of publication, the world's largest free-standing 3-D printed structure.

Mrs. Carol Davis, considered the First Lady of Raiders Nation, lit the new torch for the first time ahead of the Raiders' inaugural game at Allegiant Stadium on September 21, 2020.

Big-money Men

NO. 116

The season that began with hope, and a whole lot of money, didn't come close to what Dak Prescott predicted.

On September 8, 2024, the Dallas Cowboys' quarterback became the richest player in NFL history, signing off on a four-year contract extension that would pay him $240 million — a yearly average of $60 million. That was the high point for Prescott, who at 31 was in the prime of his career and ever so eager to lead the Cowboys to a Super

Bowl. In fact, when asked during a preseason interview to foretell what the Cowboys would do in 2024, he replied, "Win the Super Bowl."

But against the Atlanta Falcons, in Week 8, Prescott left the game in the third quarter with an injury that was later diagnosed as a partially torn hamstring. He underwent surgery and was placed on injured reserve — done for the season.

Today's NFL stars make more money than any of them, or anyone else, could have imagined 30 years ago. Consider that in 1992, there were 27 players making $2 million or more. (Joe Montana and Boomer Esiason both made $3 million a season, while Dan Marino earned $4.2 million.) The average salary was $483,900. Six years later, that number had more than doubled to $992,700, and by 1999 it had passed the $1 million level.

Compare that to what the highest-paid NFLers made in the 2024 season. In the top 10 alone, all 10 made over $50 million a year. And salary numbers are only expected to increase. The salary cap was projected to balloon from $255.4 million in 2024 to between $277.5 million and $281.5 million per club for the 2025 season.

It should come as no surprise that the highest-paid NFLers are all quarterbacks, and that's probably why the Cowboys spent as much as they did to secure Prescott for four years. They knew he could have taken the free agent route and signed for more on the open market. And that would have set the money bar even higher.

Ten Highest-Paid NFL Players in 2025

Player, Team	2025 Salary
Dak Prescott, Dallas Cowboys	$60 million
Josh Allen, Buffalo Bills	$55 million
Joe Burrow, Cincinnati Bengals	$55 million
Trevor Lawrence, Jacksonville Jaguars	$55 million
Jordan Love, Green Bay Packers	$55 million
Tua Tagovailoa, Miami Dolphins	$53.1 million
Jared Goff, Detroit Lions	$53 million
Justin Herbert, Los Angeles Chargers	$52.5 million
Lamar Jackson, Baltimore Ravens	$52 million
Jalen Hurts, Philadelphia Eagles	$51 million

The End Run

NO. 117

On April 10, 2024, O.J. Simpson was back in the headlines. One final time.

He'd been making news for four and a half decades — both very, very good and very, very bad.

The Juice, the game's first 2,000-yard rusher in a season, had died of prostate cancer at the age of 76. But the first images that sprang to mind at the news of his passing weren't of his unparalleled escapability on the football field but of June 17, 1994, when Simpson and a white Ford Bronco drove forever into infamy.

On that day, Simpson, once the superstar of all superstars, an extraordinary running back, movie-sidekick star in retirement, one of the early voices on Monday Night Football and a football Hall of Famer, was on the run from police in the most public of ways, splashed across television screens everywhere.

With Simpson's boyhood friend and former NFL teammate Al "A.C." Cowlings at the wheel, the long-retired Simpson led the constabulary on a two-hour chase across Southern California in that white Ford Bronco after being charged with murdering his ex-wife, Nicole Brown Simpson, and her friend, Ronald Goldman.

An astonished nation couldn't look away. As the *Los Angeles Times* reflected in 1995: "Ninety-five million people watched that chase, not knowing how it would end. Suicide? Arrest? Escape? Violent confrontation?"

The chase and subsequent trial became nothing less than a national obsession. A trio of lawyers hailed as the Dream Team were deployed to handle Simpson's defense in what quickly became known as "the Trial of the Century." Johnnie Cochran headed the team and delivered the famous line concerning the blood-stained glove found at the crime scene. Simpson tried to put the glove on his hand for the jurors, but it was a struggle. Cochran used that bit of theatrics to say, "If it doesn't fit, you must acquit."

And they did.

The acquittal rocked Americans along racial lines. In the ensuing wrongful death civil trial, Simpson was found guilty and ordered to pay the Brown and Goldman families more than $30 million in compensatory damages.

But his troubles were far, far from over.

On September 13, 2007, Simpson and five accomplices, two of whom were carrying guns, burst into a room at a Las Vegas hotel and confronted two men who were planning to sell O.J. sports memorabilia that Simpson claimed had been stolen from him. Simpson and his accomplices made off with boxes and pillowcases filled with sports mementos, including signed game balls, plaques and even lithographs of Joe Montana. Soon after the break-in, Simpson was arrested and charged with 12 felony counts, including armed robbery. Simpson denied having a gun and insisted he was merely reclaiming the items that had been taken from him. On October 3, 2008, he was found guilty on all counts and sentenced to 33 years in prison. He served almost nine years before being released on October 1, 2017.

When Simpson died of cancer nearly seven years after that, his once-legendary football exploits had long paled next to his troubled real-life actions.

NO. 118 Jayden Daniels and the Year of the Young Guns

No one, not even the tallest foreheads among the Washington Commanders' brain trust, could have foreseen the many miracles of Jayden Daniels. Yes, he came highly rated as a Heisman Trophy winner at Louisiana State. And yes, Washington made him the second overall pick in the 2024 NFL Draft.

But did they have it written in ink that the 23-year-old QB would be their starter from the first game of the regular season right on through to the playoffs? Did they envision him guiding Washington to a 12-5 record and its first playoff win since 2006, only to follow that with a stunning upset of the NFC's top-seeded Detroit Lions? Was anyone in Washington willing to predict all

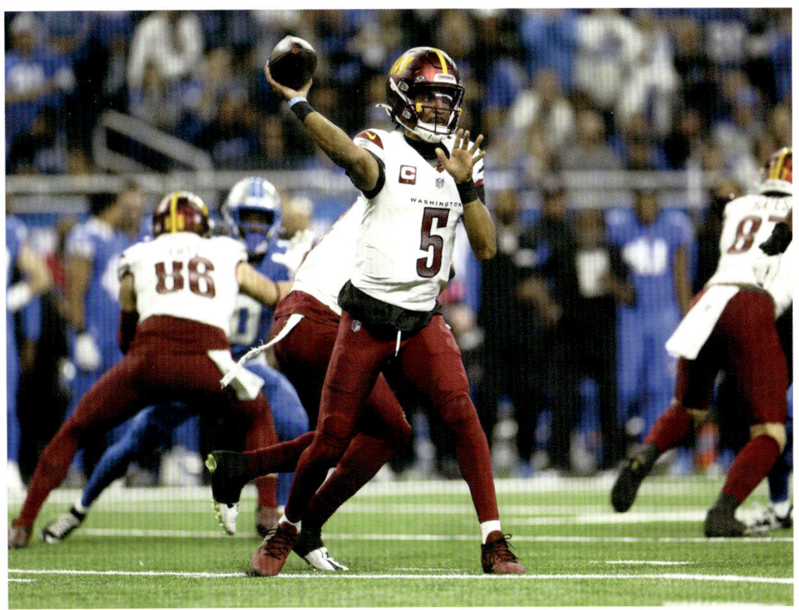

Quarterback Jayden Daniels of the Washington Commanders throws the ball in the NFC Divisional playoff game against the Detroit Lions on January 18, 2025. The Commanders would go on to defeat the Lions 45–31 and reach the NFC Championship game against the Philadelphia Eagles, only to lose 55–23.

that without fear of being fitted for a straitjacket? The answer was no, which explained why virtually everyone in the NFL began tripping over their tongues when it came to describing Daniels and his first-year accomplishments.

"The rookie rules don't apply. They don't apply to this guy," ESPN commentator Tedy Bruschi said of Daniels. "Thirteen years as a player, 16 years as an analyst, this is the best rookie quarterback I have seen."

Daniels quickly established a reputation for being an accurate passer who could run when needed and didn't flinch under pressure. In Week 3, he completed 91.3 percent of his throws against the Cincinnati Bengals, a record for NFL QBs in their first year, and was named offensive rookie for the month of September. In Week 8, he stunned the Chicago Bears with some nifty scrambling that allowed his receivers time to get downfield for a Hail Mary pass. Daniels was at his 35-yard line when he let go of the ball. It sailed 65 yards to the goal line, where it deflected off the hands of a Bears defender into the steady hands of Washington receiver Noah Brown. It went into the record books as a 52-yard game-winning, last-play touchdown. On December 22, he engineered a massive fourth-quarter comeback with his fifth TD pass of the day, clinching a 36–33 win over Philadelphia.

Daniels kept on rolling right into the NFL's wild-card weekend for Washington's game in Tampa against the Buccaneers. With the score tied at 20–20 late in the fourth quarter, Daniels assembled a 4-minute-and-41-second drive that ended with a last-play, game-winning field goal. It was another record-setting effort from the Commanders' QB, who became the first rookie to lead his team in passing and rushing yards in a playoff win. That had some deniers saying Daniels, as well as he played against the Bucs, was going to have a rude awakening when he faced the Detroit Lions at Ford Field. But it was the Lions who were left stymied — and embarrassed — after Daniels threw for 299 yards and two touchdowns, and the Washington defense created five Detroit turnovers. Suddenly all eyes were on the lanky signal-caller who had become the talk of the football world.

"I'm so proud of him," gushed Houston Texans quarterback C.J. Stroud, who grew up with Daniels in Southern California. "In my opinion, he's had the best rookie year of all-time."

Daniels was a member of what was touted as arguably the finest collection of rookie quarterbacks ever drafted in the same year — maybe even good enough to surpass the Class of '83 with its lineup of passing greats John Elway, Jim Kelly and Dan Marino. Chicago made the University of Southern California's Caleb Williams the first overall selection. The New England Patriots drafted Drake Maye third. Michael Penix Jr. went to the Atlanta Falcons with the No. 8 pick. J.J. McCarthy went to the Minnesota Vikings at No. 10 and Bo Nix was nabbed by the Denver Broncos at No. 12.

Nix was the only other freshman QB to make a playoff appearance. He sparked Denver to its first postseason date in nine seasons. Along the way, he had a masterful showing against Atlanta (307 yards passing, four touchdowns) and another against the Cleveland Browns that saw him connect with receiver Marvin Mims for a 93-yard touchdown that carried Denver to a 41–32 final.

In his AFC wild-card loss to the Buffalo Bills, Nix threw a 43-yard scoring pass on Denver's opening drive. It was the lone highlight in a 24-point defeat. Still, it was a member of the Draft Class of '83 and the Pro Football Hall of Fame who spoke of happier days to come for the young quarterback and his team.

"The sky's the limit for him," John Elway said of Nix. "He's just going to keep getting better the more comfortable he gets."

Kicking Them When They're Up and Down

NO. 119

It was during a Week 3 clash between the New York Jets and the New England Patriots that announcer Al Michaels lamented the high number of long-distance field goals that were dominating the score sheets.

"Thirty-five of 39 from 50 plus [yards out]. It's crazy now; too much," said Michaels, who then offered a tongue-in-cheek solution. "Deflate the k-ball [kicking ball]."

The numbers Michaels recited represented an 89.7 percent success rate. And that was with Baltimore Ravens mainstay Justin Tucker, claimed by many to be one of the best place kickers of all time, missing twice from beyond the 50-yard line.

But as the 2024 season unfolded, a curious conundrum occurred: while kickers were regularly hitting for more distance, some were unable to make the seemingly easier kicks, and that cost their teams wins.

Tucker, at 35, was the prime example. By December 2024, he had missed a league-leading 10 kicks. Against the Philadelphia Eagles, he botched a pair of field goals and missed an extra point in a five-point setback. Prior to that, he missed two field goals in an 18–16 loss to the Pittsburgh Steelers. His 73.3 percent success rate was the lowest in his 13 years in the NFL — and he heard the fans grumbling.

From 2021 to 2023, Philadelphia's Jake "The Make" Elliott was the league's Mr. Dependability when it came to field goals of 50 yards or more. He missed just twice in 17 attempts. It was a major reason why he was good on nearly 91 percent of his kicks overall. That number dropped to 77.8 percent in 2024 as Elliott searched for the answer to his woes. However, he was right on the money in Super Bowl LIX, making four extra points and four field goals, including one from 50 yards in the Eagles' win over the Chiefs.

Cincinnati Bengal Evan McPherson had his failings to lament. He missed kicks in four different one-score losses and was unable to explain why that had happened. "For the most part my misses have been [to the] left and for me that's interesting and kind of confusing at the same time," McPherson explained.

Washington Commanders players react to the game-winning field goal by kicker Zane Gonzalez (No. 47) in the NFC wild-card playoff game against the Tampa Bay Buccaneers on January 12, 2025.

"My whole career since I started kicking, my misses have been to the right."

The answer to McPherson's troubles was likely a groin injury that landed him on the Bengals' injured list in mid-December 2024.

No team experienced more angst over its kickers than the Washington Commanders. They started the 2024 season with Austin Seibert, who was money in the bank in a game against the New York Giants. He booted seven field goals, accounting for all his team's scoring in a 21–16 decision. Seibert's longest kick covered 45 yards, while the shortest went 26. His seven count was one shy of the NFL-best eight field goals set by former Tennessee Titans kicker Rob Bironas in 2007.

And yet Seibert was put on the Commanders' injured reserve list after several key misses, thus creating a revolving door at the position. By the time Washington faced Tampa Bay in the 2024 playoffs, the team was using its fourth kicker, Zane Gonzalez. Faced with a 37-yard field goal and mere seconds remaining on the game clock, Gonzalez's kick hit an upright, then deflected over the crossbar for the 23–20 win. It was all Washington coach Dan Quinn could do but watch, cringe and revel, all in a matter of moments.

"I felt like I was in a Bounty commercial where the cup spills. And, like, 'Nooooo!'" Quinn said at his postgame media conference. "And as it hit and went through, I just paused and probably skipped a (heart) beat, but that's the emotion."

Indeed, it was.

Rodgers, Over and Out ... of the Playoffs (Again)

NO. 120

EXPECTATIONS WERE, PUTTING it mildly, high. Higher and brighter, actually, than the star atop the Rockefeller Center Christmas tree come Yuletide.

The New York Jets had missed the playoffs an agonizing 12 seasons in a row. But everything and anything seemed possible on April 24, 2023, when the perennial doormats fashioned a deal to acquire four-time NFL MVP Aaron Rodgers from the only franchise he'd ever played for, the Green Bay Packers.

Could they have imagined what might go wrong?

The capture of a surefire first-ballot Hall of Fame quarterback was supposed to put an end to the painful postseason famine, not produce a drama worthy of Broadway.

Rodgers' first campaign as a Jet ended after just four offensive snaps and a single pass attempt, with a sack by Buffalo defensive end Leonard Floyd in the opening game rupturing the quarterback's Achilles tendon and necessitating season-ending surgery.

The build-up for his return in 2024 proved as frenzied as the year before. With a healthy Rodgers in command for an entire season, long-suffering Jets fans declared, "Watch out!"

But things got even messier. In the debris field of a season gone oh-so-very-wrong, head coach Robert Saleh was fired on October 8, 2024, and replaced by defensive coordinator Jeff Ulbrich. Eyebrows went up when Saleh was the one shown the door, rather than offensive coordinator and play-caller Nathaniel Hackett — a pal of Rodgers dating back to their time together in Green Bay.

The Jets were 2-3 at the time of Saleh's dismissal.

Things would only get worse. A lot worse.

As the malaise deepened and the losses mounted, general manager Joe Douglas was also turfed, on November 19.

Aaron Rodgers looks to pass during a Week 18 game between the New York Jets and the Miami Dolphins on January 5, 2025. The Jets won that matchup 32–20.

The accusations of entitlement and overt blame-shifting leveled at Rodgers grew. Trades, notably for old Packer pass-catching pal Davante Adams, were made to accommodate the wishes of Rodgers, who'd re-jigged his contract to a two-year, $75-million deal upon arriving in New York.

In short, implosion.

The inevitable became official in Week 14, when the Jets were, to the surprise of absolutely no one, eliminated from playoff contention — for a 14th-straight season, which is not only the longest such streak in franchise history but also the longest active postseason futility spell anywhere in North America's four biggest professional sports — in the wake of a 32–26 overtime loss to the Miami Dolphins.

Six days earlier, Rodgers had turned 41.

The loss to Miami had dropped New York's record to a subterranean 3-10. It was their fourth in a row and ninth in 10 starts.

"The expectations were high and we didn't reach them. Not anywhere close. We felt good three weeks in," Rodgers said at the postmortem. "Since then it's been a lot of difficult games with opportunities to win. We just didn't figure out how to win enough games and I didn't play well enough in some crunch times.

"That's why we are sitting here with the record we've got."

A couple of days following the Miami game, FOX Sports reported that Rodgers had been dealing with a hamstring tear, an MCL sprain and a high ankle sprain during the season.

Still, in the wake of playoff elimination and the firestorm of bad publicity, his future as a Jet, indeed in the game itself given his age, immediately became a hot topic of debate. When asked if he planned to return to football for the 2025 season, Rodgers replied, "I think so, yeah."

Given the enormity of the failed New York experiment, just where, exactly, remains a subject of conjecture.

The Brett Favre Saga

NO. **121**

Even when he was sure, Brett Favre had his doubts. Was he going to retire? Did he feel like retiring? Was his team forcing him to quit? Which team was that again — the Green Bay Packers? The New York Jets? The Minnesota Vikings? Was he too beaten up to make a sound decision?

The golden years of one of the greatest quarterbacks of the modern era were fraught with indecision and pain. In the 1990s, he was so beaten up by injuries that he became addicted to Vicodin and alcohol — and still, he played. (He would end his career with an NFL record 321 consecutive starts.) By 2005, Favre had suffered an unknown number of concussions and finished the season throwing 29 interceptions, raising speculation that he was about to retire. Instead, he announced he was considering playing beyond 2006. After a stellar 2007 season that ended with a loss in the NFC Championship game, Favre retired on March 4, 2008.

Six months later, the Packers offered him a $20-million marketing agreement to stay retired. Instead, Favre applied for reinstatement and returned to Green Bay, where team management explained it would be best if he stepped aside so Aaron Rodgers could step up and become the starter. That resulted in Favre signing with the Jets, where, after a rough 2008 season, he announced his retirement. He was released by the Jets soon after but put off retiring by signing with Minnesota. He quarterbacked the Vikings to a 12-4 record before losing to New Orleans in the NFC title game. Favre was forced to miss the final game of the 2010 season due to a concussion. Fifteen days later, he filed papers for his retirement, this time for good.

That should have made for better days ahead, but that was going to be a stretch given the number of injuries he suffered in the 321 consecutive starts (including playoffs) he made during his 20 years in the NFL. A partial list includes a first-degree shoulder separation, a severely sprained left ankle, right elbow tendinitis, a sprained lateral collateral ligament of the left knee, a broken left thumb, multiple concussions, a stress fracture of the left ankle and a sprained sternoclavicular joint of the right shoulder.

On September 24, 2024, Favre added a new item to his list of health issues when he revealed he had recently been diagnosed with Parkinson's disease, a neurological disorder that can cause uncontrollable movements. The revelation came during Favre's testimony before a U.S. congressional hearing looking into the misuse of taxpayer money in Mississippi. More than $75 million earmarked for needy families had been used in other projects, such as a new volleyball facility at the University of Southern Mississippi, where Favre played football and his daughter played on the volleyball team.

Favre explained that he had asked for state funding for a pharmaceutical company he believed was making a "breakthrough concussion drug." Favre has repeatedly said he was unaware that the money was being taken from families in need. As of this book's publication, he has not faced any criminal charges.

The T and T Watch

NO. 122

SHE IS, AT 35, among the world's richest, most popular musicians. A billionaire. *Forbes* has listed her assets as nearly $600 million from royalties and touring, plus a music catalog worth an estimated $600 million and some $125 million in real estate.

He is, at 35, a three-time Super Bowl champion, a four-time First-Team All-Pro with the Kansas City Chiefs, a lock for first-ballot Hall of Famer and the NFL's career leader in postseason catches.

Taylor and Travis.

Together, pop icon Taylor Swift and Chiefs tight end Travis Kelce have morphed into a modern-day Taylor and Burton, Charles and Di, Beyoncé and Jay-Z.

The Power Couple of a moment in time.

And while the Kelces may not match the Swifties in terms of total numbers or outright idolatry, the liaison between the two respective superstars has piqued unusual interest in both NFL and music fanbases. Apex Marketing Group reckoned the romance has brought in as much as $331.5 million to the Chiefs in terms of global visibility and merchandising.

Their liaison began with Kelce attending one of Swift's Eras Tour concerts. He then gave her a shout-out and tried to provide his phone number during one of his *New Heights* podcasts. Shortly after, in 2023, they met and suddenly had a hit-it-off connection every bit as kinetic as that of Kelce and Patrick Mahomes.

"We started hanging out right after that," Swift told *Time*. "So we actually had a significant amount of time that no one knew, which I'm grateful for, because we got to get to know each other. By the time I went to that first game, we were a couple. I think some people think that they saw our first date at that game. We would never be psychotic enough to hard-launch a first date."

Swift has become a semi-regular attendee at K.C. games (her tour dates occasionally interrupting), and he has literally followed her career as well,

Travis Kelce and Taylor Swift embrace during the on-field celebrations following the Kansas City Chiefs' Super Bowl LVIII victory in February 2024.

traveling all the way to Argentina on tour and even ambling onstage during an Eras Tour concert date at London's Wembley Stadium, decked out in top hat and tails, like a 250-pound Fred Astaire, during her performance of "I Can Do It with a Broken Heart."

The publicity and interest have only continued to swell — every move, each appearance the two make together is scrutinized. Speculation about an engagement has caught hold. The paparazzi are always on alert. The appetite for any actual news or "inside" gossip on the romance is insatiable. Why, the magazine *Elle* even printed "Taylor Swift and Travis Kelce's Complete Relationship Timeline" to appease its readers — for those that are all agog over that sort of thing, anyway.

Every Kansas City game Swift attends, she receives as much TV time interacting with, say, Kelce's mom, Donna, as No. 87 does while running routes to get open and pick up crucial third-down yardage. Swift was a very visible part of the on-field postgame celebrations following the Chiefs' 25–22 victory in Super Bowl LVIII at Allegiant Stadium in Nevada in 2024.

So much notoriety and scrutiny invariably come at a price, though.

"You want to keep things private, but at the same time, I'm not here to hide anything," Kelce said during a visit to the *Today* show. "That's my lady. It's like: I'm proud of that. I'm not sitting here trying to juggle, like, 'How can I keep this under wraps?' You just don't want to let everybody into your personal life and be able to comment on it, knowing that everything she does is getting a headline."

Wanted or unwanted, those headlines show absolutely no sign of stopping.

The Trouble with Tua

NO. 123

Tua Tagovailoa can still excite people when he runs with the football. But now there's a heightened risk of vulnerability that has the Miami Dolphins and their fans flinching whenever the 27-year-old quarterback runs upfield.

They wonder if this might be it, the last play of a mercurial talent. It's easy to understand why they think that. Tagovailoa is developing a concussion history that has alarmed many into thinking he should retire. As of the 2024 season, he had, after all, suffered four known concussions, with the three most serious coming in the span of two years. On September 29, 2022, against the Cincinnati Bengals, his head slammed off the turf and he was stretchered to the team's dressing room. On Christmas Day 2022, he suffered another brain injury and was sidelined for the rest of the season. And then on September 12, 2024, against the Buffalo Bills, Tagovailoa ran upfield and collided with defensive back Damar Hamlin. It wasn't the worst hit he had ever received but given his recent woes it had the most impact on popular opinion.

When Miami head coach Mike McDaniel announced that Tagovailoa would start against the Arizona Cardinals in Week 8, fans and media alike voiced their concerns, saying it was still too soon for a return to full-contact duty. Tagovailoa gave them all a quick dismissal, saying, "Every time we all suit up, we're all taking a risk that we could potentially get hurt whether it's a concussion, a broken bone or anything. You get up off of the bed the wrong way you potentially could risk spraining your ankle. There's just risk in any and everything and I'm willing to play the odds."

Asked if he would wear a protective Guardian Cap over his helmet, Tua replied, "Nope." When asked why not, he gave a two-word response: "Personal choice."

The pressure on Tagovailoa to return was intense. The Dolphins managed just one win — against the lowly New England Patriots — during his absence and needed an emotional lift. Tagovailoa had provided plenty of that in 2023, when he threw for a league-leading 4,624 yards. Tyreek Hill was his primary receiver, catching 119 passes for 1,799 yards and 13 touchdowns.

Hill, for one, was thrilled to see his QB back at practice prior to the Arizona game. "Felt like old times," said Hill. "Me and him connected on a few deep shots and that kind of got me feeling good. I missed that and I missed him."

Tagovailoa followed the league's six-step protocol and was examined by team doctors as well as those not connected to the Dolphins. They all gave the thumbs up on his return. As for the long-term worries, Tagovailoa said the doctors weren't 100 percent certain about what he was facing.

"I appreciate your concern," Tagovailoa said of those warning him of taking too big a risk. "I really do. I love this game. And I love it to the death of me. That's it."

He started and went the distance in Miami's loss to Arizona, then followed that with a loss to the Buffalo Bills. That defeat dropped the Dolphins' record to a dismal 2-6. They rallied after Tagovailoa's return to the lineup but were unable to make the postseason.

Running to Glory

The Battle of the Birds was a Week 13 offering between the Philadelphia Eagles and the Baltimore Ravens that was guaranteed to make feathers fly.

Leading their respective teams were none other than the NFL's No. 1 and No. 2 ball carriers, Philadelphia's Saquon Barkley and Baltimore's Derrick Henry. Both men had broken the 1,300-yard barrier after just 12 weeks of play, making their head-to-head encounter the first ever between 1,300-yard runners in Week 13 or earlier.

They had, in a sense, been spending the entire 2024 season chasing things.

First off, history — in the form of Eric Dickerson's 1984 rushing pinnacle of 2,105 yards. Then there was the prospect of combining to produce a first-ever NFL campaign populated by not one, but two 2,000-yard jackhammers.

And, of course, they were chasing each other.

It was Henry who had been garnering much of the early-season attention with his trademark power. Known as King Henry for the way he ruled the turf, the 247-pound one-man gang was celebrated for his stiff-arm assaults on tacklers of all sizes.

His 2024 pace put him on target for 2,120 yards in 17 games, which would set the new single-season standard. Henry was also looking to become the first player in NFL history to have a 2,000-yard season with different teams. He ran for 2,027 yards with the Tennessee Titans in 2020.

Henry turned 30 in 2024, and it was whispered that perhaps he had lost some of his speed. But with the Ravens looking to reduce the pressure on quarterback Lamar Jackson, Henry was signed as a free agent and quickly proved to be the right man for the job. He got off to a blazing start with Baltimore, lugging the ball 25 times for 151 yards and two touchdowns against the Dallas Cowboys in Week 3, then trampling the Buffalo Bills with 199 yards on 24 carries the following week. He offered a terse warning to any defense designed to stop him: "Doubt me? Watch me."

A meeting of two giants of the running back world: Saquon Barkley (left) and Derrick Henry (right) talk after a December 2018 game between the New York Giants and the Tennessee Titans.

Like Henry, Barkley joined a new team in 2024. When the New York Giants let him test the free-agent market, it didn't take long for the Eagles and Barkley to agree on a three-year, $37.75-million contract. In a five-game stretch, he ran for 733 yards as the Eagles won all five encounters. As a lead up to the Baltimore game, Barkley foot-stomped the LA Rams with a spectacular 255-yard performance that had Henry sending Barkley a playful message, asking him to "slow your ass down."

In their head-to-head meeting, Henry was held to 82 yards; Barkley ran for 107 aided by a 25-yard touchdown scamper that would lift the Eagles to the win while continuing to boost his status as NFL MVP. But he didn't stop there. Instead, he came out a week later and ran the Carolina Panthers ragged with his ninth 100-yard game of the season, a franchise record. He also became the Eagles' single-season rushing champ, breaking LeSean McCoy's 1,607 yards from 2013. The season-long mano-a-mano duel proved to be one of the highlights of 2024.

The final tally: Saquon Barkley 2,005; Henry 1,921. Barkley became the ninth man to reach 2,000, on a 23-yard carry, part of a 167-yard performance versus Dallas on December 29.

"I'm not going to lie," he acknowledged. "Just being a fan of the game and the running back position, to reach a milestone and put myself up there with eight other backs that I respect, and some I grew up watching, definitely means a lot."

As Philly prepared to close out its fixture-list against the woeful Giants, Barkley sat only 101 yards away from breaking Dickerson's standard.

A gimme? Hardly. Doable? Certainly.

While most football fans were relishing the opportunity to witness this assault on a milestone, one man at least had reservations.

"No, I don't want my record broken," Dickerson admitted as Barkley drew ever nearer. "When I broke that record, I didn't have kids at the time, but I said if anyone breaks it, I'd like my son to break it."

Well, even with individual immortality beckoning, Saquon Barkley never got the chance to try.

When informed by Eagles head coach Nick Sirianni that he, along with a number of other starters, would be sitting out the finale in order to freshen up for the playoffs after a long, tough grind, Barkley didn't so much as bat an eye or fire off one controversial sound bite.

"I didn't sign here to break Eric Dickerson's record," he countered. "I came here to win a Super Bowl."

And he did precisely that against the Kansas City Chiefs in Super Bowl LIX.

NO.
125 Where Eagles Dare

THE HEADLINE SPLASHED across page 1 of the *Philadelphia Inquirer* on February 10, referencing the nickname of Super Bowl LIX host city, New Orleans, told the dominating tale in two words:

"Big Easy."

And the Philadelphia Eagles had made the extremely difficult look just that — easy.

In truth, all season long in a quest for a title three-peat, the first in the Super Bowl era, the Kansas City Chiefs had wriggled out of more tough spots than Indiana Jones. Every time the Chiefs neared a precipice and looked as if they'd fall from it, they regained their balance and delivered when it mattered. The Eagles, though, wanted none of that.

Philadelphia stormed out to a 24–0 halftime lead, stunning the crowd of 65,719 at Caesars Superdome.

The final scoreline of 40–22 actually flattered the Chiefs, with two late touchdowns helping the cosmetic look of things.

In truth, it was a beatdown.

For the Eagles and quarterback Jalen Hurts, the result provided retribution for a 38–35 Super Bowl loss to K.C. two years earlier. Hurts had been superb that day in Glendale, Arizona, throwing for 304 yards and one touchdown while running for three more. Lots of great reviews, but no ring.

A wild-card loss to the Tampa Bay Buccaneers in 2023, the succeeding season, had left a sour taste, and a middling 2-2 start to 2024 started the critics cawing.

The Eagles then braced themselves. They went on a tear of 10-straight wins and 12 of 13 before dispatching Green Bay and the LA Rams in relatively close playoff games and giving a taste of what was to come on Super Sunday, demolishing Washington 55–23 in the NFC Championship to set up the Kansas City rematch.

"It's been a fun ride," Super Bowl MVP Hurts told attendees at the

Philadelphia Eagles quarterback Jalen Hurts runs the ball during Super Bowl LIX. Hurts would rush for 72 yards and one touchdown during the 40–22 beatdown of the Kansas City Chiefs.

postgame press conference. "I've embraced every step. I took great pride in never backing down from a challenge. Always turning my negatives into positives. Turning my weaknesses and making them my strengths.

"It's taken a great effort to evolve my game over time and just continue to grow and improve."

The Chiefs, who'd flirted with a perfect season and finished the regular schedule at a league-best 15-2, tied with the Detroit Lions, found they couldn't match the Eagles in virtually every department that day.

Head coach Nick Sirianni of the Philadelphia Eagles is dunked in Gatorade by teammates during the second half of Super Bowl LIX.

Running back Saquon Barkley only ran for 57 yards in the game, but that was enough to push him to 2,504 regular-season and playoff rushing yards, an NFL record; as were his 2,857 scrimmage yards at the position. The Philly defense, orchestrated by coordinator Vic Fangio, muzzled quarterback Patrick Mahomes from the outset, using just four-man pressure to keep the star quarterback decidedly off-balance and far from his improvisational best.

"There's no way around it. Anytime you lose a Super Bowl, it's the worst thing in the world … it will stick with you the rest of your career," Mahomes said postgame, referencing what had just transpired as well as K.C.'s 31–9 championship defeat by Tampa Bay in the 2020 season.

"I mean these will be the two losses that will motivate me to be even better, for the rest of my career. Because you only get so few of these (Super Bowl appearances), and you have to capitalize.

"It's going to hurt for a while, but how can you respond from it?"

The constant harassment of Mahomes — he personally turned the ball over three times and was sacked on six occasions — created a pivotal moment midway through the second quarter, when Eagles rookie DB Cooper DeJean (celebrating his 22nd birthday) picked off a Mahomes pass and bolted 38 yards for a touchdown to increase the Philly advantage to 17–0.

The drama just drained right out of the game.

"Right when I touched it," DeJean told ESPN's *SportsCenter*, "I was trying to find the open lane, find the open grass to get in the end zone. Luckily, I had some guys throwing blocks out there for me and I was able to get in there.

"It was awesome."

So much about the Eagles was on this day.

Head coach Nick Sirianni, who'd come in for his share of second guessing (and job conjecture) after the startling 2023 playoff loss and subsequent middling start out of the gate, savored the moment.

"We didn't really ever care what anyone thought about how we won … all we wanted to do is win," Sirianni, misting up, told FOX Sports. "These guys did not want to let each other down.

"This is the ultimate team game. You can't be great without the greatness of others and this was a great performance by everybody.

"I'll probably be shedding a couple happy tears tonight."

And the entire City of Brotherly Love right along with him.

Index

Page numbers in *italics* refer to illustrations.

ABC (American Broadcasting Company), 37, 65, 137, 183
Accorsi, Ernie, 150
Adkins, Nate, 208
AFC Championship game (1986), 98–99
AFC Wild Card game (1992), 121–124
AFC Wild Card game (1999), 146–147
AFL (American Football League), 15–16, 35–37
AFL–NFL world championship, 60
Alexander, Kermit, 45
Alford, Robert, 180
Ali, Muhammad, 50–51, *51*
Allegiant Stadium, 210–211, *211*
Allen, Josh, 204, *212*
Alzado, Lyle, 127, 129
Ambrosie, Randy, 125
Ameche, Alan, 15
American Professional Football Association (APFA), 11–12, 41
America's Sweethearts, 44, 197
Andersen, Morten, *71*, 185
Anderson, C.J., 182
Anderson, Dick, 73
Andrews, Mark, 208
Arizona Cardinals, 156, 158
Atlanta Falcons, 29, 72, 165–166, 174–175, 180, 198, 212, 216
Austin, Gerry, 178

Baker, Budda, 209
Baker, David, 67
Baltimore Colts, 15, 49, 58–59, 72, 183
Baltimore Ravens, 126, 141, 160–161, 193, 206, 227
Barkley, Saquon, 79, *79*, 227–229, *228*, 232
Bartkowski, Steve, 132
Barton, Harris, 110
Baskett, Hank, 167, *167*
Bass, Mike, 75
Baugh, Sammy, 22
Bednarik, Chuck, 38–39
Beebe, Don, 122
Belichick, Bill, 156, 168–169, *169*, 183, 195, 200
Bell, Bert, 12, 35, 202
Bengtson, Phil, 56, 90
Benson, Tom, 165, 168
Berwanger, Jay, 12
Bevell, Darrell, 190–191
Bidwill, Charles, 12
Biletnikoff, Fred, 57, 72, 97
Bishop, Keith, 99
Blanda, George, 39, *49*, 71–72, *71*, 185
Bountygate, 149, 170–171
Bowman, Ken, 54
Bradshaw, Terry, 63
Brady, Tom, 28, *29*, 62, *71*, 100, 149, 155–156, 164, 177–178, 180–183, *181*, 189, 200
Bramlet, Casey, 172
Brees, Drew, 16, 28, *29*, 49, *49*, 165, 167, 186
Breslin, Ed, 56
Brooklyn Dodgers, 33
Brooks, Aaron, 162
Brookshier, Tom, 38
Brown, Jim, 40, 41, 50–51, *51*, 63, 78
Brown, Larry, 56, 74
Brown, Paul, 15, 24, 108, 124
Brown, Roger, 76
Brown, Tim, 45, *104*
Bruschi, Tedy, 215
Buffalo Bills, 80, 116, 121–124, 139, 146–147, 188, 204–205, 225–227
Buoniconti, Nick, 73
Burrow, Joe, *29*, 151, *212*
Butkus, Dick, 41, 62, 76, 115
Butler, LeRoy, 142
Butler, Malcolm, 190

Campbell, Jason, 152
Canton Bears, 41
Canton Bulldogs, 11, 19
Carney, John, *71*, 162

Carolina Panthers, 60, 184, 229
Carr, Joe F., 11
Carroll, Pete, 138, 190–191
Carson, Harry, 95
Carter, Dexter, 129
Carter, Virgil, 109
Casillas, Jonathan, 167
The Catch, 100–101
CBS Broadcasting Inc., 15–16, 37, 91, 183
Celek, Garrett, 208
CFL (Canadian Football League), 125, 138, 141
Chicago Bears, 13–14, 20–22, 37, 45, 47, 61, 93–94, 105–106, 114, 130, 132–134, 140, 215
Chicago Cardinals, 21, 33
Christie, Steve, 123–124, 146–147
Cincinnati Bengals, *61,* 108–110, 126, 169, 204, 215, 225
Clark, Dwight, 100–101, *101,* 109
Clarke, Harry, 22
Cleveland Browns, 15, 24, 40, 50, 59, *61,* 65, 72, 90, 98–99, 120–121, 124, 138, 169, 206
Cleveland Rams, 23
Columbus Panhandles, 11–12
Conklin, Tyler, 208
Cook, Greg, 108–109
Corey, Walt, 122
Cosell, Howard, 65, 102–103
Cousins, Kirk, 28, *29*
Cowlings, Al, 213
Crabtree, Michael, 171
Craig, Roger, 110, *110*
Csonka, Larry, 73, 84

Dallas Cowboys, 44, 54–55, 73, 77, 80, 83, 90, 100–101, 103–104, 124, 130, 183, 194, 197, 211–212
Daniels, Jayden, 214–216, *215*
Davis, Al, 36–37, 111–112, 145, 210–211
Davis, Ernie, 39–40
Davis, Henry, 68
Davis, Kenneth, 122
Davis, Terrell, *79*
Deflategate, 177–178, 180
DeJean, Cooper, 233
Del Greco, Al, 122
Dempsey, Tom, 69–70, *70*
Dent, Richard, 105, *106*
Denver Broncos, 15, 72, 98–99, 110, 115, 128, 142–143, 163, 191, 216
Detroit Lions, 30–32, 69–70, 83, 130–131, 214, 216, 231

Dickerson, Eric, 79, *79,* 227, 229
Dilfer, Trent, 161
Ditka, Mike, 45, 105, 107, 134, 140
Dobler, Conrad, 86
Donoghue, Joe, *36*
Dorsett, Tony, 103–105
Dowler, Boyd, 53–55
Dyson, Kevin, 146–149, *147*

Edelman, Julian, 128, 183
Edwards, Herman, 84–85, *84*
Eller, Carl, 43
Elliott, Jake, 217
Elway, John, 68, 98–99, 142–143, *143,* 153, 216
Engram, Evan, 208
Esiason, Boomer, *29,* 138, 212

Facenda, John, 66–67
Favre, Brett, 62, 170–171, 221–222
Fearsome Foursome, 75–76
Fernandez, Manny, 73
Flores, Tom, 111
Floyd, Leonard, 219
Forgotten Four, 22–25
Freeman, Devonta, 180

Gage, Bob, 104
The Game, 11
Garoppolo, Jimmy, 208
Garrard, David, 83
Gault, Willie, 105
Gifford, Frank, 26, 38, 54, 66, 96, 102–103
Gleason, Steve, 166
Gonzalez, Zane, 218, *218*
Goodell, Roger, 145, 149–151, *150,* 168–169, 171, 178, 198, 202, 210
Gore, Frank, *131,* 171
Graham, Otto, 15, 202
Grange, Harold Edward, 13–14, *14,* 20–21, 93
Grant, Bud, 138–139
Greatest Game Ever Played, 15–16
Green Bay Packers, 38, 53–55, 88–90, 94, 142, 180, 193, 222
Greene, Joe, 91
Grier, Rosey, 62, 75–76
Griese, Bob, 73
Gronkowski, Rob, *177,* 195
Groza, Lou, 185
Gruden, Jon, 145
Guy, Ray, 185

Hackett, Nathaniel, 219
Halas, George, 12–14, *36,* 41, 47, 93–94

Haley, Charles, 182
Hall, Dante, 163–164, *164,* 173
Ham, Jack, 81
Hamlin, Damar, 204–205, *205,* 226
Harris, Franco, 81–82, *81*
Haslett, Jim, 162
Hayes, Lester, 97–98, *97*
Heidi Bowl, 57–58
Henderson, Jim, 162
Henderson, Mark, 112–113, *113*
Henry, Derrick, *79,* 104–105, 227–229, *228*
Hernandez, Aaron, 152–153, 195–196
Heyward, Cameron, 209
Hill, Tyreek, 226
Hines, Nyheim, 204–205
Hirsch, Elroy, 28
Honey, Stan, 125–127, *126*
Houston Oilers, *61,* 121–124
Houston Texans, 124
Hubbard, Cal, 21
Huff, Ken, 132
Hunt, Lamar, 35–37, 60, 150
Hunter, Danielle, 209
Hurts, Jalen, *212,* 230–231, *231*

Ice Bowl, 54–55, *55,* 90
Immaculate Reception, 81–82
Indianapolis Colts, 124, 153, 166–167, 177–178, 185
Ingram, Mark, 137–138

Jackson, D'Qwell, 177, *177*
Jackson, Keith, 65
Jackson, Lamar, *212,* 227
Jackson, Mark, 99
Jackson, Michael, 135, *136*
Jacksonville Jaguars, 104, 162, 188, 205
Johnson, Chris, *79*
Johnson, Keyshawn, 121
Jones, Deacon, 75–76, 179
Jones, Dub, 45
Jones, Ed, 100
Jones, Mike, 148–149
Jurgensen, Sonny, 56–57, 61

Kaepernick, Colin, 149, 191–193, *192*
Kamara, Alvin, 45
Kansas City Chiefs, 15, 53, 60, *61,* 72, 90, 163–164, 186–188, 200, 217, 230–233
Kapp, Joe, 48–49, *49*
Karlis, Rich, 99
Katcavage, Jim, 75
Kazemi, Sahel, 151–152
Kelce, Travis, 63, 198, 208, 223–225, *224*
Kelly, Jim, 121, 216
Kiick, Jim, 73
Kilgore, Adam, 128
Kilmer, Billy, 43, 74
Kincaid, Dalton, 208
Kittle, George, 208–209, *209*
Kosar, Bernie, 138
Kraft, Tucker, 208
Kramer, Jerry, 54–55, *55, 89*
Kroenke, Stan, 210

Lambeau, Earl, 12, 94
Lambert, Jack, 67–68, *68*
Lamonica, Daryle, 57–58, 71–72
Landry, Tom, 54–55, 77, 89
Lane, Dick, 41, 97, 179
LaPorta, Sam, 208
Lary, Yale, 30
Las Vegas Raiders, 210–211
Layden, Elmer, 12
Layne, Bobby, 30–32, *31*
Levy, Marv, 122, 138–139
Lewis, Jamal, *79*
Lewis, Michael, 162
Lewis, Ray, 160–161, *161,* 198
Lewis, Tommylee, 186
Lincicome, Bernie, 163
Lockette, Ricardo, 190–191
Lombardi, Vince, 41, 53, 55–57, 88–90, *89,* 154
Long, Howie, 62, 127
Los Angeles Raiders, 45
Los Angeles Rams, 23, 25, 28, 35, *61,* 75, 91, 102, 106, 182–183, 186–187, 210, 228, 230
Lowry, Alan, 146
Luck, Andrew, 153
Luckman, Sid, 21–22, 49, *49*
Lujack, Johnny, 28
Lundy, Lamar, 75
Lynch, Marshawn, 190–191

Madden, John, 86, 117–118, *118,* 203, 210
Mahomes, Patrick, 151, 187–189, *189,* 200, 223, 232–233
Mangini, Eric, 168, *169*
Manning, Eli, *29,* 203
Manning, Peyton, 32, *49,* 151, 166, 203
Mara, Tim, 12
Marino, Dan, *29,* 137–138, 212, 216
Marshall, Bobby, 22, *71*
Marshall, George Preston, 12, 22, *36,* 39–40
Marshall, Jim, 43
Mason, Derrick, 146

Maye, Drake, 216
McAllister, Deuce, 162
McCarthy, J.J., 216
McCoy, LeSean, 229
McCray, Bobby, 170
McDaniel, Mike, 226
McDowell, Bubba, 122
McGee, Max, 53
McMahon, Jim, 105
McNabb, Donovan, 175
McNair, Steve, 148, 151–152
McNally, Art, 80
McNamee, Frank, *36*
McPherson, Evan, 217–218
Meredith, Don, 65–66
Miami Dolphins, 37, 73–74, 102, 105, 112–114, 124, 137–138, 140–141, 220, 225–226
Michaels, Al, 217
Michel, Sony, 182–183
Mims, Marvin, 216
Minnesota Vikings, 43, 59–60, 83, 103, 117, 124, 133, 138–139, 222
Mitchell, Bobby, 40, 90
Modell, Art, 40, 50
Modzelewski, Dick, 75
Monday Night Football, 37, 65–66, *65,* 102–103
Montana, Joe, 100, 108–110, *110,* 142, 212, 214
Montler, Mike, 78
Moon, Warren, *29,* 121–123
Morrall, Earl, 30, 32, 59, 73
Morstead, Thomas, 167
Motley, Marion, 22, 24–25

Nagurski, Bronislau, 20–21, 41, 93
Namath, Joe, 37, 57, 58–60, *59,* 62–63, 65, 183
National Tight Ends Day, 207–209
NBC (National Broadcasting Company), 15, 33, 37, 57–58, 114, 183
Neal, Lorenzo, 146
New England Patriots, 60, 75, 85, 102–103, 106–107, 112–113, 120–121, 155–156, 164, 168–169, 177–178, 180–184, 188, 190–191, 195, 200, 204, 216, 226
New Orleans Saints, *61,* 69, 115, 132, 140, 149, 162, 165–168, 170–171, 186–187, 222
New York Giants, 12–13, 15, 22, 26, 61, *61,* 75, 84–85, 89–90, 95, 106, 115–116, 139, 160, 218, 228
New York Jets, 15, 37, 57–60, 65, 78, 120–121, 137–138, 168, 183, 219–222
NFC Championship game (1981), 100–101
NFC Championship game (2018), 186–187
NFL (National Football League): birth of, 11–12, *11*; Black players in, 22–26, 39–40, 47, 90; game changers, 179, *179*; head injuries, 152–154, *154*; and Hollywood, 62–63; instant replay, 80; lawsuits, 197; overseas leagues, 172–173, *173*; player salaries, 211–212, *212*; stadiums, 210–211; steroid era, 127–129; television broadcasts, 33, 37; tracking technology, 124–125
NFL Championship game (1960), 38
NFL Championship game (1967), 54–55, *55*
NFL Network, 159
NFL Players Association strike (1982), 37, 114
NFL–AFL merger (1966), 15–16, 37, 111
Nix, Bo, 216
Njoku, David, 206–208
Norwood, Scott, 139
Nunn, Bill, 67

Oakland Raiders, 37, 57–58, *61,* 81–82, 86, 90, 97, 111–112, 117, 145, 155–156, 184, 197, 210
Oliver, Josh, 208
Olsen, Merlin, 62, 75
Osmanski, Bill, 22
Otton, Cade, 208
Owens, Brig, 61
Owens, Terrell, 198

Page, Alan, 115
Parcells, Bill, 120
Parrish, Tony, *141*
Pathon, Jerome, 162
Payton, Sean, 149, 166–167, 171
Payton, Walter, 105–106, *131,* 132–134, *133,* 173
Pearson, Drew, 83
Penix, Michael, Jr., 216
Perry, William, *106,* 107–108, 173
Peterson, Adrian, *79, 131*
Philadelphia Eagles, 12, 33, 38–39, 84–85, 90, 112, 132, 175, 217, 227–233
Phoenix Cardinals, 120
Piccolo, Brian, 47–48
Pisarcik, Joe, 84–85, *84*
Pitts, Kyle, 208
Pittsburgh Steelers, 25, 30, 32, 67–68, 71–72, 81–82, 91, 124, 156, 180, 183, 191, 217
Pollard, Fritz, 22
Prater, Matt, 70
Prescott, Dak, *29,* 211–212, *212*
Prior, Mike, 142

Pro Bowl, 202–203, *203*
Pro Football Hall of Fame, 11, 41–42, *42,* 87–88, *87,* 104, 175, 185
Pugh, Jethro, 54
Pyle, Charles C., 14

Quin, Glover, 83
Quinn, Dan, 218

Reed, Andre, 88, 122
Reeves, Dan, 99
Reich, Frank, 121–122, *123*
Reid, Andy, 188
Reid, Eric, 192, *192*
Reis, Chris, 167, *167*
Rice, Jerry, 41, 98, 109, 110
Ridlehuber, Preston, 58
Rivers, Philip, *29*
Roberts, Gene, 24
Robey-Coleman, Nickell, 186–187
Robinson, Jack, *23*
Robustelli, Andy, 75, 85
Rodgers, Aaron, 83, 219–221, *220,* 222
Rodgers, Richard, II, 83
Roethlisberger, Ben, 28, *29,* 189
Rogers, George, 115
Romanowski, Bill, 128–129
Rooney, Art, 12, 81
Rozelle, Alvin Ray, 35–37, *36,* 52, 67, 72, 94, 111–112, 150
Ryan, Buddy, 107
Ryan, Matt, *29,* 180

Sabol, Ed, 66–67
St. Louis Cardinals, 77
St. Louis Rams, 148, 156, 164, 184, 194
Saleh, Robert, 219
Sam, Michael, 194
San Diego Chargers, 15, 72, 75
San Francisco 49ers, 15, 43, 45, 100–101, 108–110, 142, 170–171, 183, 186, 188, 191–193
Sanders, Barry, *79, 104,* 130–131, *131*
Sanders, Deion, 39, 190, 198, *199*
Sayers, Gale, 45–48, *46,* 50
Schramm, Tex, 37, 44, 77
Schroeder, Jay, *116*
Scott, Jake, 73–74
Seattle Seahawks, 180, 190–191
Seibert, Austin, 218
Shell, Donnie, 67
Shula, Don, 41, 73–74, *74,* 93
Simpson, O.J., 62–63, 78–80, *78–79, 104,* 213–214
Singletary, Mike, 105
Sirianni, Nick, 229, *232,* 233
Slater, Duke, 22
Smith, Alex, 188, 193
Smith, Charlie, 58
Smith, Emmitt, 131, *131,* 132, 190
Smith, Jerry, 90, 194
Smith, John, 103, 113
Snell, Matt, 59
Snowplow Game, 112–113
Solomon, Freddie, 100
Spears, Clarence, 20
Springs, Ron, 103
Spygate, 168–169, 178
Staley, A.E., 93
Stallworth, Donté, 162
Stallworth, John, 67
Starr, Bart, 53, 54–55, *55*
Staubach, Roger, 83, *104*
Stenerud, Jan, 185
Stingley, Darryl, 85–87
Strode, Woody, 22–23, *23,* 63
Stroud, C.J., 216
Summerall, Pat, 77, 117
Super Bowl: halftime shows, 135–137, *136*; host cities, 185–186; origin of, 37, 60
Super Bowl III, 58–59, 183
Super Bowl IV, 60
Super Bowl VII, 73–75
Super Bowl XXIII, 109–110
Super Bowl XXXIV, 148, 182
Super Bowl XLIV, 166–168
Super Bowl XLVIII, 191
Super Bowl XLIX, 190–191
Super Bowl LI, 180–182
Super Bowl LIII, 182–183
Super Bowl LIV, 188–189
Super Bowl LVIII, 186, 225
Super Bowl LIX, 185, 217, 230–233
Swann, Lynn, 41, 67
Swift, Taylor, 223–225, *224*

Tagliabue, Paul, 52, 149, *150,* 171
Tagovailoa, Tua, *212,* 225–226
Tampa Bay Buccaneers, 28, 145, 200, 216, 218, 230, 232
Tarkenton, Fran, 139
Tatum, Jack, 82, 86–87
Taylor, Jim, 38
Taylor, John, 110
Taylor, Lawrence, 95–96, 115–116, *116*
Tennessee Titans, 124, 146–148, 151, 205, 227
Testaverde, Vinny, 120

Theismann, Joe, 95–96, *95*
Thomas, Mike, 83
Thorpe, Jim, 11, 16–19, *17,* 41, 62–63
Tillman, Pat, 156–158, *157*
Tittle, Y.A., *29, 49*
Trautman, Adam, 208
Tuck Rule Game, 155–156
Tucker, Justin, 70, 217
Tunnell, Emlen, 25–27, *27*
Tupa, Tom, 120–121
Turner, Jim, 57
Tyler, Wendell, *68*
Tyree, David, 75

Ulbrich, Jeff, 219
Unitas, Johnny, 15–16, 41, 58, 59
Upshaw, Gene, 86
Uram, Andy, 104

Valdiserri, Ken, 105
Van Brocklin, Norm, 28–29, 39, 72
Veach, Brett, 187–188
Vick, Michael, 174–175
Vilma, Jonathan, 170–171
Vinatieri, Adam, 70, 156, 173, 184–185, *184*

Walker, Doak, 30, 39, *104*
Walsh, Bill, 100, 108–109, 110
Walz, Allen, 33
Warfield, Paul, 73, 138
Warner, Glenn Scobey, 18
Warner, Kurt, 148, 170, 173, 182
Warren, Jimmy, *81*
Washington, Kenny, 22–23, *23*
Washington Commanders, 32, 214–216, 218, *218,* 230
Washington Redskins, 21–22, 40, 56–57, 61, *61,* 90, 93, 95, 102, 112, 114, 130, 140, 145, 175
Wayne, John, 72
Webster, Mike, 67, 152–153
West Coast offense, 108–109
White, James, 180
White, Randy, 132
Whitfield, A.D., 61
Williams, Brian, 142
Williams, Caleb, 216
Williams, Doug, 25
Williams, Gregg, 170–171
Williams, Marcus, 128–129
Williams, Ricky, 140–141, *141*
Willis, Bill, 22, 24–25
Wilson, George, 30
Wilson, Russell, 25, 190–191
Woods, Ickey, 198
Woodson, Charles, *104,* 155
Wright, Brock, 208
Wycheck, Frank, 146

Yepremian, Garo, 74–75
Young, George, 115

Photo Credits

Associated Press: 27, 36, 51, 55, 59, 68, 70, 78, 81, 84, 87, 97, 101, 106, 110, 113, 123, 141, 143, 147, 150, 154, 164, 167, 169, 173, 177, 184, 189, 199, 203, 205, 209, 211, 215, 218, 220, 224, 228, 231, 232

Bettmann / Getty Images: 23, 31, 46, 89, 95, 116, 118

Branger / Getty Images: 17

Dennis MacDonald / Shutterstock: 42

Diamond Images / Getty Images: 133

Doug Pensinger / Getty Images: 179

Michael Zagaris / Getty Images: 192

John Biever / Icon Sportswire: 74

John Cordes / Icon Sportswire: 157

John Storey / Getty Images: 126

Paul Spinelli via AP: 136

Timoth A. Clary / Getty Images: 161, 181

Tony Tomsic / AP Images: 65

Universal History Archive / Getty Images: 14